Research Team, Advisors and National Correspondents

Research Team

Research Leader

Georges Cavalier[1] (Associate Professor, France)

Other Members

Rémi Barnéoud (Lawyer, France)
Mehdy Ben Brahim (Lawyer, France)
Pablo Guedon (Associate Professor, France)
Łukasz Stankiewicz (Professor, France)

Assistant

Jean-Kassim Ouedraogo (Senior Researcher, Lawyer, France)

Advisory Committee

Robert Danon (Professor, Switzerland)
Theodoros Fortsakis (Professor, Greece)
Csilla Andrea Heinemann (Judge, Hungary)
Michaël Karpenschif (Professor, France)
Michael Lang (Professor, Austria)
Włodzimierz Nykiel (Professor, Poland)
Jeffrey Owens (Professor, Austria)
Jean-Luc Pierre (Professor, France)
Claudio Sacchetto (Professor, Italy)

National Correspondents

Felipe Alonso Murillo (Professor, Spain)
Hrvoje Arbutina (Professor, Croatia)
Gyenge Balàzs (Associate Lecturer, Hungary)
Jasna Bogovac (Associate Professor, Croatia)

---

1. G. Cavalier answered the call for project, gathered the research team, advisors and national correspondents, liaised with them, reviewed the questionnaire drafted under his directions, analysed the answers to the questionnaire, and drafted alone the book, except the answers to the thirteen National Reports. Of course, none of this achievement could have been attained without the full team.

Klàra Gellén (Professor, Hungary)
Mario Grandinetti (Professor, Italy)
Emer Hunt (Professor, Ireland)
Karlis Ketners (Professor, Latvia)
Sabine Kirchmayr Schliesselberger (Professor, Austria)
Ziemowit Kukulski (Professor, Poland)
Steffen Lampert (Professor, Germany)
Maria Marquardsen (Assistant Professor, Germany)
Athina Moraiti (Lawyer, Greece)
Thierry Obrist (Professor, Switzerland)
Evgenia Papadopoulou (Judge, Greece)
Paloma Schwarz (Assistant Professor, Luxembourg)
Malgorzata Sek (Adjunct Professor, Poland)
Brent Springael (Lawyer, Belgium)
Tomi Viitala (Professor, Finland)

Executive Summary

The fall off in economic activity following the financial crisis of 2008 has highlighted the need to encourage new areas of economic activity. As the European Union deals with the financial and health consequences of the COVID-19 pandemic, this continues to be the case. Innovation is a possible generator of economic activity, one which many believe is underutilised in Europe. It is widely agreed that technological advances are important contributors to long-term growth, but research and development (R&D) of new technologies is risky. That is precisely why EU Member States incentivise R&D through their tax systems by supporting companies that invest in new technology.

Boosting R&D is one of the main objectives of the European Union. A majority of studies conclude that tax incentives stimulate investment in R&D and are an important component in encouraging research-oriented economic activity. However, the R&D incentives currently in place in the European Union are not always adequate and in any case piecemeal.

At the end of 2016, the European Commission proposed a Common Corporate Tax Base (CCTB) which contained some elements relating to R&D. The primary aim of the CCTB was to establish a single set of rules for calculating the corporate tax base in the EU Member States which should improve the Single Market for businesses by reducing administrative burdens, compliance costs and tax obstacles for companies operating in multiple Member States. The CCTB defined R&D, building upon statistical analysis produced by the Organisation for Economic Co-operation and Development within the so-called Frascati Manual. Nonetheless, the CCTB did not address many existing discrepancies between national tax laws, including what would constitute R&D expenditure. This lack of certainty as to what constitutes R&D means that there is no uniformity within the European Union as to what costs are eligible for R&D tax incentives. The CCTB proposal did not, therefore, remedy the theoretical and practical problems arising from varying national definitions of R&D and, in this regard, was a missed opportunity to provide a legal environment conducive to R&D.

This book proposes new solutions to the problem of lack of a uniform definition of R&D and R&D expenditure. The conceptual framework in the book is particularly apt within the context of EU tax harmonisation. The Project Team took the definition of R&D provided for in the Frascati Manual as a starting point.

The reports prepared by National Correspondents of 14 EU Members States and Switzerland detailed the legislation and practice in their respective jurisdictions. A comparative analysis of these national reports enables this book to offer a common interpretation of R&D and R&D expenditure.

The book contributes to the shaping of the new tax legal order, particularly within the EU and is addressed primarily to EU institutions, national legislatures, tax administrations and taxpayers.

Adoption of the solutions proposed in this book is designed to strengthen pan-European Union R&D activities through a uniform approach to R&D, and thereby contribute to economic activity by removing barriers to the Single Market. This is of interest to Member States, citizens, companies and professionals throughout the European Union.

Acknowledgments

Georges Cavalier wishes to express his deepest gratitude to the **European Law Institute** and to the **European Commission**. Their generous support has not only made the completion of this research possible but has also provided the broader framework within which a truly European dialogue on fiscal law can emerge. By fostering cross-border and cross-vocational exchanges of ideas and encouraging the search for shared concepts, these institutions have played an essential role in shaping the reflections contained in this book.

He is equally indebted to the **Centre for Financial and Tax Research (CERFF)** at the Lyon 3 Law School, whose guidance and institutional backing were of invaluable assistance at every stage of the project. His gratitude also extends to the **Research Department of the University Jean Moulin Lyon 3**, which provided a supportive and stimulating administrative environment.

Special acknowledgment is reserved for the **Louis Josserand Research Team**. Its long-standing tradition of rigorous scholarship and openness to comparative perspectives has been a constant source of inspiration. The author is particularly mindful of the privilege of working within such a distinguished academic community.

Beyond these institutions, the author owes an immeasurable debt to colleagues and friends across Europe who, through their reports, advice, constructive criticism, and encouragement, have accompanied him in the demanding process of producing this book. Their insights exemplify the collaborative spirit that lies at the heart of European legal scholarship, and it is to them that this work is most humbly dedicated.

Co-funded by the European Union. Views and opinions expressed are however those of the author(s) only and do not necessarily reflect those of the European Union.

Foreword

As the General Reporter on R&D tax incentives for the International Fiscal Association (IFA) at the Basel Congress in 2015, I had the opportunity to collaborate with Georges Cavalier, who authored the French national report. Ten years later, I welcome the initiative he has taken to deepen this field of inquiry by coordinating a truly pan-European project that aims not only at comparing domestic practices but also at constructing a shared conceptual foundation for R&D tax law.

This collective volume, published by Intersentia, brings together national contributions from over a dozen European jurisdictions, including Switzerland. Far from replicating the approach of Basel, this work builds upon it in a novel and ambitious manner. Its twofold ambition deserves to be emphasised.

First, the volume proposes the construction of an autonomous concept of 'research and development' for tax purposes—independent from purely administrative, accounting, or economic references such as the OECD Frascati Manual. This conceptual effort opens the door to a broader and more intellectually coherent definition of R&D. For instance, several contributions highlight that R&D activity can exist outside the technological and scientific sectors traditionally favoured by tax authorities. The inclusion of the humanities and social sciences – under specific criteria such as a formalised hypothesis, a methodological risk, or a process of knowledge creation –is one of the original and valuable proposals of this work.

Second, the volume offers a refined theory of eligible R&D expenditures. It departs from a fragmented and often inconsistent enumeration of expenses found in national tax codes, and instead seeks to identify underlying criteria justifying the fiscal benefit. These include a direct connection to the research process, the presence of scientific or methodological uncertainty, and the absence of any requirement for immediate commercial exploitation. Notably, some contributions – such as those from Germany and France – challenge the inclusion of certain software development costs or subcontracting expenses that do not meet these conceptual tests.

Coordinating such a volume required not only technical precision but also institutional support. The European Law Institute played a decisive role in funding a series of in-person meetings between contributors. As a member of the Advisory Committee, I had the opportunity to follow these exchanges closely and was impressed by their intellectual rigour and openness. This project would simply not have achieved such coherence without those shared deliberations.

By integrating legal theory, comparative methodology, and concrete fiscal implications, this work paves the way for a more principled and transparent understanding of R&D tax incentives. It deserves to be read not only by scholars, but also by policymakers and tax administrations seeking greater conceptual clarity in the design of fiscal systems that support innovation.

Robert DANON
Professor of Tax Law, University of Lausanne
Partner, Danon, Lausanne
Chair, Permanent Scientific Committee (PSC), International Fiscal Association (IFA)
Member of the Advisory Committee – European R&D Tax Incentives Project

Table of Contents

Chapter 1
Principles

The 10 Principles outlined below provide a common position on diverging interpretations of R&D and R&D expenditure.

They are the main findings of the research work detailed in the following chapters.

These Principles, and the book in general, deal only with discrepancies in interpretation amongst European Union Member States and do not deal with areas where there is a consistent approach by Member States. For example, the book notes that the requirement for novelty in the definition of R&D is broadly accepted by Member States but divergent approaches as to what is meant by novel and how such novelty must be identified.

1 R&D includes basic research, applied research and experimental developments with or without commercial objectives in all fields of knowledge, including social sciences, digital design, humanities and, when research is involved, the arts.

2 The level of novelty of the R&D is considered both from the perspective of the publicly available knowledge (world's perspective), and the company's private knowledge (firm's perspective).
To achieve a uniform interpretation of novelty, one should consider an expert body at EU level, which could, for instance, build upon the decision of the Boards of Appeal of the European Patent Office.

3 Depreciation expenses relating to assets created or acquired as new (including those used under a leasing agreement) and directly used for research operations are eligible R&D costs.

4 R&D staff include the following categories:

1. researchers educated at university-level who conduct research activities directed by the taxpayer;
2. researchers without university-level education who have a minimum of 4 years documented experience of R&D;
3. other R&D staff such as laboratory technicians who have a minimum of 2 years documented experience of R&D; and
4. support staff necessary to support the above categories of R&D staff.

Where staff participate in both R&D and non-R&D activities, staff costs are allocated to eligible R&D activities based on the proportion of time spent on such activities. All costs relating to R&D staff are eligible R&D expenditure except for profit sharing schemes or return on investment. However, to the extent that a profit-sharing scheme is based on R&D, the relevant proportion of profit-sharing may be eligible R&D expenditure.

5 Standardisation expenses are not eligible R&D expenditure, except where scientific methods are used for the purpose of standardisation. Technology watch connected to research projects is eligible [up to EUR [*amount to be decided*] per year and per taxpayer].

6 Expenses incurred in an EU member state relating to filing, maintenance and the defence of patents are eligible [within a threshold of EUR [*amount to be decided*]]; insurance costs linked to patents are eligible [within a threshold of EUR [*amount to be decided*]]. Intellectual Property (IP) consultant's fees, translation costs and taxes are examples of such expenses.

7 Other operating expenses are eligible R&D expenditure based on their link to R&D activities. Alternatively, a notional deduction of 50% of the research staff expenses could be granted. Services of tax advisors or innovation firms are tax deductible in accordance with general principles but are not eligible R&D expenditure.

8 If R&D activity is outsourced to third parties within the European Economic Area (EEA), these outsourcing expenses are eligible up to a [certain] percentage of the total R&D expenses incurred.

9 The company out-sourcing R&D has priority in claiming R&D tax incentives (if the outsourcing company can claim R&D tax incentives, the R&D contractor cannot also claim).

10 Non-refundable government, state agencies, or EU subsidies or grants related to R&D projects should be deducted from eligible expenses of the year during which these expenses are incurred, and irrespective of the payment date of the subsidies/grants. When these subsidies or grants are refundable, they are added to the basis for calculating the tax incentive for the year in which they are refunded to the organisation that paid.

Chapter 2
Theoretical framework and methodology

SECTION I
Introduction to the Research

This book proposes new solutions to cope with the diverging interpretations of the definition of R&D and of eligible R&D costs, together with a conceptual framework for R&D costs in the course of tax harmonisation, particularly in the EU. The results below are based on a comparative analysis of the reports prepared by National Correspondents of 14 EU Members States and Switzerland on the basis of the legislation and practice in their respective jurisdictions.

The scope of concepts (definitions[1]) is an important issue in international tax law. Some have clear meaning, usually when an applicable tax treaty provides a definition: for instance, Article 5 of the Model OECD Treaty defines a permanent establishment as (in short) a fixed place of business. More often this is not the case, and additionally some concepts are understood differently depending on the tax jurisdiction. While this could be an opportunity for taxpayers (for instance, a financing is considered an equity in one country and a debt in another, creating tax saving opportunities [interests are tax deductible, dividends are not] in the latter), it is also a drawback that should be avoided – situations of double taxation may result precisely from different meanings given to the same concept.

Certainty in the meaning of concepts is an objective for all parties, whether businesses, tax judges, and tax administrations. Therefore, proposing an R&D concept together of those of eligible R&D expenses, particularly in the context of the CCTB is a key task for effective management of costs in businesses and public finance control of tax administrations.

R&D tax regimes of different countries allow taxpayers to benefit, in due course and through many techniques, from a low tax rate for R&D income. Even if the possibility of using a tax advantage for a single research activity twice is carefully monitored at national levels, in a time of public austerity, citizens and

1. A definition is an attempt to describe the concept to which a word refers. See generally, M.F. Otte, L.G.X. de Barros, 'What is the Difference Between a Definition and a Concept?' (2016) 4(5) *Science Journal of Education* 159.

legislators around the globe are now more focused on the erosion of the corporate income tax bases (or rates) resulting from these tax incentive regimes.[2] Any effort to give more consistency, more flesh, to a concept must be greeted. The world is changing but tax systems have been slow to adapt in the same direction. This can hinder economic progress, lead to a loss in tax revenue for governments, and frustrate taxpayers who, in due course, elect officials.

In 2016, the European Commission decided to relaunch the Common (Consolidated) Corporate Tax Base (C(C)CTB) project in a two-step approach, with the publication on 25 October 2016 of two new interconnected proposals on a CCTB and a CCCTB. The 2016 CCTB provides for the determination of a single set of rules for the calculation of the corporate tax base. Companies operating across borders in the EU would no longer have to deal with 27 different sets of national rules when calculating their taxable profits. A single set of rules would apply with respect to the computation of taxable income. Further, the intention is that the proposed double CTB is a first step on the way towards re-establishing the link between taxation and the place where profits are made, via an apportionment formula to be introduced through a new triple CTB proposal, which is the second step.

It is unclear whether the CCTB will be adopted any time soon. Right now, the strategy is directed to a temporary 'quick fix' (such as taxing the digital economy) rather than a comprehensive solution. On 1 January 2019, the Anti-Tax Avoidance Directive (known as ATAD) entered into force. This discourages companies from using excessive interest payments to minimise taxes. It does not specifically target R&D costs. The European Commission proposal, published on 21 March 2018, to tax digital business activities has not been adopted yet.[3] That said, it seems to be the leitmotiv of the Council due to its political impact.[4] This may leave the CCTB proposal behind for some time.[5] At the end of December 2018, EU finance ministers failed to agree on this digital service tax (this requires the support of all 28 EU States, but Ireland and some Nordic countries opposed this tax). This is the reason why the EU Commission launched a debate in early January 2019 on a gradual transition to what it specified would be a more efficient and democratic decision-making in EU tax policy. This transition to qualified majority voting may increase the chance of CCTB being adopted, as it is the fourth step of the Commission's communication, which it aims to develop by the end of 2025.[6]

---

2. In general, tax incentives depart from a general and neutral tax system. See generally, M. Cotrut and K. Munyandi, *Tax Incentives in the BEPS Era*, Tax Research Series, vol. 3, Amsterdam, IBFD, 2018, p. 3 and pp. 73 et seq.
3. Proposal for a Council Directive laying down rules relating to the corporate taxation of a significant digital presence: Proposal for a Council Directive on the common system of a digital services tax on revenues resulting from the provision of certain digital services, COM/2018/0148 final – 2018/073 (CNS).
4. See report of meeting of ECOFIN on 21 January 2020, available at: https://www.consilium.europa.eu/media/42236/st05332-en20.pdf.
5. The President of the European Commission, Ursula von der Leyen, presented her priorities for the incoming European Commission on 9 October 2019 and referred to both digital taxation and the CCCTB. See https://ec.europa.eu/commission/sites/beta-political/files/political-guidelines-next-commission_en.pdf.
6. Communication from the Commission to the European Parliament, the European Council and the Council, 'Towards more efficient and democratic decision making in EU tax policy', COM(2019) 8 final.

The CCTB draft directive of 25 October 2016 provides for a 'super-deduction' for 'costs for research and development' (Article 9.3).[7] With such a 'super deduction', the taxpayer can deduct more than the expenses it incurred. A European Parliament report from 1 March 2018, proposes the deletion of the super-deduction of R&D costs and the introduction instead of a provision, according to which, for R&D costs of less than EUR 20 million that relate to staff, subcontractors, agency workers and freelancers, tax payers will receive a 10% tax credit, based on the costs incurred.[8] This report was adopted with no amendment with respect to the 10% tax credit by a European Parliament legislative resolution dated 15 March 2018 (hereafter the '2018 CCTB').[9] In doing so, the European Parliament added the important and unequivocal assertion that 'a clear definition of the genuine expenses of research and development is needed to avoid misuse of the deductions [sic].'[10]

§ 1 Basic Terminology

Basic tax terminology should be discussed, as a tax credit is not synonymous with a tax deduction.[11] The fundamental differences explained below are important as the 2016 CCTB proposed a tax deduction mechanism, whereas the 2018 CCTB version provides for a tax credit. As a reminder, one could start with the following basic tax equations:

Tax Computation = [(Tax Base x Tax Rate) – Tax Credit/Reduction]

Tax Base = [Income – Tax Deductible Expenses][12]

To determine the exact amount of income tax owed (i.e. tax computation), one multiplies the amount of taxable income (tax base) by one or several tax rates (according to tax rates charts). Roughly speaking, the tax base is gross income minus tax deductions.

The following example illustrates the above. Assume (i) the corporate income tax rate is 33.3% and (ii) R&D expenses are not tax incentivised through deduction. Assume further that a company generates 100 of gross income, and has only 10 of R&D expenses. Its tax base would be 100 – 10 = 90. This is different from its tax liability (i.e. the computation of the tax owed), which is 90 x 33.3% = 30. Assume now that the R&D expenses can be incentivised through a deduction mechanism.

For instance, the R&D effective costs of 10 could be deducted from the tax base by double their amount (i.e. 2 x 10 = 20). The tax base would no longer be of 100 – 10 = 90, but rather of 100 – 20 = 80. The resulting tax liability would be reduced from 30 initially to 26.64. Still, the incentive is computed at the level of the tax base, not of the tax liability.

7. In the 2011 CCCTB version, no R&D tax incentive was provided.
8. European Parliament Report on the draft CCTB directive, doc. No. A8-0050/2018 dated 1 March 2018, see Recital 8 and proposed amendments to Article 9.
9. European Parliament legislative resolution of 15 March 2018 on the proposal for a Council directive on a Common Corporate Tax Base (COM(2016)0685 – C8-0472/2016 – 2016/0337(CNS)).
10. 2018 CCTB, Recital 8.
11. See generally G. Cavalier, Y. Edrey and R. Avi-Yonah, Introduction au droit fiscal français – Théories économiques et droit américain (forthcoming, 2026).
12. E.g. such as R&D expenses.

This is the reason why some tax specialists refer to deductions as 'above the line',[13] i.e. applied before computing the tax liability.[14] Only tax deductions allow for the reduction of the amounts of the income (base) that is subject to income tax. These deductions depend on a variety of factors, such as the nature of the expenses paid during the year. Others are fixed by the government/State (or European bodies in the CCTB context) and may have little relation to any costs incurred. The super-deduction initially envisaged by the Commission enters into this latter category, as it provided an extra 50% deduction of R&D costs, therefore an amount that is above the actual cost incurred and effectively paid.

On the contrary, a tax credit is an amount of money that taxpayers can subtract not from the taxable base, but from the amounts of tax that they themselves owe to their government/State or Treasury (i.e. tax liability). Said otherwise, unlike tax deduction, which reduce the amount of taxable income (i.e. the tax basis), tax credits, reduce the actual amount of tax owned and applied at the tax computation level, not at the tax base computation level. Tax credits are computed 'after the line'.

In other words, a deduction reduces taxable income and the value of the deduction thus depends on the taxpayer's marginal tax rate. It usually rises with income for individual taxpayers (whereas it is usually proportional for corporate taxpayers). Credits reduce taxes directly and do not depend on tax rates. The value of credits may only depend on the taxpayer's basic tax liability: non-refundable credits can reduce tax to zero, but any credit beyond that is lost.[15]

Background

To analyse and comment upon the wording of the CCTB draft, one has to begin by consulting Recital No. 8 of the 2018 CCTB, which provides:

'Measures that incentivise private entities to invest in the real economy should be supported, as the current investment gap in the Union is one of the key sources of its economic weaknesses. At the same time, tax reliefs for companies need to be carefully constructed, and implemented only where their positive impact on jobs and growth is evident and any risk of creating new loopholes in the taxation system is excluded. Therefore, promoting innovation and investment should be done through public subsidies equally available to everybody rather than through tax exemptions'.

13. Others may say that it is tax credits which are 'above the line', i.e. they may be booked in the profit and loss statement of the company; see e.g. R. Danon, 'General report, Tax Incentives on Research and Development' in *Cahier de droit fiscal international*, vol. 100a, International Fiscal Association, Rotterdam, 2015, p 33.
14. See 'tax-deductible' in Collins English Dictionary 2018.
15. See generally, S. Holt, *The Earned Income Tax Credit at Age 30: What we Know*, Washington DC, Brookings Institutions, 2006; E. Maag, *Tax Credits, the Minimum Wage, and Inflation, Tax Policy Issues and Options brief 17*, Washington DC, Urban-Brookings Tax Policy Centre, 2006.

Surprisingly indeed, the above Recital No. 8 seems to promote the German traditional view, which is not favourable to R&D tax incentive as it clearly states that public subsidies should be preferred to 'tax exemptions'.[16] Two terminological remarks have to be made. First, the use in Recital No. 8 of the word 'exemption', which relates to the tax base, is confusing. 'Exemption' usually relates to a situation in which a person or organisation does not have to pay tax on certain income. An exemption does not refer to a deduction from the tax base, but rather to a non-inclusion in the tax base. This latter vocabulary may seem inappropriate for the type of R&D tax incentive envisaged in the CCTB which is concerned with costs, not (exempt) income.

Second, and despite the above, which seems to support the removal of the super-deduction, the 2018 CCTB does not solely remove the super-deduction; it replaces it with a tax credit. In addition, here again, from a technical standpoint, the use of the word 'exemption' (which relates to the tax base) in the Recital No. 8 above, a 'tax credit' in Article 9.3 (which relates to the tax computation) is very confusing. This probably shows the hesitations of the European Parliament, reflecting the debates between its members. Indeed, and from a technical standpoint, a tax credit is usually linked with the tax computation. However, it has been consistently advocated, whether in the 2016 CCTB version or the 2018 CCTB version, that the C(C)CTB proposals concern the corporate tax base and are not meant to harmonise national corporate tax rates which belong to tax computation. Member States would retain their sovereign right to set their own tax rates.[17] Therefore, by introducing a tax credit, it seems that the European Parliament is no longer proposing a provision relating to the tax base, despite clear announcements made and still continuously mentioned in its own European Parliament briefing.[18] This may reveal a philosophical shift.

§ 2 Philosophical Shift

The philosophical shift may result from the above variation in terminology. Does it mean that, for EU institutions, the next step would be to harmonise tax rates? This is far from sure, as the technicalities of this new European Parliament proposal may still be debated and clarified: Germany was pushing for no R&D tax incentive at all in the CCTB.[19] Until recently, Germany was (next to Estonia and Finland) an EU country that did not offer R&D tax incentives in its general rules on business taxation. However, the German National Correspondent at an early stage of this research project noted that 'the implementation of such incentives is discussed among German scholars and the German government stated in its coalition agreement, that an implementation of (not necessarily but most likely tax) incentives shall take place within this legislative period' (i.e. by 2021). A 2016 draft law providing for a tax credit limited to SMEs

16. C.ÁMALKE, I. SCHLIE and C. SPENGEL, 'German report, Tax Incentives on Research and Development' in *Cahier de Droit Fiscal International*, IFA, The Netherlands, 2015, pp. 319 et seq.
17. See e.g. European Parliament, 'Briefing, EU Legislation in Progress, Common corporate tax base (CCTB)', 14 June 2018, p. 11, available at: http://www.europarl.europa.eu/RegData/etudes/BRIE/2017/595907/EPRS_BRI(2017)595907_EN.pdf.
18. See above n. 17.
19. C.W. ERNST, *Evaluation of Tax Incentives for Research and Development in Germany*, Lohmar, EUL Verlag, 2012.

(small and medium-sized enterprises) exists in Germany. And indeed, in February 2019, the German Federal Ministry of Finance also published a draft for a discussion on the development of a bill on tax incentives for R&D, which was finally adopted on 14 December 2019. It therefore hints at what the German position now is.

The philosophical shift may also express a compromise signalling to the EU Council of Ministers the following: that the R&D tax incentive should no longer be lowered nor should it be totally eliminated.[20] The Finish presidency of the European Council (1 July – 31 December 2019), did not relaunch the CCTB process and it is not yet sure if and when it will be relaunched and if a tax incentive provision be maintained. Still, many National Correspondents expressly remained attached to their national R&D tax incentives.[21] The French Ministry of Finance was even in support of preserving the local (ie French) R&D tax credit in addition to the EU super-deduction.[22] In the meantime, some academics expressed concerns about the efficiency, and therefore maintenance, of the French R&D tax credit.[23] Others reacted by paying attention to the possibility that the EU super-deduction for R&D costs could potentially introduce new incentives for profit shifting.[24] However, the European Commission was very clear in its intention: '[If] Member States [...] give a tax credit after the computation of the tax liability [, this] would be in opposition to the spirit of the CCCTB. By granting a tax reduction after the application of formula apportionment they would not ensure a level playing field for R&D in the EU and could induce harmful competition between Member States.

Therefore this option is not retained'.[25]

Said otherwise, if a R&D tax incentive scheme is provided in a European text, such as the CCTB, one could imagine the CJEU deciding to relieve Member States of the possibility of having an additional tax incentive at national level. If nothing technically forbids the cumulate use of the French R&D tax credit (tax computation) and the super-deduction (tax base), national tax credits could become legally null and void, as constituting an obstacle to freedom of

---

20. Just before the summer 2018, German and French EU MPs reached a common position where the CCTB should not feature any tax incentives thus leaving for further discussions the possibility for Member States to provide other tax policy measures 'outside' the scope of the CCTB (e.g. tax credits) and regarding the approximation of corporate tax rates.
21. Hungarian national report.
22. B. Mauchauffé, Head of the strategy department ('sub-directorate BP1') at the Tax Legislation Directorate within the French Ministry of Finance, hearing before the Finance Commission of the French Senate, reported by Albéric de Montgolfier during the 14 December 2016 hearing of the same Commission, available at: http://www.senat.fr/compte-rendu-commissions/201612126fin.html.
23. J.L. Pierre, 'Crédit d'impôt recherche : observations et interrogations sur une dépense fiscale majeure' in *Mélanges Patrick Serlooten*, Paris, Dalloz, 2015, p. 709 (specifically, paras. 18 et seq. on the concept of R&D); *contra*: see 'Études d'impact du crédit d'impôt recherche (CIR) – une revue de la littérature, Rapport à l'attention de Monsieur Thierry Mandon, Secrétaire d'Etat chargé de l'enseignement supérieur et de la recherche', MENESR, 2017, available at : https://cache.media.enseignementsup-recherche.gouv.fr/file/CIR/83/9/Evaluation_CIR_OFCE_avril_2017_755839.pdf.
24. Eurodad, 'Survival of the Richest – Europe's role in supporting an unjust global tax system 2016', 7 December 2016.
25. EU Commission Staff Working Document Impact Assessment, Accompanying the document Proposals for a Council Directive on a Common Corporate Tax Base and a Common Consolidated Corporate Tax Base (CCCTB), 24 October 2016, No. SWD(2016) 341 final, p. 29, § 4.4.2.2 entitled 'Tax credit for R&D expenses'.

establishment. This would be even more accurate if the European Parliament proposal of a tax credit were kept, since it would weaken the argument that the CCTB impacts should only be 'above the line'.

It is therefore probably advisable to adopt an intermediary approach that the 2018 CCTB replaced the super-deduction initially available for a vast variety of research (2016 CCTB), with a 10% tax credit on a very limited number of research costs (notably R&D staff costs) – (Article 9.3, 2018 CCTB). One could make two immediate comments of unequal importance on this 10% tax credit. First, the 10% rate is low compared to most common EU tax credit rates in existing regimes. To list just a few, these tax credits rates are: 14% in Austria, 13.5% at least, in Belgium, 30% in France, 25% in Ireland, 14% in The Netherlands,[26] 32.5% in Portugal,[27] and 25%, at least, in Spain.

Second and more decisively, this proposed tax credit entails a breach of the general policy option laid down by the EU Commission clearly providing that 'a minimum requirement should be that the preferred option maintains the current tax incentives for R&D expenses. Incentives going beyond the current levels in the EU need to be balanced against the revenue costs for providing such incentives'.[28]

Even more clearly, the same document concluded that 'tax credits reduce directly the tax bill and therefore do not vary with the tax rate. However, tax credits go beyond the scope of the common base'.[29] This is the reason why the tax credit option was not kept initially, taking into consideration the different approaches in Europe and other parts of the world.

§ 3 Different Approaches

As a preliminary point, it should be noted that the current book does not deal with the decision to opt, at EU level, for a super deduction or for a tax credit. It only addresses the more general and conceptual question of 'what notion of R&D activity should be, and the costs associated thereto' at European level. This question was valid for the super-deduction of R&D expenses. It is still valid for a R&D tax credit and for many tax incentives. The research focuses on input incentives (e.g. R&D tax credits and super-deductions), but increasingly EU countries also have very attractive special IP tax regimes, and in particular the patent box[30] also known as IP box regime, the innovation box or the IP box. These special tax IP regimes aim at fostering R&D by providing preferential treatment for income from qualified intangible assets.[31] This is why there

26. For expenses above EUR 350,000.
27. And 47.5% for start-ups (see https://www.oecd.org/sti/rd-tax-stats-portugal.pdf).
28. Commission Staff Working Document. Impact Assessment – Accompanying the document 'Proposals for a Council Directive on a Common Corporate Tax Base and a Common Consolidated Corporate Tax Base (CCCTB)', (COM(2016) 683 final), (SWD(2016) 342 final), p. 23.
29. *Ibid.*, p. 28.
30. So-called because there is a box to tick on the patent boxes tax qualifying profits.
31. R. Danon, 'General report, Tax Incentives on Research and Development' in *Cahier de droit fiscal international*, vol. 100a, 2015, p. 33.

are so-called 'output tax incentives'.[32] In the early 1970s, Ireland introduced an exemption from tax on patent royalties for Irish-resident companies and individuals. Section 34 Finance Act 1973 allowed total tax relief in respect of royalties and other sums from Irish patents. This regime was criticised by the Code of Conduct Group on Business Taxation – the so-called Primarolo group – in 1999.[33] The exemption was the subject of progressive anti-avoidance measures in Ireland until its eventual abolition in 2011 as a result of a review which concluded that it had been used as a tax-efficient way of remunerating employees.[34] Several countries followed Ireland's example, including France in the early 1980s. This system was criticised both by the EU (Economic and Financial Affairs Council (Ecofin) assessment 2014) and the OECD under its Base Erosion and Profit Shifting (BEPS) project, since it was suspected of being used as a BEPS tool, to lower corporate taxes. Therefore, the OECD and the BEPS Action item 5 promoted the so-called 'modified nexus approach' under which there must be a direct link between the income benefiting from the preferential treatment in that country and the R&D expenditure incurred there and contributing to that income. In other words, the favourable tax treatment of IP income must be linked to the underlying R&D activities undertaken by the taxpayer in the country where it obtains preferential tax treatment. These incentives have been (or should have been) amended in order to comply with this approach. This was the case in France with respect to its Finance Law of 2019, which offers a reduced (10%) tax rate applicable on annual net income calculated after deducting R&D expenses for the year related to the assets generating this income. Even more importantly, it is only a fraction of the net result which is intended to be effectively subject to a reduced rate; that is where the nexus approach makes sense, because it is not enough to have research revenue and research expenditures: it is still necessary that these expenses and revenues be well connected to the research activity of the taxpayer that receives the income.

Generally, therefore, such output incentives' tax benefits are applied on revenues, and not on expenses as for R&D tax credit or tax deduction. The Frascati Manual's definition comes into play of course, but as a starting point as it is not always the same definition of research as for input incentives, even in the same countries. However, in order to define 'research' for purposes of this output tax incentive, the French draft administrative guidelines make direct reference to its R&D tax credit guidelines (i.e. input tax incentive).[35] This makes even more relevant the efforts to encourage a common understanding within Europe.

32. See § 3.I in this section.
33. See https://ec.europa.eu/taxation_customs/sites/taxation/files/resources/documents/primarolo_en.pdf. Section 32 Finance Act 1996 imposed an arm's length test for the exemption of royalties.
34. Minister for Finance, Michael Noonan, on 16 February 2012 https://www.kildarestreet.com/wrans/?id=2012-02-16.725.0.
35. See BOI-BIC-BASE-110-10-20190717, No. 140.

I. Europe and Other Parts of the World

The European Commission issued a 2014 report entitled 'A Study on R&D Tax Incentives'.[36] It stressed that 'R&D tax incentives schemes are widely adopted in advanced economies, including innovation leaders like the United States and Japan'.[37] Trying to decrease its innovation gap against these two countries, the EU aimed at becoming more innovative.[38] Among the tools used, in most EU countries are tax incentives. Indeed, from an economic standpoint, tax incentives for R&D expenditure reward firms for the social benefits that they themselves are unable to appropriate from innovation. Firms in industries with high R&D orientation and in sectors with high market concentration are on average more responsive to fiscal incentives to R&D.[39]

R&D process can be divided into two phases, the one requiring expenditure (identification of a problem, development of a solution), and the one bringing revenue (launch of the product into the market) to the taxpayer. Accordingly, there are two types of tax incentives depending on the timing of their effect in the R&D process, they focus either on cost deduction, or on lowering of tax on income generated by the research (e.g. patent income).

The first category of tax incentives includes the so-called 'input incentives' and comes into play when expenses are incurred. These incentives typically include super-deductions (enhanced allowances), tax credits, and accelerated depreciations. Super-deduction and tax credit have been discussed above. Accelerated depreciation is an incentive that allows the taxpayer to depreciate qualified purchased assets at a higher rate in earlier fiscal periods. As a result, this will reduce the taxable base or generate, as the case may be, carry forward losses.

The second category of tax incentives are called 'output incentive', commonly known as 'patent boxes'.[40] They would typically provide a preferential treatment for income from qualified intangible assets. Since the debate around patent boxes now focuses on revenue losses for the Treasury without a commensurate increase in innovation and R&D for society,[41] the European Commission concluded that patent boxes, which introduce a preferential rate for income from innovations that are already protected by IP rights ('IPRs'),

36. European Commission, 'A Study on R&D Tax Incentives, Final Report', November 2014, available at: https://ec.europa.eu/futurium/en/system/files/ged/28-taxud-study_on_rnd_tax_incentives_-_2014.pdf.
37. *Ibid.*, p. 5.
38. Eurostat, 'Smarter, greener, more inclusive? – Indicators to support the Europe 2020 strategy', 2015, p. 68, available at: http://ec.europa.eu/eurostat/documents/3217494/6655013/KS-EZ-14-001-EN-N.pdf/a5452f6e-8190-4f30-8996-41b1306f7367.
39. I. Bodas Freitas, F. Castellacci, R. Fontana, F. Malerba and A. Vezzulli, 'The additionality effects of R&D tax credits across sectors: A cross-country microeconometric analysis', Working Papers on Innovation Studies, Centre for Technology, Innovation and Culture, University of Oslo, 2015.
40. See *supra*, p. 11, under § 3 Different Approaches.
41. See generally, M.A. Sullivan, 01-A History Lesson for a Future Patent Box', *Tax Notes International*, 7 September 2015, p. 823; A. Gupta, 'Boxing the Box: Patent boxes Take Center Stage at IFA Congress' , *Tax Notes International*, 7 September 2015; in French: W. Chaiehloudj, 'Les stratégies fiscales de l'industrie pharmaceutique. Regard sur l'attractivité des Patent Boxes et la pratique des corporate inversion tax deals' (2016) 1 *Propriété industrielle*, study No. 2.

raise concerns when they are used as a tool for profit shifting. IPRs enable firms to capture a large part of the social benefits their products offer; as such, the need for a tax incentive for protected innovations becomes unclear. The issue was partially addressed in the OECD/G20 BEPS action plan, aiming at reconciling substance and form. The 'modified nexus approach' specifically reunites income and substantial activity. More precisely, the tax benefit for income derived from IPRs should be proportional to the IPRs owner's own R&D expenditures. Tax benefits from IPRs acquisitions and outsourced R&D can also be claimed but are limited to a combined 30% of the IPRs owner's own R&D expenditures. Therefore, the current book does not address 'output incentives' further.

II. Super-Deduction, Tax Credit, or Accelerated Depreciation

The relative benefits and drawbacks of a super-deduction, versus a tax credit or accelerated depreciation could be assessed through the practice of the Member States in the EU. The European Commission analysed and benchmarked more than 80 tax incentives schemes in 31 countries.[42] Tax credits are the most widely used tax incentive (in 21 countries), while super-deductions can be found in 16 countries, and accelerated depreciations in 13 countries. The reason why these numbers differ might arguably be that popularity of each incentive depends on its impact on public finance.

The underlying issue relates to public finance theories.[43] In order to assess whether public funds should support R&D, the question is how such support such as Adam Smith's Wealth of Nations (1776): the ability to pay, fairness, simplicity, and efficiency are the four basic tenets of a 'good tax system'.[44] In addition, and linked to the more modern theories on public choice,[45] there is a need for a tax system to minimise interference with economic decisions (the 'neutrality' principle): participants of the tax system should face the same choice options and decisions – on sums to invest, location, the employment of more or less labour, etc. – should be made on their economic merits and not for tax reasons. However, a neutral tax system is not always efficient.[46] Indeed, the encouragement of certain behaviour may have high social returns justifying the discriminatory treatment of certain activities. This is the reason why Germany requests full accounting of revenue losses attributable to provisions of federal income tax laws.[47]

---

42. European Commission, 'A Study on R&D Tax Incentives', Final Report, 28 November 2014, p. 56.
43. See section II of this book, 'Theoretical Framework'.
44. M. Myrsky, What Does a Good Tax System Require?, Yearbook for Nordic Tax Research 2012, p 169.
45. R. Musgrave and A. Peacock, *Classics in the Theory of Public Finance*, New York, St Martin's Press, 1958; D. Mueller, 'Public Choice: A Survey' (1976) *Journal of Economic Leterature*, p. 395.
46. An opposite reason for departing from neutrality is when private actors in the economy do not bear the full social cost of their activities (e.g. environmentally harmful activities).
47. See B. Bittker, 'Accounting for federal "tax subsidies" in the National Budget' (1969) *National Tax Journal*, p. 244; S. Surrey and W. Hellmuth, 'The Tax Expenditure Report – Response to Professor Bittker' (1969) *National Tax Journal*, p. 528.

This also explains why the European Commission concluded that tax incentives should ideally apply to those types of expenditures that bring about strong knowledge spill-overs. More notably, it recommended, as regards the type of incentive and its tax basis, 'to provide a carry-over facility and an option to receive the benefit even in case a company is not profitable (cash refunds)'.

Since some types of expenses are likely to generate higher knowledge spill-overs than other types of R&D expenditure, the European Commission concluded that it is good practice to provide for '[t]ax incentives based on the wage bill paid to researchers [...] because [...] researchers move from one employer to another and take their former's employers knowledge with them'.[48]

The European Commission concluded in terms of 'best practice principles' that 'volume-based R&D tax should be designed to be efficient and to comply with the legal requirements of EU law and in national laws. This question is not only relevant in EU law. It originates in the works of early social philosophers, credits are preferred over incremental ones'.[49] The 2018 CCTB proposal introducing a 10% tax credit in lieu of the initial super-deduction is in line with such good practices. Another reason to prefer a tax credit is that, unlike a super-deduction that may affect tax rates, tax credits do not lead to tax-rate adjustment.[50] As to the basis for the tax credit, the 2018 CCTB proposal preferred to limit it to wage costs, probably bearing in mind the general trend of lowering corporate tax rates in Europe.[51] Indeed, it is generally considered that a tax system using a broad tax base with a low tax rate is more efficient than a system with higher tax rates on smaller bases. This is certainly an argument for minimising tax expenditures.

The design of the above tax incentives currently raises several other concerns that are not addressed in the current book.[52] One of these concerns is linked with the increasingly cross-border context in which intangible and new business models operate in Europe. Often, one can observe a split within a company between R&D functions or incomes and production or commercial

48. European Commission, 'A Study on R&D', p. 6.
49. *Ibid.*, indeed, tax credits are implemented in two different ways: volume-based or incremental. Volume-based schemes apply to all qualified R&D expenditure, while incremental schemes only apply to increases in R&D expenditure. In the latter case, the base amount on which the increment is calculated is a firm's average expenditure either in some fixed period of time (for example between 2010 and 2012) or during the past few years (for example the last 3 years).
50. *Ibid.*, p. 75.
51. E.g. France; the UK. In general, corporate tax rate in the European Union is expected to decrease: see https://tradingeconomics.com/european-union/corporate-tax-rate (accessed on 20 January 2019).
52. For a review of the literature, see P. Arginelli, 'Innovation through R&D Tax Incentives: Some Ideas for a Fair and Transparent Tax Policy' (2015) 7(1) *World Tax Journal* 3; N. Noked, *Integrated Tax Policy Approach to Designing Research & Development Tax Benefits*, Discussion paper No. 57, 2014, Harvard John M Olin Fellow's Discussion Paper Series (available at http://www.law.harvard.edu/programs/olin_center/fellows_papers/pdf/Noked_57.pdf (accessed on 16 August 2018); M. Graetz and R. Doud, 'Technological innovation, international competition and the challenges of international income taxation' (2010) *Columbia Law Review*, p. 407.

activities.[53] This issue is targeted by transfer pricing rules,[54] but may also be addressed by other tax rules, to be designed, and that may pave the way for future ELI work.

Bearing in mind the aforementioned, the 2018 CCTB provision that '[a] clear definition of genuine expenses of research and development is needed to avoid misuse of the deductions'[55] is noteworthy. This assertion should remain true whether a super-deduction mechanism or a tax credit one is adopted, and even whether the CCTB is adopted or not: a theoretical framework is indeed necessary.

Section II
Theoretical Framework

By providing an R&D tax incentive, the 2016 and 2018 CCTBs seek to promote a European view of what the EU considers a 'fair' distribution of public goods in the innovation sector. Although the 2016 CCTB defines 'research and development' (Article 4.11) as including basic research, applied research, and experimental development, there is no precise list of costs which should, or should not, be taken into account for purposes of the 'super deduction'. Should research in the social sciences, humanities or even the arts be viewed in Europe as a better social good and be promoted though public finance? This could be a highly debatable question. In the drafting phase of the 2011 proposal for a directive for a CCTB, the Commission did not consider seeking consensus on an EU-wide definition of R&D for tax purposes: R&D support is marginally mentioned in a 2007 CCCTB working group paper, but no R&D incentive was found in due course in the 2011 proposal.[56]

This contrasts sharply with discussions nowadays. First, patent box regimes were not as common and widespread then as today. Second, as the 2011 proposal was 'only' optional for companies and not intended to increase tax charges for companies or lower tax revenues for EU Member State, simplicity and the ease of administration (for both companies and tax administrations) was a high priority for the work on the CCCTB. It was also an important

53. For example, in the famous 'Conversant International Ltd case' (Supreme Administrative Court (Conseil d'État, 11 December 2020, case no. 420174), and although no R&D was particularly involved, a company which seat was in Ireland provided online marketing services in Europe and for which its French subsidiary providing assistance including the identification and prospection of potential French customers, for a cost plus 8% remuneration.

54. These rules ensure that the price at which related parties located in different tax jurisdictions transact is a market price (arm's length principle).

55. See Recital 8. The word 'deductions' may be replaced by the ones of 'tax credits'. The French version of the document uses the word 'charges' which shows a certain inconsistency in the terminology.

56. CCCTB working group paper dated 27 July 2011 and entitled 'CCCTB: possible elements of a technical outline' (CCCTB/WP057/doc/en), especially p. 9, n. 14 providing: 'This effectively gives 100% deduction of research and development expenditure even when of a capital nature'. See generally the background documents for the preparation of the 2011 CCCTB proposal, available at: https://ec.europa.eu/taxation_customs/business/company-tax/common-consolidated-corporate-tax-base-ccctb/preparation-2011-ccctb-proposal_en.

objective to tackle obstacles for doing business in the Single Market and making the EU an attractive and competitive place for EU companies and foreign direct investors.

Since then, however, a lot of water has flowed under the bridge: Rules introduced by BEPS, in general, and from the ATAD 1 and 2, in particular on the Common Base, triggered the need for a balanced approach. It was therefore decided to insert new measures into the CCTB project, such as temporary loss set-off, notional interest (Allowance for Growth and Investment) and the R&D super reduction.[57]

Today, across countries, the input incentive bases typically used are R&D costs (most countries), especially wages, and IP costs.[58] A distinction is usually drawn between current expenditure (wages, salaries of R&D staff, cost of materials, etc.) and capital expenditure (cost of equipment and facilities used for R&D purposes). For instance, in Finland, only wages and salaries of R&D staff are taken into account, other current (cost of materials, etc.) and capital expenditures being excluded. However, many questions remain. For R&D staff cost? How should staff costs be defined? Do they include bonuses, benefits in kind and compulsory social security contributions? What happens to assets, which are only partly used for R&D eligible projects? A further distinction could be made based on sub contracted R&D expenses and expenses for R&D that were directly and personally carried out by the taxpayer.

Along with the inquiry as to which costs should be included, one could request some precision as to the definition of R&D itself. Indeed, one recital of the proposed CCTB directive mentions the goals of the 'super-deduction' as being '[t]o support innovation in the economy and modernise the internal market'.[59] Therefore, national tax administrations could argue that costs associated with research which do not have any particular application or use that benefits the economy or leads to the modernisation of the internal market, may not qualify for the 'super-deduction'. However, taxpayers may well argue the contrary, based on some European national tax heritages, which foster basic research with no commercial objective. This is one example of the debates that may occur as regards the goal (impacting the definition) of 'research and development' for CCTB purposes.

Each different national interpretation will probably guide each national tax administration in construing Article 9.3 of the proposed CCTB directive. The result may well be very different approach in construing the super-deduction. Of course, the ECJ may in due course unify the diverging interpretations, but this may take years whereas certainty is needed now in a very sensitive area for business and national budgets.

57. Thanks are due to Uwe Ihli, Head of Section – Corporate Tax Directives and Common Consolidated Corporate Tax Base with the European Commission for very useful insights.
58. European Commission, A Study on R&D Tax Incentives, Final Report, November 2014, https://ec.europa.eu/futurium/en/system/files/ged/28-taxud-study_on_rndtax_incentives_-_2014.pdf, Tables 5.2 & 5.3, pp 57–58.
59. Recital No. 8.

As a preliminary issue, why use tax incentives rather than direct subsidies? Financing R&D projects that would have been undertaken by an enterprise even without external financing is a waste of resource, as public spending will not help to create new R&D. 'Hence, the most cost-effective way would be to single out those projects where the social but not the private benefit exceeds the social costs.'[60] This may support direct subsidies where governmental agencies evaluate each R&D projects by weighing private and social return. However, there is no guarantee that the government is in a better position to make that assessment than the market. On the contrary, the market would be less vulnerable to the demands of special interest groups than the government. Besides, direct subsidies are associated with more uncertainty and higher administrative costs. The conclusion is that it is difficult to favour direct subsidies over tax incentives or not. However, this choice in Europe has to be made bearing in mind the State aid prohibition. In certain cases, tax incentive will make it possible to avoid a State Aid characterisation whereas a direct subsidy would clearly be within the scope off the prohibition. This can induce Member States to develop a bias in favour of implementing economic policies through tax incentives rather than direct subsidy.[61]

The purpose of this book is neither to decide whether to favour direct subsidies over tax incentives, nor is it to decide, from among the various tax incentives, which one should prevail. Its main purpose is to propose new solution to solve the diverging interpretations of the definition of R&D for tax purposes and the definition of eligible R&D costs. How to promote such uniform interpretation in Europe?

Section III
Methodology

In this methodology section, an emphasis is placed on short answers to several questions; the first is: why compare national approach with respect to R&D tax incentives? Comparative law has been considered to be the necessary instrument for a desirable harmonisation of law in general within the EU.[62] With respect to tax law, this is not always expressly mentioned in legislative works, due perhaps to the need to preserve sovereignty.[63]

---

60. A. Hansson and C. Brokelind, 'Tax Incentives, Tax Expenditures Theories in R&D: the Case of Sweden' (2014) 6(2) *World Tax Journal* 168, p. 170, at 176.
61. For this view, see G. Tar, 'Considérations sur le choix, par un Etat membre de l'Union européenne ou de l'Espace économique européen, entre une réduction d'impôt ou une subvention pour mener à bien une politique économique' (2016) 2 *Eur & Int'l J'l of Tax Law*, p. 256.
62. M. Van Hoecke, 'Methodology of Comparative Legal Research' (2015) *Law and Method*; R. Saleilles, 'Droit civil et droit comparé' (1911) *Revue inter. enseignement*, p. 22; E. Rabel, 'Aufgabe und Notwendigkeit der Rechtsvergleichung' (1924) *Rheinische Zeitschrift für Zivil-und Prozessrecht*, p. 279–301, reprinted in H.G. Leser (ed.), *Ernst Rabel Gesammelte Aufsätze*, vol. III, *Arbeiten zur Rechtsvergleichung und zur Rechtsvereinheitlichung 1919–1954*, Tübingen, J.C.B. Mohr, 1967, pp. 1–21; P. Pescatore, 'Le recours dans la jurisprudence de la Cour de justice des Communautés européennes à des normes déduites de la comparaison des droits des Etats membres' (1980) *Rev. int'l dr. comp.*, p. 337.
63. In the French language, see J.-F. Boudet, *Manuel de droit fiscal comparé*, Brussels, Bruylant, 2021. See also P. Di Malta, *Droit fiscal européen comparé*, Paris, PUF, 1995.

From a methodological point of view, the interpretation of the concepts can be based on existing (preparatory) work (this method is developing in the European Union), but also as a law that keeps pace the international evolutions (notably the OECD)[64] and perhaps not only tax work for the case of R&D: indeed the Frascati's manual is a tool primarily statistical. This methodology would aim to improve the quality of European tax law.[65]

Questionnaires are common tools in comparative work.

The next methodological question is about selecting the tax systems to be compared. Usually, researchers in comparative law make a choice partly on the basis of their knowledge of languages: this explains why most comparative research in the Anglo-Saxon world is focusing on comparing common-law countries that still use English as their (main) official language. This would not be relevant for a European comparative tax research, but the English language is still a federative device to pursue harmonisation of law. The methodology therefore consisted in contacting local scholars, judges or lawyers primarily able to carry out research in the English language. A well-elaborated and valuable network of tax experts has thus been built. Each respondent has the qualification to answer the questionnaire: most are tax academics, but the team members also include tax judges and other tax practitioners. All these team members have been selected based on their expertise in the tax field, notably tax incentives, and based on their command of the English language. Such diverse participation is not always easy to reach as involving so many people in a still time-consuming task remains a challenge. One very active team member is a transfer pricing expert involved in academic research. The communication within the team was intense and qualitatively good.

A country selection was made in order to focus the available resources on the most meaningful jurisdictions. Thirteen (13) EU countries and Switzerland were selected based on their R&D spending in 2014. This is easily accessible through Eurostat data.[66] These Eurostat's statistics on R&D expenditure are compiled using guidelines laid out in the Frascati Manual. Based on the R&D spending, it is not necessary at this stage to have Cyprus or Malta represented in the study.[67] 'Innovation leaders' include Germany and Finland in Europe.[68] Portugal, Estonia and Latvia have shown the most improvement over the past few years, but are not classified as 'regional innovation leaders'.[69] These regional innovation leaders are located in only eight Member States, and consist

64. D. Gutmann, *Sources et ressources de l'interprétation juridique – Étude de droit fiscal*, Paris, LGDJ, 2023, e.g. no. 120.
65. See generally B. Ricou (dir.), *Regards croisés sur la qualité de la législation fiscale*, Paris, LexisNexis, 2022.
66. Eurostat, 'R&D expenditure in the EU stable at slightly over 2% of GDP in 2014', 209/2015, 30 November 2015.
67. Cyprus (83 million euro) and Malta (67 million euro). The highest shares of R&D expenditure performed in the business sector were observed in Slovenia (77%), Ireland (73%), Hungary (72%), Belgium and Austria (both 71%), Germany and Finland (both 68%), Sweden (67%), Bulgaria and France (both 65%), Denmark and the United Kingdom (both 64%).
68. Eurostat, 'Smarter, greener, more inclusive? – Indicators to support the Europe 2020 strategy', 2015, p. 68, available at http://ec.europa.eu/eurostat/documents/3217494/6655013/KS-EZ-14-001-EN-N.pdf/a5452f6e-8190-4f30-8996-41b1306f7367.
69. Their innovation performance index increased by more than 25% between 2006 and 2013. *Ibid.*

of Denmark, Germany, Finland, France, Ireland, the Netherlands, Sweden and the United Kingdom. Although the UK is a large R&D spender, it is not represented in our study. The reason has not to be found in the Brexit. Although this project is primarily sponsored by the ELI which is a European institute, not an EU institution, and despite the fact that the UK is in Europe, it is also true that the Brexit should not make the CCTB as relevant to the UK as for France, Germany, or Ireland. Switzerland is included as a good comparative indicator for both practical and scientific reasons: our preface writer, Prof. Robert Danon, was the general reporter of the 69th Congress of the International Fiscal Association (Basel, 2015) on the subject No. 1 entitled 'Tax incentives on research and development (R&D)'. Switzerland is a country where EU law is closely followed, even sometimes in its tax developments. However, the availability of specific national R&D tax incentive was not a criteria, as the EU-designed tax incentive would, in due course and if adopted, be applied in these countries as well. Germany, Estonia, or Switzerland for instance, have or had no specific tax incentive for R&D and Germany especially is nonetheless a major player in Europe in innovation. Although an increasing number of States currently favour tax incentives over direct subsidies to support R&D, and Switzerland may follow this trend[70], one should not underweight Germany in the design of this EU tax incentive, since tax convergence within the EU in the field of direct taxation of corporation is the initiative of both France and Germany.[71] Represented countries are therefore: Austria, Belgium, Croatia, France, Germany, Greece, Hungary, Ireland, Italy, Luxembourg, Poland, Spain, and Switzerland.

In these countries, the questionnaire was sent to our team members.

The third methodological question was to inquire about what has to be compared. Not only 'tax legislation' was taken into account, but much attention was paid to judicial decisions and the way tax R&D incentives apply in practice. Therefore, and largely because of time constraints which did not allow the research team to do a full comparative work in the drafting phase of the questionnaire, the latter was drafted essentially based on existing case law and administrative guidelines available to the reporters. Given the time frame and team resource availability, the French R&D tax credit (*crédit d'impôt recherche*) was worthy of an example. First because this corpus is well known to the core members of the group, and also because France has a very well-advanced system working for several decades now. The questionnaire listed possible R&D expenses that could be viewed as eligible to the CCTB super deduction.

Each item of this list has then been subject to comments, approval or refusal by our team members across Europe. Based on these initial answers, a refined list has been produced, and sent for further comments.

---

70. *Switzerland* is considering introducing by 2020 a R&D tax incentive in *Tax Proposal 17* at cantonal level (still being discussed at the time of drafting of this *Statement*).
71. See for instance, R. Kruse and F. Riester, 'Pour un code européen des affaires', *Le Monde*, 5 May 2018, Chapter 'Idées', p. 7 and also published in the *Handelsblatt* journal, 5 May 2018, No. 92, p. 15. In the European Business Code project leaded by France and Germany, a tax section is envisaged.

Finally, the comparison has used the so-called 'functional method'.[72] It offers one concrete guideline in that it suggests focusing on (common) legal problems and legal solutions in the compared legal systems, rather than on the (diverging) rules and doctrinal frameworks. Based on their national law (this being understood as comprising also case law and tax administrative guidelines), each respondent answers to the best of their knowledge the attached questionnaire for the purpose of interpretation of Articles 4(11) and 9.3 of the CCTB directive. Therefore, in reporting their national law system, they have assessed (positively and/or negatively) and explained their position with respect to particular expenses, and therefore they have proposed their own interpretation of Article 9.3 with their own tax background.

72. K. Zweigert and H. Kötz (translation T. Weir), *An introduction to Comparative Law*, Oxford, Clarendon Press, 1998, p. 35.

Chapter 3
Commentaries

Section I
The Notion of R&D

> Principle No. 1:
>
> R&D includes basic research, applied research and experimental developments with or without commercial objectives in all fields of knowledge, including social sciences, digital design, humanities and, where research is involved, the arts.

Research is usually presented as a legal concept as soon as a result is found. It is only when the researcher becomes a finder that the benefit from certain legal protection is available and/or that the finder is subject to legal duties (e.g. confidentiality). However, as regards tax law, a researcher that is not yet a finder may well benefit from certain tax incentives. A tax credit is also a mean to compensate the taxpayers for the technical risks they are willing to take and the associated development efforts. In most jurisdictions, a R&D project that is stopped because of technical difficulties can still be eligible for a tax credit. For instance, many pharmaceutical R&D projects do not yield results. Research is therefore a tax concept not only during the results phase, but also during the activity phase. What does R&D mean precisely?

The Frascati Manual provides the definition of research and experimental development (R&D) and of its three components: basic research, applied research, and experimental developments. These definitions have been criticised for not being sufficiently clear and objective. For instance, the central distinction between basic and applied research appears highly dependent on the subjective attitude of the researcher. In addition, many projects may often include both basic (synonymous for fundamental) and applied aspects that do not easily fit in either category.

§ 1 No Commercial Objective?

I. Background

As mentioned above, the Frascati Manual[73] provides that R&D covers three types of activity: basic research, applied research and experimental development.

Basic research (also known as 'fundamental research') is experimental or theoretical work undertaken primarily to acquire new knowledge of the underlying foundations of phenomena and observable facts, without any particular application or use in view. Applied research is an original investigation undertaken in order to acquire new knowledge. Experimental development is systematic work, drawing on knowledge gained from research and practical experience and producing additional knowledge, directed to creating new products or processes or to improving existing products or processes. Most R&D tax credit claims fall in that last category. Public scientific organisations (i.e. receiving public funding and not subject to corporate tax) pursue usually fundamental (i.e. basic) and applied research programs. However, among the above main categories, some refinements could be proposed.

Should research for tax incentive purposes be limited to applied research and experimental development, thus excluding fundamental research? In other words, should a commercial objective be a condition of the R&D tax incentive? Half a century ago, basic research was often called 'pure science' or simply 'science'. Scientific research is then perceived as a search for truth that ought to be as free as possible from the interference not only of particular economic, but also of political, ideological and religious interests. Of course, resources for basic research could be justified because of possible 'positive output consequences' but also simply 'because it is a pleasurable activity'. This Weberian ideal type science was championed right after World War II. The defenders were people like the Austrian Karl Popper, or the American Robert Merton. In Europe, the scientific tradition was more seen as a crucial support for liberal democracy against totalitarian regimes or as a barrier against the latter. This was the original view.

This classical liberal ideal of science was eroded in the sixties. At that time, a new theory primarily interested in contributing to economic growth emerged. The focus of science policy had shifted to economic growth and development. Science was recognised as a fundamental motor in economic growth and supported by public money on a scale unknown before the War. Therefore, the democratic control of science then appeared more important than its autonomy. In addition, the distinction between basic and applied research reflects the difference between science and politics as social institutions. Science is dedicated to managing and increasing knowledge of overall validity, whereas politics' role is to produce agreement and ensure collective action. It is in

73. Frascati Manual, §2.9.

applied science that science and politics best interact. Applied science depends highly on advanced scientific knowledge and methods, but it is dedicated to the solution of practical economics.[74]

II. Should Research with No Commercial Objective Qualify for Tax Incentives?

In the US for instance, such a direct link with a commercial objective is necessary to benefit from a US tax credit.[75] Indeed, research qualifying for the purposes of section 41 of the Internal Revenue Code means research which 'is undertaken for the purpose of discovering information which is technological in nature, and the application of which is intended to be useful in the development of a new or improved business component of the taxpayer'.[76] However, R&D expenditure that initially is 'unsuccessful', whether in terms of the research objective or commercially, may nonetheless result in an advance in knowledge. This intermediate knowledge could be later used in projects that yield advances in other areas, processes, or practical applications and even result in commercial success. Even in the US, there is no absolute opposition to provide some kind of tax incentive to fundamental research.[77] The German Correspondents even confirmed that '[t]he closer R&D comes to improvement of existing technology, the less it qualifies as really innovative'. This is also the view taken by the French Correspondent.

For the same reasons, all National Correspondents believe that the position taken by Article 4 of the CCTB proposal is correct in so far as it includes fundamental research. This is not the case though for all EU domestic legislations.

III. Discussion

According to the jurisdictions under review, and unlike in the US, a 'commercial objective' requirement to qualify for R&D incentives would not be necessary in Europe. Most of the National Correspondents answered that R&D should include basic (fundamental) research, which expands to pure basic research. R&D for CCTB should therefore generate new knowledge as an output, irrespective of its purpose, which could be the generation of economic benefits, addressing societal challenges or simply generating knowledge in itself.[78] The Finnish Correspondent mentions that in order to apply (or likely construe) the Finnish R&D super-deduction that was only applicable between the 2013-2014 tax years, it is required that the R&D activity is carried on for the benefit of (one's own) business but no other conditions regarding the intended or realised application were set. This view is closer to the US approach

74. N. Roll-Hansen, 'Why the distinction between basic (theoretical) and applied (practical) research is important in the politics of science?', AHRC, 2009.
75. US IRC, §41 ('in carrying on any trade or business') or §174 ('in connection with his trade or business').
76. US IRC, section 41 (d)(1)(B).
77. S. Shay, J. Clifton Fleming and R.J. Peroni, 'R&D Tax Incentives: Growth Panacea or Budget Trojan Horse?' (2016) 69 *Tax Law Rev*, pp. 419–432.
78. Frascati Manual, §1.16.

where it should be 'in connection with his trade or business'. The Italian Correspondent added that it is difficult to determine *a priori* the result of R&D activities, and therefore R&D should include all activities, irrespective of their application or use. Such unanimity is interesting as this would distinguish the European approach of R&D, which will include fundamental research, from the American tax concept of R&D.[79]

§ 2 Social Sciences, Humanities (Including the Arts?)

Should R&D be limited to the industrial sector or also include social sciences, humanities, and the arts? The latter group should not be confused with the 'service sector', which is much broader (for instance communications or energy supply belong to the service sector, but not necessarily to social sciences, humanities, or the arts).[80] The service sector amounts to 60% of the world economy, and more than 75% in most developed national economies. Is it thus not surprising that the largest portion of research expenses for the US R&D tax credit is for services.[81] To be precise, the question is usually not the inclusion of services into the R&D credit but rather the inclusion of part of the service sector, i.e. social sciences, humanities and arts, within the R&D tax credit.

One could consider, for instance, the following activities: the development of new theories of financial risks (basic research activity); the study of new types of algorithms enabling insurance or savings contracts to cover risks linked to different markets in a new way (applied research); the development of a software or risk management service based on a new financial algorithm (experimental development). Should all or only some of these activities pertaining to social sciences, humanities, and the arts be included in the definition of R&D for tax purposes?[82] Alternatively, should a distinction be made for tax purposes between social sciences and humanities on the one hand, or the arts on the other hand?

I. Background

If these endeavours, together with all scientific and technological developments, are subject to tax subsidies through the R&D allowance, it could mean that almost every activity potentially qualifies for R&D tax credits. If this is the case, the financial burden of R&D could become unsustainable and the

79. S. Shay, J. Clifton Fleming and R.J. Peroni, 'R&D Tax Incentives: Growth Panacea or Budget Trojan Horse?' (2016) 69 *Tax Law Rev*, p 419.
80. §2.41. Moreover, p. 59 of the Frascati Manual (2015 edition) provides the following classification of 'Social sciences': '(1) Psychology and cognitive sciences, (2) Economics and business, (3) Education, (4) Sociology, (5) Law, (6) Political sciences, (7) Social and economic geography, (8) Media and communications, (9) Other social sciences. As to 'Humanities and the arts', it distinguishes (1) History and archaeology, (2) Languages and literature, (4) Philosophy, ethics and religion, (5) Arts (arts, history of arts, performing arts, music), (6) Other humanities'. For further differences between these terms, see also below.
81. E.g. S. Shay, J. Clifton Fleming and R.J. Peroni, 'R&D Tax Incentives: Growth Panacea or Budget Trojan Horse?' (2016) 69 *Tax Law Rev*, p. 428.
82. See discussion below with respect to definition of 'services'.

policy may not achieve its aim of encouraging scientific and technological innovation. It also lacks transparency because such a wide coverage of R&D tax credits would be better substituted by a reduction in tax rates.

However, as stressed by the German Correspondent, the tax privilege needs 'to be as neutral as possible. In modern economies, it is almost impossible to draw a clear demarcation between industry and services'.This is the reason why the R&D definition should cover all sectors of business, including service providers of all kinds. This does not mean, however, that all sectors are equally innovative, whether actually nor potentially.

II. Issue

Some voices among the National Correspondents suggested excluding banking and insurance from the definition of R&D for policy reasons. Banks (some of them at least) were at the origin of the financial crisis of 2007–2008 and should not be helped further through tax incentives. However, the Project Team considered that this reason alone, but also the principle of equality before tax, does not justify a differentiation for R&D tax incentives purposes. More precisely, the Project Team confirmed the view that the expression 'service sector' includes not only activities performed within social sciences, humanities, and the arts, but also the 'servitisation' of industry. Except for Ireland, all National Correspondents agreed to include the service sector in the concept of R&D.[83]

When it comes to the status of arts, should it be differentiated from humanities? The majority of the Project Team believed that art works involving research should not be rejected, as a matter of principle. This being said, and although art involves some level of creation,[84] this creativity is not enough to qualify as R&D: the other criteria have to be confirmed (e.g. uncertainty, systematicity, transferability and/or reproducibility).[85] There are definitely relationships between the arts and sciences.[86]

On the one hand, Irish law statutorily excludes'arts and humanities' for the definition of R&D for tax purposes and similar exclusions exist in the US,[87] Canadian, and Australian law.[88] French law, on the other hand, does not specifically exclude 'arts and humanities'. There is also a technical argument for inclusion of arts in the definition of R&D for tax purposes, namely that EU law and in particular State aid law should preclude discrimination based on activities. It is worth noting that the Swiss National Correspondents indeed emphasised the neutrality principle.

83. In Ireland, advancement or improvement of materials, processes and services could qualify as research. Public health services are also a relevant category of activity for R&D.
84. R. Untereiner, 'Réflexions sur la création artistique', *Bulletin de l'Association Guillaume Budé*, No. 2, June 1960, pp 285–293.
85. Frascati Manual, §2.17.
86. See generally, Y. Kreplak, 'Retour sur les relations entre art, science et recherche, "Entre arts et sciences"' (2013) 19 *Culture & Musées*.
87. IRC section 41(d)(4)(G).
88. See generally, M. Bowler-Smith, 'Comparing R&D tax regimes: Australia, Canada, UK and US' (2017) 1 *B.T.R.*, 34–59.

Based on this last technical argument alone, the view taken by the Project Team was that 'services, including social sciences, humanities, and the arts' should be part of the European concept of R&D.

The second question discussed was the 'digital design'. Indeed, the digital revolution gave birth to a digital economy that challenges the traditional concept of value creation. In this new world, the innovative nature of start-ups and global companies' business models and the continuous improvement of the design of their interfaces and the experiences they offer through their applications is fueled by data, especially personal data. Data allow companies that collect them to measure and improve the performance of an application, to customise the service rendered, to recommend purchases to their customers, to support innovation efforts which give rise to other applications, or still make strategic decisions. Users of a service become quasi-collaborators, volunteers, of businesses, and contribute to the blurring of the border between production and consumption. Users thus become, through such data, auxiliaries of the production and create value generating profits on different faces of the business models. More specifically, users in the digital economy are auxiliaries of R&D activities.

It is not clear if such R&D involving users is compatible with the definitions given in the Frascati Manual. On the one hand, the Manual excludes from the scope of R&D 'systems or programs that were available to the public before the beginning of the said work'. It thus seems to favour the idea of an R&D confined in the organisation, remote from users and even characterised by the absence of interactions with them. However, as mentioned above, R&D in the digital economy in many cases involves contact with users. On the other hand, several elements of the Frascati Manual suggest a wider meaning, since among the R&D activities are for example: 'advances in operating systems, programming languages, data management, or software development tools.'

It is therefore difficult to resolve these uncertainties and reach a conclusion on the exact delineation of R&D activities in the digital economy. The difficulties of interpreting and applying R&D tax rules curb growth and innovation in the digital economy. One of the theoretical bases of R&D tax incentives is grounded on the idea that knowledge derived from R&D and indirect long-term macroeconomic effects is generally impossible to fully appropriate. In the digital economy, this theoretical foundation should lead one to reconsider the scope of R&D and move it clearly from technology to 'business models' and 'designs'. There are three reasons for reconsidering such scope.

First, Europe needs digital champions, like the US or China. Business models and designs are decisive for the success or failure of digital economy companies. However, they are subject to the same characteristic as traditional knowledge resulting from R&D: a company cannot keep all the research results to itself. Once the activity is started, these elements, even radically innovative, can largely be imitated by competitors, especially by large companies that have sufficient resources to very quickly counter the entry of a disruptive competitor on the market.

The second reason for extending the notion of R&D to business models and designs is that these companies perform R&D activities through their users. These companies in the digital sector operate under a 'traction' characteristic. Traction is defined as the ability to quickly establish a privileged relationship with users and then use data from regular and systematic monitoring of their activity. This monitoring has the purpose of enriching the offer and accelerating the conquest of market share. It is true that this meeting as early as possible with the market, allows a company to protect its R&D thanks to the speed of execution and especially to feed this R&D with user contribution. That said, the precocity of the encounter with the market makes such a business model and the design of the experience more vulnerable to imitations by competitors.

Finally, the third reason for the necessary extension of the R&D notion to business models and design is the speed with which applications are launched in the digital economy. This rapidity can be explained by the radical changes in the role of technology in value creation. Most innovative technologies from the digital economy are born within communities of developers. The dominance of free software is one of the factors of the considerable decline in the cost of technology. The fact that technological R&D has moved from the inside to the outside of organisations is leading companies to concentrate their R&D efforts on other areas: the business model, design, 'the traction', and the processing of data from regular and systematic monitoring of user activity.

Design, business models, and 'traction' are therefore as much a matter of R&D as data collection and processing, algorithmic and software architecture. The obsolescence of the European concept of R&D compared to the reality of the digital economy is a strategic threat to competitiveness. This question is all the more important at a moment when Europe is becoming aware that unlike other regions such as China or the United States, it has not seen the birth of a digital giant such as Google or Alibaba. Moreover, if arts include design and architecture, one must consider opening the R&D category to include digital design.

§ 3 Novelty

Principle No. 2:

The level of novelty of the R&D is considered both from the perspective of the publicly available knowledge (world's perspective), and the company's private knowledge (firm's perspective).

To achieve a uniform interpretation of novelty, one should consider an expert body at EU level, which could, for instance, build upon the decision of the Boards of Appeal of the European Patent Office.

Following the Frascati Manual, R&D activities must be novel, creative, uncertain, systematic, transferable and/or reproducible.[89] Among these criteria, the most important is the first on the list, the novelty.

89. Frascati Manual, §2.7.

I. Background

Research projects are expected to pursue entirely new advancements in knowledge. This includes novelty, which is different from an inventive activity. Indeed, a research activity could qualify for tax incentives despite the fact that it does not lead to an invention, whether patentable or not. Patents are heterogeneous in terms of the novelty and value of the underlying invention. Research is a process independent from its effective findings. The need to 'aim at' findings should be sufficient. Should the research be new to the public, irrespective of territory boundaries? Also, should it be absolutely or relatively new? According to the Frascati Manual, the potential novelty of R&D projects in the business enterprise sector has to be assessed by comparison with the existing state of knowledge in the industry.[90] This requirement should go beyond country borders as long as it belongs to the same industry. It is therefore broader than a novelty, which is solely new 'to the product market'. There are further levels of novelty, for instance 'new to the world', which supports R&D with the largest potential social returns. Indeed, such requirement provides benefits to taxpayers involved in basic research, rather than imitating another country's new knowledge. An R&D activity is 'new to the firm' when it entails the diffusion of existing knowledge to a firm. Proprietary knowledge may have already been acquired by other firms, but it is not publicly available and is new to this particular firm.

Similarly, with respect to innovation, the 2018 Oslo Manual provides that 'a local or regional market novelty could be based on imitating what is already available in other geographical markets, whereas a world-first innovation will be a market leader'.[91] More precisely, a 'world-first product innovation implies a qualitatively greater degree of novelty that a new-to-market innovation'.[92] The 2014 EU Commission Paper recommended, as a best practice, first 'new to the world', and second 'new to the country' levels of novelty with regard to R&D.

II. Issue

Which level of novelty should be included in the definition of R&D? Should R&D activities be new (i) 'to the firm'; (ii)'to the product market'; (iii)'to the country'; or (iv) 'to the world'? Or perhaps, since the CCTB tax incentive aims to promote European R&D activities, (v) 'to the Internal Market'? The first option was supported by Austrian, Croatian, Finnish, French, Italian and Latvian National Correspondents. Austrian (also) and Greek Correspondents supported the second option, whereas no National Correspondent supported the third. Belgian, French, German, Luxembourgish and Irish National Correspondents supported the fourth option while Spanish and Hungarian the fifth. In fact, in Spain the 'new to the world' level of the novelty is required

90. Frascati Manual, §2.15. The same approach is taken by the 2018 Oslo Manual for innovation (§3.57.).
91. Frascati Manual, §3.58.
92. Frascati Manual, §3.59.

by the tax administration. However, courts have sometimes accepted a lesser degree of novelty for these tax credits, but the correspondent believes that it should be new to the Internal Market given the scope of the draft directive.[93]

In practice, it is generally assumed that the level of novelty should be both new to the world and new to the firm. An eligible project would be 'new to the world' for a company with no prior R&D experience in the domain of the project and for which knowledge gained by competitors is not publicly available (but still above publicly available knowledge, otherwise this is not R&D but training), and 'new to the firm and the world' if the company has prior acquired and proprietary knowledge in that domain and it is trying to gain further knowledge in that domain.

This can be seen from the following example. Many companies carry out activities abroad: for a French-based research project, a group may have its Asian or US subsidiaries involved. Therefore, a territorial definition of novelty (i.e. 'new to the country' criterion) may not make sense. It is therefore not surprising that no country applies a territorial definition, and that most countries refer to the 'new to the world' and/or 'new to the firm' criteria. Assume a technology has been developed by a US company, but this company keeps this development secret. Many companies, such as Oracle or SAP, do not reveal the source code nor detailed algorithms of their software program for instance. Therefore, a competing company willing to develop this technology could claim the R&D tax incentive, because it would not have access in its own state of the art to this technology. In the meantime, the novelty criteria could not be simply 'new to the firm' since such criterion would involve huge costs for public finance. Indeed, if the 'new to the firm' criterion was the sole and unique criterion, virtually all training expenses could be included as R&D costs, which would be unbearable from a public finance standpoint. If is therefore the combination of the two criteria ('new to the world' and/or 'new to the firm') which has to be retained. This is the main difference with the novelty criterion as required for a patent.[94]

The 'new to the market of the firm' criterion is retained, for instance by France, for the innovation tax credit: for an innovative product to be eligible, there is no need to look at the state of the art. What is important is to carry out a market study: is this product available on the relevant market segment?[95]

The level of novelty of 'Internal Market' would fall between new 'to the firm' or 'to the market of the firm' and new 'to the world'. Indeed, a strict 'new to the world' novelty requirement would imply high administrative and compliance

93. European Commission, 'A Study on R&D Tax Incentives', Final Report, 28 November 2014, figure 5.3, p. 59.

94. Under French patent law, novelty should be strictly 'new to the world': see F. Pollaud-Dulian, *La propriété industrielle*, Paris, Economica, 2011, para. 264. Indeed, in the French law of 5 July 1844, the requirement of novelty appeared in Articles 1 and 2 and was defined in Article 31: 'Will not be deemed new any discovery, invention or application that in France or abroad and prior to the date of filing the application, will have received sufficient publicity to be enforced'. See J. Schmidt-Szalewski, JCI Brevets, fasc. 4260 (nouveauté), updated on 8 September 2018 (see No. 1).

95. See French administrative guidelines, BOI-BIC-RICI-10-10-45-10-20160302, paras. 50, 90 et seq.

costs, and would not stimulate adoption of foreign technologies. A 'new to the Internal Market' novelty requirement would not permit imitation between firms located in the Internal Market and is easier to implement.

Replacement of the 'new to the world' level by the 'new to the Internal Market' one will make it easier for taxpayers to demonstrate the element of novelty, which would mean more burden on national budgets. Therefore, the 'new to the Internal Market' level may not yet be an option to consider for the EU liberal economies. Should the general landscape evolve, further consideration may be given to that criterion, but only after carrying out an economic study to assess the impact on each local budget and firm's innovation of such standard, in particular in countries like France, Belgium, Luxembourg, or Ireland.

Section II
Definition of Eligible Costs

Eligible costs definition is usually the second condition for input tax incentives, whether EU or national, or whether structured as a super-deduction or a tax credit. In business and accounting,[96] cost is the monetary value that a company has spent in order to produce something. Cost denotes the amount of money that a company spends on the creation or production of goods or services. It does not include the mark-up of profit. If producers were to sell their products at the production price, their costs and income would break even, meaning that they would not lose money on the sales. However, they would not make a profit either. From a buyer's point of view, the price is the cost of a product. It is also the amount charged for a product by a seller, and it includes both the production cost and the mark-up, added by the seller in order to make a profit.

The term cost sometimes refers to the monetary value of expenditures for raw materials, equipment, supplies, services, labour, products, etc. It is true that cost most closely equates to the term expenditure. However, the definition is much more difficult, as it depends on the adopted point of view (accounting or economy generally) and the jurisdiction in question.[97] In accounting, and while there are exceptions, it is generally true that costs are related to business assets and they are shown on the balance sheet. Expenses are related to business expenditures usually over time or with no financial benefit, and they are shown on the business net income (profit and loss) statement. An expense

96. A branch of accounting is very much concerned with costs. It is cost accounting (or analytical accounting – comptabilité analytique in French), which is the process of recording, classifying, analysing, summarising, and allocating costs associated with a process, and then developing various courses of action to control the costs. Its goal is to advise the management on how to optimize business practices and processes based on cost efficiency and capability. See generally, S. Bragg, *Cost Accounting Fundamentals*, 5th ed, Accounting Tools, 2016.

97. Definitions are not universally accepted: see already L. Perridon, 'Quelques concepts fondamentaux de l'économie de l'entreprise dans la littérature étrangère' (1961) 102 *Journal de la société statistique de Paris* 40, p. 70, at 58 et seq.

may refer to the consumption of the item acquired, while an expenditure is a payment or disbursement.[98] For instance, a company makes an expenditure of 10,000 to purchase equipment. Assuming the equipment use is for ten years, the income statement reports the asset's expenditure as depreciation expense of 1,000 per year.

Costs are however often treated exactly as an expense because most expenditures are consumed at once: for instance, when the expenditure relates to a specific period (monthly bill, salaries, rent, office supplies), the expenditure immediately converts from a cost to an expense.

Bearing in mind the above distinctions, this book uses the terms cost, expenditure, and expense interchangeably.

There are a number of different types of costs for a R&D activity. Accounting rules may provide further clarification for their definition. For instance, the Latvian Annual Financial Statements and Consolidated Financial Statements define research costs as 'costs which are directly applicable to research measures, as well as such costs which have arisen in the project development stage of creation of a particular intangible investment object, if the undertaking cannot separate the research stage of such project from its development stage'. However, the financial statements report these R&D costs in several ways;[99] for instance, Belgian domestic tax law follows Belgian GAAP, and not EU accounting rules.[100]

In the effort of clarifying a tax concept for R&D purposes, it is therefore fundamental to define these costs with precision in order to avoid/limit future litigation.

There are three general heading of Operating Expenses, also known as OPEX: general and administrative expense (G&A), sales and marketing costs (S&M), and R&D. R&D expenses are often long-term investments, and sometimes treated as capital expenditure, defined as those expenditures that are likely to create benefits over multiple periods. For instance, International Accounting Standard No. 9 requires the expensing of research cost but allows for the capitalisation of development expenses. Similarly, in France, the UK or Canada, firms are permitted to capitalise development's costs as the research gets closer to commercial exploitation.[101] However, this permission is not a requirement. In general, though, most companies in most countries expense R&D costs.

98. An expense is reported on the income statement in the period in which the cost matches the related sales, has expired, was used up, or had no future value. In other words, expenditure will generate future economic benefits for a company, whereas expenses will generate the benefit for the current period only.
99. K.T. Szilagyi, 'Accounting Problems of Research and Development' (2010) *Periodica Oeconomica*, p. 140.
100. See the general remark in the introduction concerning the relationship between accounting and tax: see section II in This chapter.
101. Prior to 1975, US companies were allowed to capitalise R&D expenses. Accounting rule SFAS 2, which has governed the treatment of research and development expenses since 1975, requires that all R&D expenses be expensed in the period incurred. Once and SFAS is published, it becomes part of the FASB accounting standards, known as generally accepted accounting principles, that govern the preparation of corporate financial reports. Some argue that, for

However, when an innovative company uses its capital assets for R&D purposes, the capital expenditure may enter into the tax incentive basis. This is probably why the Frascati Manual, in its new chapter on government tax R&D[102] provides that their scope cover 'all types of R&D costs, including current and capital expenditure'.[103]

§ 1 Capital Expenditure

> **Principle No. 3:**
> Depreciation expenses relating to assets created or acquired as new (including those used under a leasing agreement) and directly used for research operations are eligible R&D costs.

Capital expenditure, also known as CAPEX, are funds used by a company to acquire, upgrade, and maintain physical assets, such as property, industrial buildings, or equipment. A taxpayer cannot generally deduct spending on capital assets immediately; instead, the taxpayer claims the cost over time, reflecting the asset's depreciation (or decline in value): this 'depreciation allowance' corresponds to this deduction over a period.

I. Depreciation Expenses in General

In general, depreciation expenses corresponding to assets created or acquired as new directly and exclusively for research operations are eligible R&D costs.[104] In the case of mixed use of research and manufacturing, only the research part must be used to calculate the depreciation allowance for R&D tax incentive purposes. The taxpayer shall determine the allocation in proportion to the time used. For instance, a company acquired an equipment amortised during a five-year period. If taxpayers use this equipment for research operations conducted the first year alone, they will only take into account the first depreciation allowance for tax incentive purposes. In subsequent years, the taxpayer shall not retain the depreciation expenses of this equipment since it is not using the equipment for research operations.

Depreciable capital assets of the taxpayer comprise also assets leased under a leasing agreement for tax incentive purposes, subject to providing the amount of depreciation computed for these assets by the leasing company. This straightforward usual treatment is not the one provided in the 2016 CCTB proposal, which is difficult to grasp.

---

purposes of valuation, R&D expenses should be treated as tax-deductible capital expenditures: A. Damodaran, Research and Development Expenses: Implications for Profitability Measurement and Valuation, Paper Stern School of Business, 2009 (available at: http://people.stern.nyu.edu/adamodar/pdfiles/papers/R&D.pdf).

102. Chapter 13 entitled 'Measurement of government tax relief for R&D'.
103. Frascati Manual, §13.26.
104. For instance in France: see French administrative guidelines BOI-BIC-RICI-10-10-20-10-20140404.

II. Depreciation Expenses in the 2016 CCTB Proposal

A. Background

The tax treatment of movable tangible assets and immovable property, as regulated in Articles 9, 10 and 12 of the 2016 CCTB proposal is different.

Its Article 9 provides: 'In addition to the amounts which are deductible as costs for research and development in accordance with paragraph 2, the taxpayer may also deduct, per tax year, an extra 50% of such costs, with the exception of the cost related to movable tangible fixed assets, that it incurred during that year. To the extent that costs for research and development reach beyond EUR 20,000,000, the taxpayer may deduct 25% of the exceeding amount.'[105]

In addition, the Explanatory Memorandum further provides that 'R&D costs will be fully expensed in the year incurred (with the exception of immovable property)'.[106]

Further, the CCTB proposal, under the 'Other deductible items' heading (Article 10) provides that '[a] deduction shall be made in respect of the depreciation of fixed assets referred to in Articles 30 to 40'.[107]

Its Article 12 also provides that '[b]y way of derogation from Articles 9 and 10, the following items shall be non-deductible: [...] (i) acquisition or construction costs or cost connected with the improvement of fixed assets which are deductible under Articles 10 and 18, except for the cost related to research and development. The costs referred to in point (a) of Article 33(1) and points (a) and (b) of Article 33(2) shall not be treated as costs related to research and development; [...]'.[108]

What seems clear from the above articles, is that costs relative to movable property are fully expensed in the year incurred (Article 10), but they do not give rise to the super-deduction (Article 9).

With respect to building costs and financing expenses related to the acquisition of immovable (property)/immovable fixed assets,[109] costs related to acquisition or construction of new or second-hand commercial or industrial immovable assets are excluded from the super-deduction, and these costs should be fully deductible in the year they are incurred.

Concerning the issue of which criteria for proportional eligibility applies if the asset is used both for R&D and manufacturing purposes (e.g. an equipment used both to manufacture prototypes and serial products), most National

105. Art 9.3 (emphasis added).
106. Frascati Manual, §8.
107. Art 10. Arts. 30 to 40 constitutes a Chapter IV entitled 'Depreciation of Fixed Assets' and details rules for depreciation (fixed assets register, depreciation base, timing, etc.). Art. 38: provides that certain category of fixed tangible assets will not be eligible for a depreciation allowance. These are fixed tangible assets, which not subject to wear and tear and obsolescence, such as land, fine art, antiques, or jewelry, and financial assets.
108. Art 12. For additional context, see Annex.
109. Art 12(i).

Correspondents agree that there should be a *pro rata* calculation. In France the 'time spent' criteria for the pro rata calculation is used, while in Greece, Italy, or Switzerland it is left to the taxpayer to decide which criteria should be used, as no guidance is provided.

B. Discussion

For the purpose of consistency, the Project Team suggests to replace 'property', by 'assets' in Recital 8 of the CCTB Proposal. Usually, 'properties' which are used in the course of a business or profession become 'assets'. Further, for accounting purposes, the term 'asset' is usually preferred, rather than 'property'. Also, a definition of asset and intangible asset should be provided.

For clarification purposes, the tax treatment of movable tangible assets and immovable property should be better explained, for instance in a new Recital 8(a). As the Project Team understands the proposal, the tax treatment of depreciation expenses has to be distinguished depending on whether the assets concerned are movable or immovable.

For movable fixed assets, depreciation expenses are not available since the costs of these assets are fully expensed in the year incurred, and are not eligible for the super-deduction.

For immovable fixed assets, depreciation expenses remain available, since the costs of these assets cannot be fully expensed in the year they were incurred, and depreciation expenses are eligible for the super-deduction.

Further clarification would be beneficial for a situation where an asset is used both for R&D and manufacturing purposes (e.g. an equipment used both to manufacture prototypes and serial products). Some National Correspondents suggested that the criteria for proportional eligibility should be based on a time spent *pro rata* calculation and others mentioned that their tax systems leave it to the taxpayer. The production of prototypes and the construction of a pilot plant/or pilot facilities could be considered as R&D activities.

Finally, the question of the extent to which an asset is used for R&D purposes has to be further clarified. A possible formulation would be: 'An asset is considered directly used for R&D purposes if such is used to carry out research programs of the business.' More precisely, 'indirect use' of assets for R&D purposes can be included if indirect costs can be determined. Examples of indirect use of assets for R&D purposes are: (i) handling devices; (ii) calculation tools; (iii) computers; (iv) machines used to manufacture components of a prototype; or (v) telephones, small office appliances, office furniture.

Indirect costs can be included in the tax base of the super-deduction, when allocated – if possible – to a cost unit or a cost centre proportionally. Indirect costs (or other overhead costs) would have to be estimated if no applied cost accounting method is available (as is the case in Austria).

§ 2 Current Expenditure

The OECD defines current expenditure as 'expenditure on goods and services consumed within the current year, which needs to be made recurrently to sustain the production [...]'.[110]

Current expenditure could include final consumption expenditure, property income paid, subsidies and other current transfers (e.g. social security, social assistance, pensions and other welfare benefits).

While the 2016 CCTB proposal could potentially encompass a vast variety of current expenditure (R&D staff cost, standardisation expenses,[111] patent related expenses, and other current expenditure related to R&D) in the super-deduction, the 2018 CCTB proposal reduced the scope of the costs that are eligible to R&D staff costs. However, since these costs usually represent more than 60% of total R&D costs, such reduction is not drastic.

I. R&D Staff Cost Background

Principle No. 4:

R&D staff include the following categories:

1. researchers educated at university level who conduct research activities directed by the taxpayer;
2. researchers without university level education who have a minimum of years documented experience of R&D;
3. other R&D staff such as laboratory technicians who have a minimum of 2 years documented experience of R&D; and
4. support staff necessary to support the above categories of R&D staff.

Where staff participate in both R&D and non R&D activities, staff costs are allocated to eligible R&D activities based on the proportion of time spent on such activities.

All costs relating to R&D staff are eligible R&D expenditure except for profit sharing schemes or return on investment. However, to the extent that a profit-sharing scheme is based on R&D, the relevant proportion of profit-sharing may be eligible R&D expenditure.

The 2015 Frascati Manual provides guidance on defining and identifying R&D personnel, that is the people who perform R&D activities, whether highly trained scientists and engineers, or technicians with high levels of technical experience and training, or supporting staff contributing to directly carrying out R&D projects.[112] The Manual treats as R&D personnel any individual undertaking one or more of the above tasks 'contributing to the intramural R&D activities [...] irrespective of their function (formal role) or their employment status [...]'.[113] Such a comprehensive view, adopted for statistical measurement of R&D personnel, cannot, without precaution, be transposed for tax incentives purposes as it does not take into account the legal aspects of the relationship between the R&D provider and the beneficiary (who is paying the personnel?), and would impair significantly national budgets with possible abuse of deductions or tax credits.

110. See: https://stats.oecd.org/glossary/detail.asp?ID=5570.
111. See point II in this section.
112. Chapter 5 (2015 ed.), pp. 149 et seq.
113. Chapter 5 (2015 ed.), p. 150.

This is the reason why the Frascati Manual also limits the above by providing that not all of the personnel contributing to or facilitating the performance of R&D activities are to be included in the R&D personnel totals, but only those who make a direct contribution to R&D activities.

Therefore, the Manual excludes from the R&D personnel the 'individuals undertaking indirect support or ancillary activities in R&D-performing units'.[114] However, 'their related costs (including the remuneration of the personnel providing such services) should be included in the statistical unit's R&D expenditures and be reported as other current costs'.[115]

A. Definition of R&D Staff

Methodology (Formal and/or Functional Approach?)

The main methodological question is whether researchers should be defined according to a formal criterion (i.e. a black letter list (including degrees/diplomas (e.g. PhDs), qualifications) or a functional approach. Many countries (for instance Belgium, France, Greece) use the formal criteria. Some, however, use both formal and functional definition, for instance Latvia:[116]

'Scientific staff – scientists who have acquired a scientific qualification (a scientific doctoral degree) and professionals with an academic degree or a higher education diploma, who perform research activities in order to acquire new knowledge, products, processes, methods and systems, as well as project managers who are engaged in planning and the management of scientific and technical aspects of research activities.

Research technical staff – persons who have the necessary technical knowledge and experience in one or several areas and who participate in research activities by performing technical tasks under the guidance of the scientific staff. Engineers, technicians, laboratory assistants, technologists, and operators are included in the research technical staff bracket.

Research assistants – persons who perform assisting functions in the execution of scientific technical works (employees of planning, economic, financial, and scientific technical information structural units, employees of special and scientific technical libraries, patent service specialists, archivists, as well as qualified workers who ensure the assemblage, adjustment, maintenance and repair of the equipment and devices necessary for the performance of scientific activity. A scientist is defined as an individual who performs scientific activity and who has acquired scientific qualifications in accordance with the procedures specified in this Law.'

114. Frascati Manual, §5.4 (emphasis added).
115. Frascati Manual, §5.5 (emphasis added).
116. Latvian national report.

The above definition is interesting as it uses both a formal criterion and a functional criterion. However, should there be an inconsistency between the formal and the functional criteria, the latter should prevail. This approach should be supported.

Other countries (e.g. Poland) seem to refer to the wording of the employment contract[117] and effective research, but legal doctrine challenges this approach as too restrictive.[118]

Some National Correspondents (e.g. Austrian and Irish) consider that the R&D staff category can be broader than researchers and scientists since the phrase is not defined in their legislation but through reference to a more open definition including all staff and employees involved in the R&D process (for instance Austrian regulation BGBl II 2015/515, and Irish Tax and Duty Manual, Part 29-02-03, p. 22). The current approach under Irish legislation focuses on the activity performed, not on academic or professional qualifications.

Since the educational structure is converging in the EU, one has a better sense across Europe of which specific diploma evidences research capacities and qualities. Nevertheless, the Project Team is of the opinion that formal qualifications should not preclude somebody who has learned to be a researcher from experience, but without having a formal degree, to qualify as R&D staff.

In Spain, there is a specific additional tax credit for 'qualified researchers' exclusively dedicated to R&D activities. The Spanish tax administration understands that research technicians and other supported staff cannot be considered 'qualified researchers'. This approach is not supported by the Project Team, who support the view that research technicians may be considered R&D staff, as, although the formal criterion is an indication, the functional criterion should prevail. This raises the question of which staff should qualify as R&D staff.

1. Which Staff Should Qualify (R&D Related Personnel)?

R&D-related personnel are those performing R&D-related tasks. The Frascati Manual provides a list of these key tasks. According to this basic categorisation, R&D personnel not only perform scientific and technical work for an R&D project (setting up and carrying out experiments or surveys, building prototypes, etc.), but also 'plan and manage R&D projects, prepare interim and final reports for R&D projects, provide internal services for R&D projects (e.g. dedicating computing or library and documentation work), and [...] support [...] the administration [for] the financial and personnel aspects of R&D projects'.[119]

117. See Head of the Tax Chamber in Katowice, private ruling of 25 January 2017, No. 2461-IBPB-1-2.4510.934.2016.3.
118. P. Wyrwa, *Ulga na działalność badawczo-rozwojowa wpraktyce*, Lex/el, Warsaw, 2017.
119. Frascati Manual (2015), §5.2.

2. Research Technicians

Should research technicians be included in the category of R&D-related personnel? One reason to support their inclusion in the fact that without them, the principal researcher cannot carry out the research. For instance, under French regulations, research technicians are staff who provide indispensable support to actual researchers, such as preparation of substances, material and appliances for experimentation; assistance to researchers during experimentations or actual performance of experimentations; maintenance and controlling of the functioning of the appliances and equipment required. This group is considered research staff also in Belgium, Croatia, Greece, Italy, Luxembourg, as well as Ireland, which evaluate the activity, not the qualifications.

3. More Remotely Involved R&D Staff

An important question arises as to whether the inclusion of research technicians extends to other employees who, though not official researchers, still indirectly contribute to R&D activities (e.g. a manager overseeing a research program or unit, a secretary, administrative staff, or cleaning personnel, etc.). In order to answer, it is important to determine where the R&D activity starts (i.e. does the submission of an R&D proposal constitutes a qualifying R&D function?) and ends (does typing out a final research report still qualify for the tax incentive?).

Some National Correspondents (e.g. from France, Hungary, Italy) believe that including indirect research staff or staff performing ancillary activities could be a source of uncertainty and potential abuse. For example, under this approach, general managers should not qualify, unless they directly contribute to the research itself. In Austria, Greece, and Luxembourg, the costs of administrative staff running the project are clearly included as R&D related (but not the costs of cleaning staff).[120] This seems to also be the case in Italy. In France, this category of staff is not openly recognised as conducting research, but it is indirectly included as a percentage allowance pertaining to administrative costs. In Ireland, Poland and Belgium, however, they are excluded, since administrative tasks are not considered as eligible costs, even if they are necessary and may constitute a prerequisite to a research project.

For the reasons above, all National Correspondents supported the inclusion of research managers and all but Spanish NCs supported the inclusion of technicians in the category of R&D staff. With regard to secretaries, HR and cleaning staff, NCs were against their inclusion. When it comes to general managers of businesses with a R&D department, National Correspondents did not agree to include them in the category of research personnel, unless they are actually performing research activities.

120. Greek Law 4310/2014 (Art. 18) and the Ministerial Decision 109/2017, Art. 3, para. d.

4. Partial Involvement

In case the staff participates both in R&D and non-R&D activities, the Project Team suggests to allow for proportional eligibility based on time spent on various activities, proved by a detailed timesheet. There is a clear unanimity in responses. As an example, Greek law provides for a legal basis for that proposal.[121]

B. Definition of R&D Staff Cost

Certain costs including wages and compulsory social security contributions qualify as R&D staff costs. Other potential costs do not qualify in such a straightforward manner. For instance, non-compulsory social contribution schemes qualify in Austria or Greece, but not in France.

With respect to employers' contribution in the form of the participation of employees of the enterprise in a profit-sharing scheme (employee share-ownership), the answer is more complicated as not all Member States recognise such a scheme. While the Polish legal system does not recognise such category of payments, in France the *'intéressement et participation'* is eligible personnel expenses.[122] One possible reason to exclude profit sharing is that it is in principle based on a return on investment and does not qualify as staff costs. However, the company issuing the profit-sharing shares could base its profit upon the amount of research (e.g. a group subsidiary dedicating its operations to R&D activities). If profit sharing is based on research, then the Project Team sees no reason for excluding these costs.

The application of the above criterion becomes more complicated with regard to bonuses and/or benefits in kind. When a researcher receives stock/shares based on performance, one could still consider that this remuneration arises directly from the research activity. The right answer depends on the particular situation and the drafting of the contract or motivation for the unilateral decision of the employer to grant a bonus.

With respect to indirect R&D costs (e.g. support staff indirectly and partially effected), and if an analytical accounting document provides details of expenses based on time spent on a certain activity, it is suggested that a percentage allowance would be a preferred solution to cope with a somehow time consuming calculation.

Finally, some countries covered in this research provide that compensation paid to PhD holders of should count more (e.g. double) than other costs for a limited period of time, in order to promote their hiring. Since such measure is contrary to the harmonisation objective of the proposed directive it is believed that it should not apply on a European level.

---

121. Relevant provision is Art. 3, para. d of the Greek Ministerial Decision 109/2017.
122. This position results from a French Supreme Administrative Court decision of 12 March 2014, overriding French administrative guidelines.

II. Standardisation and Technological Watch Expenses

> **Principle No. 5:**
> Standardisation expenses are not eligible R&D expenditure, except where scientific methods are used for the purpose of standardisation. Technology watch connected to research projects is eligible [up to EUR [*amount to be decided*] per year and per taxpayer].

Standardisation expenses are expenses related to the establishment of technical standards concerning products. Standards are rules, guidelines or characteristics for activities or their results, for common and repeated use, aimed at achieving an optimum degree of order in a given technical context.[123] Standardisation is the process of formulating, drafting, publishing and reviewing appropriate technical standards for the benefit of individuals, businesses, governments and/or society, together with implementing them through relevant regulations, testing and certification, marking and labelling, inspection and surveillance.

Should expenses related to the establishment of technical standards concerning the products of a business be eligible for the super-deduction (e.g. expenses incurred on participation of employees in official meetings of standardisation bodies)? The answers given by National Correspondents span a whole range of options. France and Greece seem to be in favour of eligibility of such costs, while Luxembourg and Spain seem to be against. The Austrian, Irish, Italian and Polish National Correspondents proposed a compromise: standardisation expenses should not be included with the exception of research activities that use scientific methods for the purpose of standardisation.

The French position qualifying standardisation meeting costs as R&D related costs irrespective of the fact whether such meetings include research activity, should not be supported, as such meetings may only be coordination of views or dealing with administrative issues not related to standardisation research. However, standardisation could sometimes take the form of a research activity. First and formally, it is true that standards developers are primarily research and testing bodies. Second, and from a more substantive standpoint, as research matures, standardisation provides a bridge between research results, implementation, and widespread deployment of such results. Standardisation can effectively reduce the proliferation of innovations, but by limiting the field, promotes the emergence of more robust technological infrastructures at the same time.

123. See, ISUG, Study into the Impact of Standardisation (2002), p. 4, and Annex 2. The European Directive No 98/34/EEC (formerly 83/189), defines a standard as a subspecies of a 'technical specification'. It is a technical specification approved by a recognised standardisation body for repeated or continuous application, with which compliance is not compulsory. The WTO Agreement on Technical Barriers to Trade defines a standard as: 'A document approved by a recognized body, that provides, for common and repeated use, rules, guidelines or characteristics for products or related processes and production methods, with which compliance is not mandatory. It may also include or deal exclusively with terminology, symbols, packaging, marking or labelling requirements as they apply to a product, process or production method'.

In an effort to establish a common R&D concept for tax purposes, one should support the answers of Austrian, Irish, Italian, and Polish National Correspondents, according to which only standardisation that uses scientific methods should qualify as cost eligible for R&D tax incentives. The French (and Greek) position disconnecting standardisation from research activities is not defendable, even though the Project Team agrees that standardisation should be promoted in research activities generally. This promotion could take other forms, such as its integration in a researcher's career assessment.

The remaining issue is whether expenses related to technical monitoring/ technological watch should be taken into account?

Technology watch (*veille technologique* in French) is intended to provide an up-to-date assessment of new technologies. It 'consists in systematically capturing, analysing, disseminating and exploiting useful technical information for the watch and growth of a company. Watch must be ready for any scientific or technical innovation susceptible to creating opportunities or threats'.[124]

The answers to this question by National Correspondents varied, including that many jurisdictions did not reply (Austrian, Belgian, Hungarian, and Swiss), probably because there is no local view on the subject. Some considered that if connected to a research project, expenses related to technical monitoring should be taken into account (Luxembourgish), including with no limit (Croatian, Greek, Italian, and Spanish) or within a yearly limit (EUR 60,000 in France).

Therefore, one can conclude that a moderate approach would be to consider technology watch costs as eligible for R&D tax incentives, if linked to the carrying out of a research project. In addition, depending on public expenditure impact (to be assessed by economists) these costs could be limited to a certain amount (to be determined) to avoid abuse,[125] or not.

A. Patent Related Expenses

Principle No. 6:

Expenses incurred in an EU member state relating to filing, maintenance and the defence of patents are eligible [within a threshold of EUR [*amount to be decided*]]; insurance costs linked to patents are eligible [within a threshold of EUR [*amount to be decided*]]. Intellectual Property (IP) consultant's fees, translation costs, taxes are examples of such expenses.

Patent related expenses are expenses linked to the filing, maintenance and defence of patents incurred in a Member State (for instance, IP consultant's fees, translation costs, taxes). Taxes refer to miscellaneous taxes/fees levied for the benefit of the IP National Protection Agency for the grant of patents and for the benefit of foreign states or international bodies which ensure the protection of the invention. There is considerable difference in patent costs between Member States. For example, fees paid for a patent maintained for 20 years

124. C. Rovira, Technology Watch and Competitive Intelligence for SEM-SEO, No. 6, 2008.
125. French national report.

in Germany can be more than five times higher than in Malta. However, the cost of a German patent relative to the size of the German market is nearly 75 times lower than for Malta.[126]

Some National Correspondents replied that expenses linked to patents should be eligible for the R&D tax incentives (Austrian, Belgian, French, Greek, Irish and Italian). Spanish and Luxembourgish Correspondents supported the approach of the Frascati Manual, according to which R&D would typically not include administrative and legal work connected with patents, routine tests or data collection. Polish Correspondent explained that patent related costs are eligible only for micro, small and medium entrepreneurs. Therefore, for larger companies typically targeted at this stage by the super-deduction, this should not be eligible.

In the United States, many patent-related expenses are deductible, including attorney's fees. Such legal fees are considered part of research and experimental costs, as defined by the Internal Revenue Service.[127] Other deductible expenses include the costs of applying for the patent and the research required for patent development. The costs of obtaining a patent, including attorneys' fees paid or incurred in making and perfecting a patent application, are research and experimental costs. However, costs paid or incurred to obtain a patent developed by a third party or another taxpayer are not research and experimental costs.

Some National Correspondents suggested that to ensure consistency with the above Principle and R&D concept, patent-related costs should not be included as research costs. This is the case even if patents impact research investments.[128] Overall however, since patents are often a necessity to secure the output of R&D operations, it was decided to consider some patent-related expenses as eligible for R&D tax incentives, in full or up to a limit.

Similarly, premiums and contributions or the share of premiums or contributions relating to legal protection insurance contracts providing for the inclusion of expenditure incurred in disputes relating to a patent owned by the taxpayer should be eligible. However, premiums and insurance contributions related to a contract underwritten by a company to cover itself for the taxpayer's own infringements are not eligible, since it is not related to a patent defense trial. Similarly, premiums or the share of insurance premiums relating to contracts providing for the assumption of expenses resulting from a possible breach of law (damages and interest, fines, costs, etc.) are not eligible expenses.

126. European Commission, *Patent costs and impact on innovation*, study: an international comparison and analysis of the impact on the exploitation of R&D results by SMEs, Universities and Public Research Organisations, 2015.
127. Publication 535 (2019), Business Expenses, available at: https://www.irs.gov/publications/p535#en_US_2019_publink100078332.
128. H.L. Williams, 'How do patents affect research investments?' (2017) *Ann Rev Econom*, pp. 441–469.

B. Related to R&D

> **Principle No. 7:**
> Other operating expenses are eligible R&D expenditure based on their link to R&D activities. Alternatively, a notional deduction of 50% of the research staff expenses could be granted. Services of tax advisors or innovation firms are tax deductible in accordance with general principles but are not eligible R&D expenditure.

1. Identification of Such Residual Category Expenses

The majority of National Correspondents were in favour of identifying such residual category of expenses (Austrian, Croatian, French, Greek, Irish, Italian, and Spanish). In Hungary the law provides that the costs such as compensation payments or wages, income taxes, social security contributions paid during the period, shall not be considered as direct costs of R&D activities. Other operating expenses relating to R&D are considered 'indirect costs' and are thus not eligible. The Hungarian National Correspondent stressed, however, that a non-inclusive list would be useful for tax authorities. Belgian and Swiss National Correspondents had no particular view on the question, while the Polish legislation suggests that there should be an exhaustive list of eligible R&D expenses, in line with respective national system.

2. List of Other Expenses

National Correspondents were more divided as to whether a detailed list of possible expenses is advisable. Austrian, Belgian, Croatian, Greek, Irish, Polish, and Spanish National Correspondents answered positively, but seem (it is clear for Croatia and Poland) to favour a non-exhaustive list due to the vast variety of R&D projects in different industries. The Greek National Correspondents share a similar opinion, although their national law has an exhaustive list. The Irish and Luxembourgish approaches where, respectively, that 'it would be impossible to have a complete list; a residual category would be required. Therefore, a detailed list is not useful' and 'there should be a certain degree of flexibility'.[129]

The French National Correspondent explained that a lump sum (*forfait* in French) should be computed based on other expenses, and no detailed list is therefore necessary, while the Italian, and Swiss National Correspondents had no particular view on this question.

Since none of the National Correspondents supported the view that an exhaustive list of (other) eligible expenses is advisable, it is recommended that such a list is not required. However, should tax administrations or national legislators be willing to maintain such list, they are free to do so. The only requirement should be that these expenses be computed based on the involvement in R&D activities. Of course, this may create burdensome monitoring

129. Irish and Luxembourg national reports.

costs. To alleviate these costs, as the need may be, these other operating expenses related to R&D activities may be computed as a percentage of other eligible expenses.

3. Percentage of Expenses

Concerning the issue of whether it is appropriate to assess these expenses notionally by reference to other precisely defined eligible expenses (e.g. 15% of immovable [property] depreciation expenses, and/or 50% of eligible staff expenses), National Correspondents were also divided in their approaches. Belgian, Hungarian and Irish explained that there is no guidance on this issue in their jurisdictions.

French regulations evaluate general and administrative expenses at 75% of the amortisation of assets directly affected to the research and 43% of the research staff expenses (as of 1 January 2020).

Croatian National Correspondent proposed an interesting alternative: together with such notional expenses, taxpayers should also have the possibility to provide a detailed and precise list of the other operating expenses they incurred during an eligible R&D project and were necessary for research as well as reasonably and consistently allocated directly to the research. Due to the development of IT and sophisticated programmes for record keeping, this would not create additional costs for the business. If taxpayers find it reasonable, in accordance with their appraisal of the cost effectiveness of such compliance, the exact calculations should be accepted as an alternative. Austrian and Greek National Correspondents seemed to agree.

Italian, Luxembourgish, and Polish National Correspondents were of the contrary opinion.

The Croatian alternative offers the advantage of reconciling various views: the lump sum costs could be substituted for actual costs, depending on which is (i) easier to maintain or more favourable to the taxpayer, or (ii) easier to control for the tax administration. This is therefore the view supported in this book.

4. External Consultants' Fees

As to whether fees paid to external consultants assisting the company to determine its R&D super-deduction should be eligible, and to what extent, only the Italian National Correspondents believed that these expenses should be deductible as part of an amount eligible for R&D tax incentives. In Austria, services of state-certified tax advisors are tax deductible as a special expense, regardless of any R&D activity. This is also the case in Croatia, Greece, Ireland, and Luxembourg.

The French and Spanish National Correspondents seemed to have a different view. In France there is a different system, external consultants' fees are taken into consideration to decrease the amount of the tax credit. If the remuneration is a proportion of the tax credit obtained, it comes fully at a reduction of the tax basis for the credit. Otherwise, the amount is deductible after reduction of the higher between 5% of the tax basis before this reduction or EUR 15,000.

Polish and Swiss National Correspondents didn't express any particular view on the issue.

Apart from the Italian NCs, the remaining NCs were against the view that these costs should be eligible for purposes of the R&D tax incentives. Due to the fact that such consultants are not performing R&D activities, the recommendation is that remuneration for services of tax advisors or innovation firms are regularly tax deductible but should not be eligible as 'costs for R&D'.

§ 3 Contracted Expenditure

Principle No. 8:

If R&D activity is outsourced to third parties within the European Economic Area (EEA), these outsourcing expenses are eligible, up to a [certain] percentage of the total R&D expenses incurred.

Principle No. 9:

The company out-sourcing R&D has priority in claiming R&D tax incentives (if the outsourcing company can claim R&D tax incentives, the R&D contractor cannot also claim).

Principle No. 10:

Non-refundable government, state agencies, or EU subsidies or grants related to R&D projects should be *deducted* from eligible expenses of the year during which these expenses are incurred, and irrespective of the payment date of the subsidies/grants.

When these subsidies or grants are refundable, they are *added* to the basis for calculating the tax incentive for the year in which they are refunded to the organisation that paid them.

Contracted expenditure relates to subcontracting R&D tasks. To understand the context, one needs to identify the main (tax) questions of whether a taxpayer can subcontract costs in respect of qualifying R&D activities? If they can, who can claim the costs in respect of qualifying R&D activities: the general contracting company (or 'principal') or its subcontractor? Indeed, when the principal company is considering claiming for subcontracted R&D expenses, it is crucial to establish whether, or not, the subcontractor has already claimed R&D tax incentives for the project it has undertook on behalf of the principal company. If the subcontractor has already claimed such expenses, can the principal company claim too? A positive answer (i.e. double claim) to this last question would support the so called 'double-dipping', '[t]he usually illicit practice of accepting income from two mutually exclusive sources (as from a government pension and a government salary or from two insurers for the same loss)'.[130]

The tax world implements this legal definition as follows: double dips refer to the achievement of a tax deduction in two countries for what is, in fact, the same interest payment. However, double dips do not only concern interest

130. Literally, the expression means 'putting food into a dip for a second time after it has already been bitten'.

payments, they prevent multinational corporations from using tax havens and other tax avoidance structures to generate two expense deductions for only one investment.[131] Concerning R&D activities, should a single research activity give rise to two tax incentive claims?

I. Context

Numerous contract research organisations are emerging from the academic world or elsewhere offering their expertise in specific processes. In the R&D industry, a subcontractor is an individual or company hired by a general contractor (or prime contractor, main contractor, or principal) to perform a specific task as part of the overall R&D project. The general contractor ordinarily pays for services provided to the project. The main features of subcontracting are risks, deliverables, autonomy, and IPRs.

Concerning risks, in subcontracted R&D, the general contractor pays the subcontractor for the outcome of the R&D, regardless of the project's success. Therefore, it is the principal company, not the subcontractor, which incurs any failures or overruns. For deliverables, the principal company should be carrying out an R&D project and contracting out a specific part of that project to the subcontractor. The principal company is therefore knowledgeable in the area of development and outlines a detailed specification of the work. The level of autonomy is also key to the understanding of the subcontracting relationship. If there is a very low level of autonomy and high level of supervision, one could suspect difficulty in characterizing the relationship as subcontracting: in this case indeed, the scales will tip in favour of an externally provided worker. If the principal company is subcontracting qualifying activities, the subcontractor will enjoy a degree of autonomy in resolving the uncertainties despite the fact that the principal company keeps interest in the R&D. Finally, with respect to IP, and if the principal company's R&D is subcontracted, it is generally expected that the IPRs will rest with the principal company. However, all the above features are complex and are used as indicators rather than being conclusive of the status of the relationship.

Let us illustrate the above on the following example. Assume a lab is developing a diagnostic kit for the COVID virus. Researchers would need partners from another lab specialised in biomarkers to ask them for specific synthesis or tests. Working with a second team of experts will increase the scientific value of the project. Each lab has its own expertise, the necessary knowledge and equipment that relates to it. In-house research does not always allow for some specific experiments. Outsourcing is then a serious option to consider. Other options would be partnerships or training, but they are more lengthy process, whereas hiring a subcontractor is probably more cost effective.[132]

131. See for instance, M. Huynh, E. Lockwood and M. Maikawa, 'The Anti-Tax-Haven Initiative and the Foreign Affiliate Rules' (2007) 55(3) *Rev Fisc Canadienne*, p. 657.

132. It avoids investment costs (and maintenance costs of some equipment) and enhance strategic alliances, allowing the principal R&D company to focus on its core business.

In this way, the general contractor receives the same or better service than the general contractor could have provided itself. Subcontracting opens doors to working with different companies and academic groups. It offers different expertise to better pursue R&D through partnerships and the benefit of external experts' knowledge. From the subcontractors' point of views, this allows further specialisation.

Concerning the above, the Frascati Manual distinguishes internal and external R&D personnel.[133] However, this distinction is for statistical purposes only. From a legal perspective, internal R&D personnel are usually employees, whereas external R&D personnel are usually subcontractors.[134] It is well established in comparative labour law that the main test used to distinguish the two situations usually relies on who sets the working rules?[135] Employees must follow rules set by their employer; independent contractors set their own rules.

II. Are Subcontracted Costs Qualifying Expenses?

Costs of subcontracting are currently treated differently in Member States.

On the one hand, there is the UK regulation, according to which one cannot claim twice for the same expenses. For R&D expenses other than staff costs, the UK distinguishes two situations: the first involves a large company ordering from a Small or Medium Enterprise (SME). In this case the ordering company cannot claim R&D expenses subcontracted to a private company. The large ordering company can only claim 100% of the expenses for work subcontracted to public entities (e.g. universities, health bodies) or individuals.[136] The rationale being that large companies may afford a private lab. If it does not do so, it is then the one (the UK subcontractor) doing the work who can claim the tax credit. The second situation is when the ordering company is a SME, in which case it can claim subcontracted R&D expenses (i.e. invoices) to a non-related private company up to 65%, or up to 100% to a related company.[137] In this case, the UK subcontractor cannot claim the R&D expenses. In both cases one cannot claim for the same expenses twice.

The UK makes a particular case for staff costs: UK large and SME companies may claim staff costs for contracted employees working under the supervision, direction, or control off the claimant, where their services are provided through a third-party staff provider (restricted to 65% of the costs) or up to

133. Chapter 5 (2015 ed.), pp. 149 et seq.
134. This is not always the case: one can distinguish the externally provided workers, who are temporary workers sourced from an external agency. They work like regular employees, but their contract is with the agency, not with the R&D company performing the R&D-related tasks.
135. G. Cavalier (with R. Upex), 'The Concept of Employment Contract in European Union Private Law' (2006) 55 *International Comparative Law Quarterly*, pp. 587–608.
136. See generally, HM Revenue & Customs, Research and development tax relief, available at: http://www.hmrc.gov.uk/gds/cird/attachments/rdsimpleguide.pdf (consulted on 1 December 2019).
137. *Ibid.*

100% if provided through a related party staff provider. In this case, the UK subcontractor cannot claim the R&D staff expenses. The rationale being that the subcontractor is merely acting as a staff provider.

On the other hand, a French company can claim R&D expenses subcontracted to a private EU company, if the private subcontractor has a valid agreement from the French Ministry of Research and if the R&D work is actually driven by the company. In this case, French private subcontractors with a valid agreement cannot claim the R&D expenses paid for by another French company, whether the sub-contractor has actually claimed the R&D expenses or not.[138] From these two sides of the spectrum, one can easily see the possibility of double-dips at the EU level.

There are also further solutions in place. For instance in Belgium the following principle applies: who owns the assets benefits from the tax incentive. Indeed, and with regards to the R&D tax credit or investment deduction, Belgian law usually requires that the following general conditions are met: (i) activation of expenses (i.e. it must be an asset for use within the company); (ii) new assets not having been used for professional purposes in Belgium before; and (iii) used for 'own use' (i.e. not acquired in order to lease out).

Because of these requirements, and where the same asset is used by both principal and subcontractor, it is impossible to claim a R&D tax allowance. Economically however, an overlap at the subcontractor level may occur when acquiring (tangible) R&D assets to complete the subcontracted work. The salary expenses will not benefit from the tax allowance since these expenses are not linked with an asset owned and used by the subcontractor; at the principal level, the activation of the subcontracting costs will, to some extent, be reflecting the subcontractor's expenses.

Most National Correspondents agreed that such contracted expenses should be qualified for purposes of the R&D tax incentive (Austrian, Belgian, Croatian, French, Greek, Hungarian, Irish, Italian, Latvian, Luxembourgish, Polish, Spanish, and Swiss).

Limits

The above could be limited with respect to the amount (to be determined) or territorial scope.

The amount claimed may be limited to an absolute value or to a percentage of the total costs of the research project or of the payments made to the sub-contractor. For example, in Greece, such sub-contracted payments qualify for up to 70% of the whole cost of the research project. It is also true in the UK, if the company and the subcontractor are not connected, the company can only claim R&D tax relief on 65% of the payment it makes to the sub-contractor.[139]

138. Versailles Administrative Court of Appeal, Altran, 15 October 2015.
139. HMRC Internal Manual, Corporate Intangibles Research and Development Manual, R&D tax relief: categories of qualifying expenditure: subcontracted activities – CTA09/ Ss 1078, 1133-1136, available at: https://www.gov.uk/hmrc-internal-manuals/corporate-intangibles-research-and-development-manual/cird84200.

In other countries absolute value limits are preferred, for instance in Austria, where R&D tax credit is only available for expenses in the amount of EUR 1 million per financial year. This amount has to be reduced proportionately if the fiscal year covers less than 12 years. This applies both for situations of subcontracting, and non-subcontracting.

Under current French law, R&D costs invoiced by accredited private subcontractors can be kept within the limit of three times the total amount of all the other R&D eligible expenses incurred by the company.[140]

Overall, the Project Team proposes to give priority to the principle described above. Therefore, the eligibility is up to a (certain) percentage of the total R&D expenses incurred.

Finally, the question whether a tax incentive (whether a super-deduction as provided for in the CCTB proposal or another tax incentive) should be excluded if the subcontractor or the company itself benefits from another incentive scheme under national or European law should also be further investigated, as it is another research project on its own.

The next limit is whether there should be a territorial scope in order to exclude payments to subcontractors outside European Economic Area (EEA), which cannot invoke the freedom to provide services.[141] Most National Correspondents agree that subcontractors should be located within the EEA (Austrian, French, Greek, Italian, Luxembourgish, Polish, and Spanish). Swiss Correspondent concurred (as it limits its own tax incentive to expenses carried out in Switzerland).

However, the Belgian and Croatian National Correspondents are of the opposite view and emphasise that there is no point in punishing companies relying on service providers located outside the EEA. Another argument would be that by contracting R&D activities outside the EEA creates spill over effects within broader Europe.

In the United States, section 174 expensing rule is not limited to R&D performed in the United States.[142] For instance, R&D performed through a foreign branch or by a foreign service provider is eligible for tax deduction. This is also the case under the UK R&D tax credit.

Only Irish Correspondent considered the answer to the question relating to territorial scope as being 'a pure policy decision'.

---

140. French national report.
141. The European Free Trade Association (EFTA) was established on 3 May 1960 following the signing of the Stockholm Convention on 4 January 1960. Its purpose was to serve as an alternative trade bloc for those European states that were unable or unwilling to join the then European Economic Community (EEC), now the European Union (EU). Of all previous members (Austria, Denmark, Norway, Portugal, Sweden, Switzerland, and the United Kingdom (UK), and later on Finland, Iceland, and Liechtenstein), only four remain part of EFTA today: Iceland, Liechtenstein, Norway and Switzerland. In order to extend the EU's Single Market to EFTA States, the European Economic Area (EEA) was established in 1994. Of the four EFTA states, Iceland, Liechtenstein and Norway are a part of the EEA while Switzerland is not. Instead, Switzerland has a series of complex bilateral agreements with the EU. The same basic rules governs the EEA Internal Market: for instance, the EEA Agreement guarantees the freedom to provide services on a non-discriminatory basis anywhere in the European Economic Area.
142. 26 U.S. Code para. 174.

Taking into consideration that Europe aims at being 'the most competitive and dynamic knowledge-based economy in the world capable of sustainable economic growth with more and better jobs and greater social cohesion',[143] the idea was that Europe should provide in its area all necessary tools for R&D success. Therefore, the notion of a territorial limit was kept in this book.

III. Who Claims R&D Tax Incentives (Principal vs Subcontractor)?

Assuming the subcontracted costs qualify as R&D expenses for the given tax incentive, the determination of who claims the R&D tax incentive (the principal company or its subcontractor) becomes crucial. It usually depends on who takes on the financial burden of the project and who holds the IP of the subcontracted work.

The following example illustrates the problem. A US company makes an investment in Europe through a Dutch company owning the IP, and pursuing R&D costs in Denmark, Spain, and France, the latter subcontracting R&D works in Romania. Who should be able to claim R&D expenses? Is it the US company bearing the financial risk of the project? Or the Dutch company owning the IP? Or even the French company supervising the R&D activity? And what about the Romanian company whose employees are realising the R&D activity?

The general idea is that only one entity can claim the deduction. The view of the Swiss National Correspondent reflects this general principle that should be adopted at EU level: if the ordering company can benefit from the super-deduction, the R&D subcontractor is not entitled to any super-deduction.

This is currently true from a national perspective, but not from a European-level perspective: R&D personnel expenses in country A that are invoiced in country B may be claimed in both countries under different regimes (France, Belgium, etc.). This is often seen as a competitive advantage of Europe as compared to the US for instance. However, the question of whether this should still be the case in the future remains within the framework of a European incentive scheme.

This is part of a general limitation for a double deduction in case of a unique R&D activity. In Spain for instance, there is also a limit as to the acquisition of the rights to the eventual results of the R&D activity by the subcontractor and ordering company, in order to avoid unjustified double or multiple tax incentives for the same R&D activity.

Other countries have provisions to prevent double use of expenses. For example, in Austria neither the agent can be controlled by the principal, nor can they be in the same group of companies, while in France, Spain, and Hungary, this applies to both the principal, and the sub-contractor levels. This may clearly be addressed by the draft CCTB directive or any European

143. Lisbon Strategy followed by the Europe 2020 Strategy.

tax incentive concept. Therefore, the proposed Principle would include the following: 'If the ordering company can benefit from the tax incentive, the R&D supplier is not entitled to this tax incentive.'

§ 4 Reimbursed Expenditure (Governmental, State and EU Funding)

The last inquiry concerns the tax treatment of expenditure reimbursed by the government or the state and/or the EU. The key to using innovation grants and R&D tax incentives together is careful cohabitation. These two sources of funding are not mutually exclusive but their relationship can be complicated. One important distinction between the two is the timing around when the taxpayer will receive a cash boost. Whereas grants tend to constitute up-front funding for which the taxpayer has to pitch, R&D tax incentives constitute retrospective funding that are claimed after having begun the R&D operations.

Almost all National Correspondents (except those from Belgium and Italy) agreed that governmental and State agency subsidies/grants related to R&D eligible projects should be deducted from the eligible expenses of the year during which these expenses are incurred.

Where these grants are refundable, they are added to the basis for calculating the tax incentive for the year in which they are refunded to the organisation that paid them.

There are usually important time delays (up to one to two years in some cases) between subsidy/grants payments and related R&D activities and associated expenses. Therefore, the taxpayer should consider when the grants are received, and when they are effectively paid. For instance, once a project is finished, the taxpayer receives the last payments of the grant the following year. When the taxpayer no longer has any expenses to match these grant payments, they retain them to match future expenses originating from another project. The French administration accepts that in the event a public subsidy is paid in a year and the expenditure eligible for the tax credit, which that subsidy is intended to cover, is exposed by the recipient in subsequent years, the subsidy must be deducted from the expenditure incurred in the year or years in which the eligible expenditure is incurred.[144] The final question is whether EU institution subsidies should be encompassed in the deduction from eligible expenses. An argument for deduction is that it would ensure an equal playing field with national subsidies.

The Project Team believes this question has to be further addressed by competition law specialist, since EU State aid rules require deduction and monitoring of cascading State aids.[145] In particular, the *de minimis* rule limits aid to firms

144. See French administrative guidelines, BOI-BIC- RICI-10-10-30-20-20140404, No. 10.
145. See in particular, Commission Notice on the notion of State aid as referred to in Art. 107(1) of the Treaty on the Functioning of the European Union, C/2016/2946, paras. 44 et seq.

so as to not hinder competition in the EU: over three years, the taxpayer cannot obtain more than EUR 200,000 from a certain type of aid. It is up to the taxpayer to ensure it does not exceed this ceiling, by taking stock of the various aids collected. On the one hand, certain incentives are not included in the *de minimis* calculation.[146] On the other hand, other aids are included: usually, the regulation indicates whether the aid fits into the *de minimis* regulation.[147]

146. E.g. the research tax credit in France.
147. This is expressly the case in France for the collection tax credit (designed for companies in the textiles, clothing and leather sector and related to the expenses of designing new collections. The resulting credit is known as 'collection tax credit', which is subject to the '*de minimis*' rule: see BOI-BIC- RICI-10-10-40-20190213, §380).

Chapter 4
National Reports

SECTION I
Austria

		Answers and comments	Technical source (when necessary)
1.	'RESEARCH AND DEVELOPMENT' – DEFINITION		
1.1.	As indicated in Section I (*supra*), should 'research and development' be excluded if there is no particular application or use in view for the economy or the internal market?	A study by the Institute for Advanced Studies Vienna in collaboration with the Austrian Institute for SME Research and WPZ Research published by the Austrian Federal Ministry of Finance (*Bundesministerium für Finanzen*) on the evaluation of the R&D premium (*Forschungsprämie*) – since its introduction in 2002 – shows that (i) R&D activity was intensified from those companies which already had a focus on R&D and (ii) R&D activity was transferred to Austria. (iii) On the downside, the R&D premium did not promote R&D activities in those companies which showed little or no interest in R&D. The study was published in March 2017 and is publicly available.	Study on the evaluation of the R&D premium as set out in Section 108c of the Austrian Income Tax Act 1988: https://www.bmf.gv.at/budget/aktuelle-berichte/BMF_Evaluierung_der_Forschungspraemie_Endbericht.pdf?5wmav6.
1.2.	Should the level of novelty be new 'to the world', 'to the internal market (EU)', 'to the market', or 'to the firm'?	For the purposes of the R&D premium, the Austrian R&D definition is related to the R&D definition in the OECD Frascati Manual (basic research, applied research and experimental development). The level on novelty is linked as to whether the underlying R&D question is readily apparent to someone familiar with the basic stock of common knowledge and techniques in the area concerned (see para. 84 Frascati Manual); this assumes a level of novelty which is new *'to the market'*. However, the Supreme Administrative Court (*Verwaltungsgerichtshof – VwGH*) denied a R&D premium in two cases relating to 'social sciences' and 'data collection' without any accompanied data analysis.	Section 108c of the Austrian Income Tax Act 1988 Decree (*Verordnung*) of the Austrian Federal Ministry of Finance (BGBl II 2002/506) VwGH 30.9.15, Ro 2014/15/0018 ('social sciences'); 26.6.13, 2009/13/0060 ('data collection').

1.3.	Should R&D be limited to the industrial sector, or also include the service industry (banking and insurance, but also humanities)?	In Austria, there is no such limitation, apart from the above mentioned VwGH jurisdiction in the research field of 'social sciences'.	VwGH 30.9.15, Ro 2014/15/0018 ("social sciences")
1.3.1.	In the latter case, which criteria help to identify the presence of R&D in services activities?	In Austria, in-house R&D activities must be confirmed by the Austrian Research Promotion Agency (*Forschungsförderungsgesellschaft* or *FFG*) or by a ruling according to Section 118a Federal Fiscal Code (*Bundesabgabenordnung*). In the case of contract R&D, the principal must inform the agent, if, and to what extent, he plans to claim the R&D premium for contract R&D. This information exchange must be documented. (The agent is then not allowed to claim a premium for in-house R&D for the expense, which form the principal's basis for the R&D premium for contract R&D).	https://www.ffg.at
1.3.1.1.	Links with public research laboratories;	For all criteria, please refer to 1.3.1. (confirmation by the Austrian Research Promotion Agency or an advance ruling is required).	
1.3.1.2.	Involvement of staff with PhDs or PhD students;		
1.3.1.3.	Publication of research findings in scientific journals;		
1.3.1.4.	Organisation of scientific conferences;		
1.3.1.5.	Involvement in scientific reviews;		
1.3.1.6.	Others?		
2.	'COSTS' (FOR RESEARCH AND DEVELOPMENT) – DEFINITION		
A.	**Capital expenditure**		
2.1.	**Depreciation allowances**		
a.	<u>*General Principles*</u>	<u>**Draft Art. 9-3**</u> provides: '*In addition to the amounts which are deductible as costs for research and development in accordance with paragraph 2, the taxpayer may also deduct, per tax year, an extra 50% of such costs, with the exception of the cost related to movable tangible fixed assets, that it incurred during that year. To the extent that costs for research and development reach beyond EUR 20,000,000, the taxpayer may deduct 25% of the exceeding amount.*' In addition, the Explanatory Memorandum (**para. 8**) provides: '*R&D costs will be fully expensed in the year incurred (with the exception of immovable property).*'	

		Draft Art. 10 (Other deductible items) provides: *"A deduction shall be made in respect of the depreciation of fixed assets referred to in Articles 30 to 40.* [...]" **Draft Art. 12** (Non-deductible items) provides: *'By way of derogation from Articles 9 and 10, the following items shall be non-deductible:* [...] *(i) acquisition or construction costs or cost connected with the improvement of fixed assets which are deductible under Articles 10 and 18, except for the cost related to research and development. The costs referred to in point (a) of Article 33(1) and points (a) and (b) of Article 33(2) shall not be treated as costs related to research and development;* [...]" – **For additional context, see Annex**. *Based on your national tax background:*	
		General remark: *The acquisition of or costs relating to immovable or movable assets can be fully added to the tax base of the Austrian R&D premium.*	
2.1.1.	Do you share our understanding that depreciation allowances have to be distinguished depending on the assets concerned, whether they are movable or immovable?	In Austria, assets are distinguished between depreciable and non-depreciable assets: since direct investments (investment costs) in R&D are included in the R&D tax base, a depreciation allowance is not eligible in the case of depreciable assets are directly serving R&D purposes (no double consideration of investment costs). Hence depreciation-allowances can only be included in the R&D tax base within the scope of the allocation of overhead costs. In consideration of overhead costs, depreciation-allowances are not excluded from the R&D tax base, in contrary to direct investments; a clear distinction must be drawn: directly R&D serving investments do not qualify for the consideration of a depreciation allowance, and/whereas not directly serving R&D investments qualify for a depreciation allowance on a pro-rated basis (according to the use for R&D purposes).	Para. 8208g Austrian Income Tax Regulations (*Einkommens-steuerrichtlinien*)
2.1.2.	Do you share our understanding that depreciation allowances are not available for movable fixed assets, because they are fully expensed in the year incurred, and not eligible to the super-deduction?	Regarding depreciation allowances that are not available for movable fixed assets, because they are fully expensed in the year incurred: if the background is the avoidance of double R&D tax incentives, this is agreed.	Decree (*Verordnung*) of the Austrian Federal Ministry of Finance on the R&D premium (BGBl II 2002/506)

		Regarding depreciation allowances not being eligible to the super-deduction, this is agreed. However, besides a full expense of movable fixed assets in the year incurred (by means of a full write-off in the year of acquisition), there is in the end only limited (or little) R&D tax incentive for the acquisition of movable fixed assets for R&D purposes (cf. currently in Austria expenses, such as capital investments including investments into properties, can be added to the tax base for the R&D premium. If such assets (properties) were added to the tax base, depreciation allowances in subsequent years are not available for the R&D tax base). Currently, Austria does not have a super-deduction regulation.	Para. 8208g Austrian Income Tax Regulations (*Einkommenssteuerrichtlinien*)
2.1.3.	Do you share our understanding that depreciation allowances remain available for immovable (property), because it cannot be fully expensed in the year incurred, and is eligible to the super-deduction?	Yes, in principle we do. However, as stated above, the Austrian R&D premium is granted without any limitations of deductibility of depreciation allowances in the year incurred as well as in subsequent years (although as stated above – to avoid double tax incentives – allowances for depreciation cannot be added to the tax base of the R&D premium in subsequent years).	Para. 8208g and 8208i Austrian Income Tax Regulations (*Einkommenssteuerrichtlinien*)
2.1.4.	What if an asset is used both for research and non-research purposes (such as manufacturing)?	If an asset serves R&D purposes in the long-term (*nachhaltige Nutzung*), acquisition costs are added to the tax base of R&D premium on a pro-rated basis. 'Long-term use for R&D purposes' is given if (i) depreciable assets (excluding buildings) with a useful life of up to ten years for a period of more than half of their useful life and (ii) land, buildings and other depreciable assets with a useful life of more than ten years for a period of at least 10 years, are used for R&D.	Para. 8208i Austrian Income Tax Regulations

2.1.5.	If eligible, which criteria for proportional eligibility if asset used both for R&D and manufacturing purposes (e.g. an equipment used both to manufacture prototypes and serial products)?	Whether an asset is used for R&D is determined pursuant to the 'principle of predominance' (*Überwiegensprinzip*).	
2.1.6.	What if the asset is 'indirectly' used for R&D purposes?	'Direct use' of assets for R&D purposes can be included if indirect costs can be determined. Indirect costs can be included in the tax base of the Austrian R&D premium, when allocated – if possible – to a cost unit or a cost center proportionally. According to the VwGH, indirect costs (or other overhead costs) are to be estimated if no applied cost accounting method is available.	VwGH 30.1.2014, 2011/15/0156 Para. 8208g Austrian Income Tax Regulations
2.1.7.	What do you think of the following definition: 'Is considered directly used for R&D purposes an asset permitting, in and of itself, to carry out research programs of the business'?	For Austria, in addition, an 'indirect use' of assets should be reflected.	
2.1.8.	Is the production of the following assets an R&D activity? (i) production of prototypes; (ii) construction of a pilot plant/or pilot facilities.	Both (i) and (ii) are R&D activities	
2.1.9.	Would you characterise the following assets as, potentially, directly used for R&D activities: (i) Handling devices; (ii) Calculation tools; (iii) Computers; (iv) Machines used to manufacture components of a prototype; (v) Telephones, small office appliances, office furniture?	If such assets are not deemed as direct costs attributable to a R&D project, the usage of such assets, (i) to (v), would be allocable to the R&D tax base as indirect costs under application of a standard cost accounting method. If a cost accounting is not in place, costs can be estimated proportionally and allocated accordingly (see answer to question 2.1.6.).	
b.	*Specific Rules*		
(i)	*Intangible Assets*	**Draft Art. 33.1(e)** provides: '*Without prejudice to paragraph 2 and Articles 37 and 38, fixed assets shall be depreciated individually over their useful lives on a straight-line basis. The useful life of a fixed asset shall be determined as follows: […] (e) fixed intangible assets: the period for which the asset enjoys legal protection or for which the right has been granted or, where that period cannot be determined, 15 years.*'	

		The problem is that not all intangible items (e.g. intellectual property, brand names), meet the definition of an intangible asset. If an item does meet the definition of an intangible asset, expenditure to acquire it or generate it internally should be recognised as an expense when it is incurred. Therefore, *based on your national tax background*:	
2.1.10.	Should we use the European Union Accounting Rule 6 defining intangible asset (i.e. identifiability, control over a resource, and existence of future economic benefits or service potential)?	Yes, a homogeneous definition is favourable.	
2.1.11.	If not, what should be the definition of intangible assets?		
2.1.12.	Are intangible fixed assets (including intellectual property (IP)) costs fully expensed in the year incurred and included in the CCTB super-deduction?	Yes, IP is an integral part of R&D expenses.	
	The inclusion of mere intellectual property costs is not advisable: it may create a bias in favour of patented research compared to that stemming from unpatented technology.	*An independent body (such as the Austrian Research Promotion Agency) could avoid such a bias by confirming the fulfilment of the eligibility requirement for R&D activities.*	
2.1.13.	Will in practice this provision be limited to patents costs acquired with a view to carry on new experimental research and development?	Reference is made to question 1.2 (level of novelty). In Austria, there is currently no such limitation.	
2.1.14.	What if these patents are (also) used in the manufacturing process?	Reference is made to question 2.1.6 (indirect costs). If patents are also used in the manufacturing process, those costs allocable to R&D are attributable to the R&D tax base.	
2.1.15.	Should plant variety rights be treated in the same manner as patents?	Yes, if a single intellectual property right is received when applying to the Community Plant Variety Office (CPVO).	http://cpvo.europa.eu
2.1.16.	What about outlays incurred to acquire licences or know-how?	Outlays are generally considered as incidental acquisition costs and are part of the acquisition costs.	Section 6 of the Austrian Income Tax Act 1988
(ii)	*Immovable (property)*		
	In any case, not covered by exclusion in Art. 9-3		
	In Austria, building costs and financing expenses related to R&D activity may be taken into account.		

2.1.17.	Should the concept of 'immovable property' (Recital No. 8) be preferred to the one of 'immovable fixed asset' (as opposed to Art. 9.3 CCTB)?		
2.1.18.	Would building costs and financing expenses related to the acquisition of immovable [property] be eligible to the super-deduction?	Apart from the fact that Austria currently has no super-deduction regulation, building costs and finance costs attributable to R&D activities can be added to the tax base for the R&D premium.	
2.1.19.	What is your understanding of Art. 12(i): 1st meaning: that costs related to acquisition or construction of new commercial or second-hand commercial or industrial immovable [property] is excluded from the super-deduction? Or 2nd meaning: that costs related to acquisition or construction of new commercial or second-hand commercial or industrial immovable [property] is not fully deductible the year incurred but should be depreciated and such depreciation allowances are eligible to the super-deduction?		
(iii)	*Lease payments*		
2.1.20.	What if equipment is used according to the terms of a leasing-type transaction?	If attributable to R&D activities, yes.	
2.1.21.	Are leasing instalments eligible for super-deduction under current wording of Art. 9-3?	In case of a finance lease: no (argument: same consideration should apply as for depreciation allowances of movable fixed assets). In case of an operating lease: in principle, yes.	Para. 135 Austrian Income Tax Regulations
2.1.22.	Should they be?	Depending on the fact, which lease contract is at stake? Finance lease should be treated equivalent to an acquisition of assets, whereas the tax treatment of operating lease expenses is open to discussion.	

(iv)	*Alternative readings*		
2.1.23.	Please feel free to add any alternative readings you may have of relevant CCTB provisions and that has not yet been discussed.	No other alternative readings are to be added.	
B.	**Current expenditure**		
2.2.	**R&D staff cost**		
a.	*What is meant by R&D staff?*		
2.2.1.	Should eligibility be limited to staff directly-involved in R&D?	Staff, who is 'indirectly' serving R&D purposes or only 'partially', should be included as well.	Decree (*Verordnung*) of the Austrian Federal Ministry of Finance on the R&D premium (BGBl II 2002/506)
2.2.2.	In case the staff participates both in R&D and non R&D activities, should the text allow for proportional eligibility based on time spent (or other criteria)?		
2.2.3.	How can researchers or scientists be defined? Should the text use black letter criteria (list diplomas (PhDs), qualifications…) or a more open definition?	There should be a more open definition. Main criteria should not be a job description and/or a definition of 'R&D staff'; main criterion should be the time invested and served for 'R&D purposes' which is independent from job description or any other 'formal' aspects.	
2.2.4.	Are research technicians R&D staff?		
2.2.5.	What about other employees (not 'official researchers') which still have contributed to a patented invention?	If directly or indirectly attributable to R&D activities, yes.	
2.2.6.	What about the managers of the business (e.g. running a research program)?	If directly or indirectly attributable to R&D activities, yes.	
2.2.7.	What about other staff (secretariat, cleaning, etc.)? Can, in the alternative, their compensation be taken into account, proportionally, as other operating R&D expenses (cf. I-3 below)?	If directly or indirectly attributable to R&D activities, yes.	

<u>*b.*</u>	<u>*What is meant by R&D staff cost?*</u>	All actual salaries and wages including incidental wage costs.	Decree (*Verordnung*) of the Austrian Federal Ministry of Finance on the R&D premium (BGBl II 2002/506)
2.2.8.	Wages, bonuses, benefits in kind?		
2.2.9.	Social security contributions (compulsory and/or non-compulsory)?	Yes, including non-compulsory social security contributions.	
2.2.10.	Employer's contribution to participation of employees in profits of the enterprise by means of profit-sharing plan, employee share-ownership?	Yes, in case of a written, legally binding and irrevocable commitment.	Cf. Section 14(12) of the Austrian Income Tax Act 1988
2.2.11.	Can a Member State provide that compensation paid to holders of PhD will count more (e.g. double) for a limited period of time (in order to promote hiring of PhD holders)?	Only costs, which actually incurred are allocable.	
2.3.	**Standardisation expenses**		
	Based on your national tax background:		
2.3.1.	Should expenses related to the establishment of technical standards concerning products of the business be eligible for the super-deduction (e.g. expenses incurred on participation of employees in official meetings of standardisation bodies)?	Standardisation expenses should not be included with the exception of research activities using scientific methods for the purpose of standardisation.	Decree (*Verordnung*) of the Austrian Federal Ministry of Finance on the R&D premium (BGBl II 2002/506)
2.3.2.	If yes, should it still be the case even if these employees are not scientists or research technicians?		
2.3.3.	How should these expenses be assessed (e.g. as portion of employee compensation related to the time spent in connection with such meetings)?		
2.3.4.	Should expenses related to technical monitoring/ technological watch be taken into account?		

2.4.	**Patent related expenses**		
2.4.1.	Are expenses linked to patents eligible? Please define NB: *under current French tax law, expenses linked to the filing, the maintenance and the defence of patents incurred in France or in another State (IP consultant's fees, translation costs taxes...) are eligible to the R&D tax credit; insurance costs linked to patents are eligible within a threshold of EUR 60,000. However, under the Frascati criterion, R&D would typically not include administrative and legal work connected with patents, routine tests or data collection.*	Administrative and legal work related to patents – so-called security costs – can be claimed under the Austrian R&D premium. However, such costs must be directly related to specific R&D projects. Thus, for example, costs incurred during the patenting of an invention in the form of registration or annual fees can be added to the tax base of the R&D premium. The fact that security costs do not have a direct impact on the development or improvement process (but rather primarily on the exploitation phase) does not have a negative impact on the Austrian R&D premium.	Decree (*Verordnung*) of the Austrian Federal Ministry of Finance on the R&D premium (BGBl II 2002/506)
2.5.	**Other operating expenses related to R&D**		
2.5.1.	Should such category be identified?	Austria distinguishes between direct and indirect costs allocable to R&D. Whether or not such costs are defined as 'other operating costs' or according to any other P/L position is not relevant for the categorization as 'R&D expense'.	Decree (*Verordnung*) of the Austrian Federal Ministry of Finance on the R&D premium (BGBl II 2002/506)
2.5.2.	Is a detailed list possible of expenses advisable?	Yes, the annex of the Decree (*Verordnung*) of the Austrian Federal Ministry of Finance on the R&D premium (BGBl II 2002/506) outlines a delimitation of R&D expenses (e.g. data collection, documentation, unsuccessful R&D).	
2.5.3.	Is it appropriate to assess these expenses notionally by reference to other precisely defined eligible expenses (e.g. 15% of immovable [property] depreciation allowances, and/or 50% of eligible staff expenses)?	As stated above, costs should be allocable to the R&D tax base depending whether or not costs are directly or indirectly incurred by R&D and according to a standard cost accounting method (proportionally) allocable to R&D expenses.	

2.5.4.	Should fees paid to external consultants assisting the company to determine its R&D super deduction be eligible, and to what extent?	In Austria, services of state-certified tax advisors are tax deductible as a special expense; regardless of any R&D activity.	Section 18(1)(6) of the Austrian Income Tax Act 1988
C.	**Contracted Expenditure**		
2.6.	**Subcontracting expenses**		
2.6.1.	What if R&D activity is outsourced? *Currently in France, payments to R&D service suppliers, public or private, accredited by the French Ministry of research and located in the EU or the EEA, qualify as eligible expenses.*	If R&D activity is outsourced (in Austria it is called 'contract R&D'), such subcontracting expenses can be added to the tax base of the R&D premium. In the case of contract R&D, the principal must inform the agent until the end of the financial year, if, and to what extent, the principal is planning to claim R&D premium for contract R&D. This information exchange must be documented. The agent is then not allowed to claim a premium for in-house R&D for the expense, which form the principal's basis for the R&D premium for contract R&D.	Section 108c(2)(2) of the Austrian Income Tax Act 1988
2.6.2.	Should there be a territorial limit to exclude payments to subcontractors outside the EEA (which cannot invoke the freedom to provide services).	In the case of contract research (outsourcing) the following rules must be observed accordingly: i. The R&D order must be assigned by an Austrian entity, permanent establishment or branch. ii. Only expenses to companies or organisations based in the EU or EEA can be included. iii. Neither the agent can be controlled by the principal; nor can they be in the same group of companies. iv. The R&D tax credit is only available for expenses in the amount of EUR 1 million per financial year. This amount has to be reduced proportionately if the fiscal year covers less than 12 years	

2.6.3.	Should there be other limits? *Under current French law for instance, R&D costs invoiced by accredited private subcontractors can be retained within the limit of three times the total amount of all the other R&D eligible expenses incurred by the company; and such expenses can be retained by the company subcontracting R&D works within a yearly limit of EUR 12 or 10 million and EUR 2 million when the parties (i.e. ordering company and R&D supplier) are related companies.*	See above, R&D tax credit is only available for expenses in the amount of EUR 1 million per financial year. This amount has to be reduced proportionately if the fiscal year covers less than 12 years.	
B.	**Reimbursed expenditure**		
2.7.	**Treatment of public subsidies**		
2.7.1.	Should governmental and other State agencies subsidies/grants related to R&D eligible projects be deducted from eligible expenses of the year during which these expenses are incurred?	In Austria, tax free grants from public funds (Section 3(4) of the Austrian Income Tax Act 1988) reduce the tax base for the R&D premium.	VwGH 22.10.2002, 2002/14/0030.

Section II
Belgium

		Answers and comments	Technical source (when necessary)
1.	'Research and Development' – Definition		
1.1.	As indicated in Section I (*supra*), should 'research and development' be excluded if there is no particular application or use in view for the economy or the internal market?	Currently, Belgian R&D tax incentives do not have a distinct definition of R&D. Tax administration usually relies on the Frascati Manual. As a result, also basic or fundamental research will usually be covered by the R&D incentives.	
1.2.	Should the level of novelty be new 'to the world', 'to the internal market (EU)', 'to the market', or 'to the firm'?	The answer depends on the type of tax incentive. Generally, the level of novelty should be interpreted as new 'to the world'. However, for some incentives, it may be sufficient to be 'new to the market' (or sector).	
1.3.	Should R&D be limited to the industrial sector, or also include the service industry (banking and insurance, but also humanities)?	R&D should also include the service industry. Some tax incentives (e.g. the exemption for payroll tax for researchers), however, require specific degrees of the researchers which do not include the services industry.	
1.3.1.	In the latter case, which criteria help to identify the presence of R&D in services activities?		
1.3.1.1.	Links with public research laboratories;	Yes	
1.3.1.2.	Involvement of staff with PhDs or PhD students;	Yes	
1.3.1.3.	Publication of research findings in scientific journals;	Yes	
1.3.1.4.	Organisation of scientific conferences;	Yes	
1.3.1.5.	Involvement in scientific reviews;	Yes	
1.3.1.6.	Others?		

2.	'COSTS' (FOR RESEARCH AND DEVELOPMENT) – DEFINITION		
A.	**Capital expenditure**		
2.1.	**Depreciation allowances**		
a.	*General Principles*	**Draft Art. 9-3** provides: *'In addition to the amounts which are deductible as costs for research and development in accordance with paragraph 2, the taxpayer may also deduct, per tax year, an extra 50% of such costs, with the exception of the cost related to movable tangible fixed assets, that it incurred during that year. To the extent that costs for research and development reach beyond EUR 20,000,000, the taxpayer may deduct 25% of the exceeding amount.'* In addition, the Explanatory Memorandum (**para. 8**) provides: *'R&D costs will be fully expensed in the year incurred (with the exception of immovable property).'* **Draft Art. 10** (Other deductible items) provides: *'A deduction shall be made in respect of the depreciation of fixed assets referred to in Articles 30 to 40. [...]"* **Draft Art. 12** (Non-deductible items) provides: *'By way of derogation from Articles 9 and 10, the following items shall be non-deductible:* [...] *(i) acquisition or construction costs or cost connected with the improvement of fixed assets which are deductible under Articles 10 and 18, except for the cost related to research and development. The costs referred to in point (a) of Article 33(1) and points (a) and (b) of Article 33(2) shall not be treated as costs related to research and development;* [...]" – **For additional context, see Annex**. *Based on your national tax background:*	
2.1.1.	Do you share our understanding that depreciation allowances have to be distinguished depending on the assets concerned, whether they are movable or immovable?	Belgian law provides no guidance regarding this question. However, no distinction is made in particular for R&D depreciation (stipulating a minimum of three year depreciation scheme for R&D expenses).	
2.1.2.	Do you share our understanding that depreciation allowances are not available for movable fixed assets, because they are fully expensed in the year incurred, and not eligible to the super-deduction?	The super deduction is available to both movable and intangible fixed assets. Both tax incentives can be combined.	

2.1.3.	Do you share our understanding that depreciation allowances remain available for immovable [property], because it cannot be fully expensed in the year incurred, and is eligible to the super-deduction?	Both tax incentives can be combined.	Arts. 68 et seq. of the Belgian Income Tax Code ('BITC') and Arts. 47 et seq. Royal Decree implementing the BITC (esp. Art. 48 Royal Decree implementing the BITC) Arts. 205/1 et seq. BITC
2.1.4.	What if an asset is used both for research and non-research purposes (such as manufacturing)?	It depends on the Belgian domestic tax measures and on the situation (e.g. for the R&D deduction and the R&D tax credit, there could be proportional eligibility (if the assets are allocated to a research centre constituting a branch of activity) or no eligibility; for the innovation deduction, there should be a proportional eligibility).	
2.1.5.	If eligible, which criteria for proportional eligibility if asset used both for R&D and manufacturing purposes (e.g. an equipment used both to manufacture prototypes and serial products)?	For the R&D deduction and the R&D tax credit, if the assets are allocated to a research centre constituting a branch of activity, they are only eligible to the extent they do not exceed what is needed for the good functioning of this centre.	Art. 48 Royal Decree implementing the BITC
2.1.6.	What if the asset is 'indirectly' used for R&D purposes?	Such assets are, in principle, not eligible (except, for the R&D deduction or the R&D tax credit, if the assets are allocated to a research centre constituting a branch of activity and do not exceed what is needed for the good functioning of this centre).	Art. 48 Royal Decree implementing the BITC Arts. 205/1 et seq. BITC
2.1.7.	What do you think of the following definition: 'Is considered directly used for R&D purposes an asset permitting, in and of itself, to carry out research programs of the business'?	This definition is based on the essence of the asset, where it should instead be based on its effective use.	
2.1.8.	Is the production of the following assets an R&D activity? (i) production of prototypes; (ii) construction of a pilot plant/or pilot facilities.	(i) Yes (ii) Yes, assuming that (a) no commercial use is made of the goods produced in the pilot plant/facilities and (b) the pilot plant/facilities production capacity is insufficient to assure a normal profitability.	Art. 48 Royal Decree implementing the BITC

2.1.9.	Would you characterise the following assets as, potentially, directly used for R&D activities: (i) Handling devices; (ii) Calculation tools; (iii) Computers; (iv) Machines used to manufacture components of a prototype; (v) Telephones, small office appliances, office furniture?	(i) to (iv) yes (v) no (except, for the R&D deduction or the R&D tax credit, if the assets are allocated to a research centre constituting a branch of activity and do not exceed what is needed for the good functioning of this centre).	Art. 48 Royal Decree implementing the BITC Arts. 205/1 et seq. BITC
b.	*Specific Rules*		
(i)	*Intangible Assets*	**Draft Art. 33.1(e)** provides: '*Without prejudice to paragraph 2 and Articles 37 and 38, fixed assets shall be depreciated individually over their useful lives on a straight-line basis. The useful life of a fixed asset shall be determined as follows: [...] (e) fixed intangible assets: the period for which the asset enjoys legal protection or for which the right has been granted or, where that period cannot be determined, 15 years".* The problem is that not all intangible items (e.g. intellectual property, brand names), meet the definition of an intangible asset. If an item does meet the definition of an intangible asset, expenditure to acquire it or generate it internally should be recognised as an expense when it is incurred. Therefore, *based on your national tax background*:	
2.1.10.	Should we use the European Union Accounting Rule 6 defining intangible asset (i.e. identifiability, control over a resource, and existence of future economic benefits or service potential)?	Belgian domestic tax law is based on Belgian GAAP, which do not follow EU Accounting Rule 6.	
2.1.11.	If not, what should be the definition of intangible assets?	Under Belgian GAAP, intangible assets are defined as: i. R&D costs that are useful for the future activities of the company ii. Patents, licences, know-how, trademarks and other similar rights; iii. Goodwill. However, for the application of the Belgian tax incentives, only the R&D costs, patents, licences and know-how will generally be eligible.	Art. 95 Royal Decree implementing the Belgian Companies Code Arts. 68 et seq. BITC and Arts. 47 et seq. Royal Decree implementing the BITC Arts. 205/1 et seq. BITC

2.1.12.	Are intangible fixed assets (including intellectual property (IP)) costs fully expensed in the year incurred and included in the CCTB super-deduction?	Belgian law provides no guidance regarding this question.	
	The inclusion of mere intellectual property costs is not advisable: it may create a bias in favour of patented research compared to that stemming from unpatented technology.		
2.1.13.	Will in practice this provision be limited to patents costs acquired with a view to carry on new experimental research and development?	Belgian law provides no guidance regarding this question, but we would assume not.	
2.1.14.	What if these patents are (also) used in the manufacturing process?	N/A	
2.1.15.	Should plant variety rights be treated in the same manner as patents?	It depends from the Belgian domestic tax measures (no for the R&D deduction and the R&D tax credit; yes for the innovation deduction).	Arts. 68 et s. BITC and Arts. 47 et seq. Royal Decree implementing the BITC Arts. 205/1 et seq. BITC
2.1.16.	What about outlays incurred to acquire licences or know-how?	It depends from the Belgian domestic tax measures (in principle, yes for the R&D deduction and the R&D tax credit; in principle, yes for the innovation deduction, except for know-how unless related to a patent or functionally equivalent IP right).	Arts. 68 et s. BITC and Arts. 47 et seq. Royal Decree implementing the BITC Arts. 205/1 et seq. BITC
(ii)	*Immovable (property)*		
	In any case, not covered by exclusion in Art. 9-3		
	In Austria, building costs and financing expenses related to R&D activity may be taken into account.		
2.1.17.	Should the concept of 'immovable property' (Recital No. 8) be preferred to the one of 'immovable fixed asset' (as opposed to Art. 9.3 CCTB)?	Belgian law provides no guidance regarding this question. However, both concepts are slightly different under Belgian law (immovable property can in some circumstances not be a fixed asset, e.g. a building to be sold could be a stock).	

2.1.18.	Would building costs and financing expenses related to the acquisition of immovable [property] be eligible to the super-deduction?	It depends from the Belgian domestic tax measures (yes for the R&D deduction and R&D tax credit; no for the innovation deduction).	Art. 48 Royal Decree implementing the BITC Arts. 205/1 et seq. BITC
2.1.19.	What is your understanding of Art. 12(i): 1st meaning: that costs related to acquisition or construction of new commercial or second-hand commercial or industrial immovable [property] is excluded from the super-deduction? Or 2nd meaning: that costs related to acquisition or construction of new commercial or second-hand commercial or industrial immovable [property] is not fully deductible the year incurred but should be depreciated and such depreciation allowances are eligible to the super-deduction?	Belgian law provides no guidance regarding this question.	
(iii)	*Lease payments*		
2.1.20.	What if equipment is used according to the terms of a leasing-type transaction?	Belgian law provides no guidance regarding this question.	
2.1.21.	Are leasing instalments eligible for super-deduction under current wording of Art. 9-3?	Belgian law provides no guidance regarding this question. However, they will likely not if these expenses are not activated and amortised (e.g. an operational lease would not qualify).	
2.1.22.	Should they be?	Belgian law provides no guidance regarding this question.	
(iv)	*Alternative readings*		
2.1.23.	Please feel free to add any alternative readings you may have of relevant CCTB provisions and that has not yet been discussed.		

B.	**Current expenditure**	**N.B.: although only assets are, in principle, taken into account for the Belgian R&D deduction and Belgian R&D tax credit, expenditures also have to be taken into account to determine the value of some intangible assets (e.g. the R&D costs)**	
2.2.	**R&D staff cost**		
<u>a.</u>	<u>*What is meant by R&D staff?*</u>		
2.2.1.	Should eligibility be limited to staff directly-involved in R&D?	Yes	
2.2.2.	In case the staff participates both in R&D and non R&D activities, should the text allow for proportional eligibility based on time spent (or other criteria)?	Yes	
2.2.3.	How can researchers or scientists be defined? Should the text use black letter criteria (list diplomas (PhDs), qualifications…) or a more open definition?	For some Belgian domestic tax measures, there is a list of diplomas, but not for all.	For an example of such list, see Art. 275/3 BITC
2.2.4.	Are research technicians R&D staff?	Generally yes (for some domestic tax measures, provided that they have a qualifying diploma).	
2.2.5.	What about other employees (not 'official researchers') which still have contributed to a patented invention?	Generally yes (for some domestic tax measures, provided that they have a qualifying diploma).	
2.2.6.	What about the managers of the business (e.g. running a research program)?	Generally yes (for some domestic tax measures, provided that they have a qualifying diploma).	
2.2.7.	What about other staff (secretariat, cleaning, etc.)? Can, in the alternative, their compensation be taken into account, proportionally, as other operating R&D expenses (cf. I-3 below)?	No	
<u>b.</u>	<u>*What is meant by R&D staff cost?*</u>		
2.2.8.	Wages, bonuses, benefits in kind?	All of them.	

2.2.9.	Social security contributions (compulsory and/or non-compulsory)?	Yes	
2.2.10.	Employer's contribution to participation of employees in profits of the enterprise by means of profit-sharing plan, employee share-ownership?	All of them.	
2.2.11.	Can a Member State provide that compensation paid to holders of PhD will count more (e.g. double) for a limited period of time (in order to promote hiring of PhD holders)?	Belgian domestic legislation currently does not provide for such measure.	
2.3.	**Standardisation expenses**		
	Based on your national tax background:		
2.3.1.	Should expenses related to the establishment of technical standards concerning products of the business be eligible for the super-deduction (e.g. expenses incurred on participation of employees in official meetings of standardisation bodies)?	Belgian law provides no guidance regarding this question. However, in our view, likely not.	
2.3.2.	If yes, should it still be the case even if these employees are not scientists or research technicians?	N/A	
2.3.3.	How should these expenses be assessed (e.g. as portion of employee compensation related to the time spent in connection with such meetings)?	N/A	
2.3.4.	Should expenses related to technical monitoring/ technological watch be taken into account?	Belgian law provides no guidance regarding this question. However, tax administration's view is that routine testing or data collection does not constitute qualifying expenditure for the purposes of the R&D tax credit.	

2.4.	**Patent related expenses**		
2.4.1.	Are expenses linked to patents eligible? Please define NB: *under current French tax law, expenses linked to the filing, the maintenance and the defence of patents incurred in France or in another State (IP consultant's fees, translation costs taxes...) are eligible to the R&D tax credit; insurance costs linked to patents are eligible within a threshold of EUR 60,000. However, under the Frascati criterion, R&D would typically not include administrative and legal work connected with patents, routine tests or data collection.*	Administrative expenses related to patents are generally not eligible.	
2.5.	**Other operating expenses related to R&D**		
2.5.1.	Should such category be identified?	Belgian law provides no guidance regarding this question.	
2.5.2.	Is a detailed list possible of expenses advisable?	Presumably yes, but Belgian law provides no guidance regarding this question.	
2.5.3.	Is it appropriate to assess these expenses notionally by reference to other precisely defined eligible expenses (e.g. 15% of immovable [property] depreciation allowances, and/or 50% of eligible staff expenses)?	Belgian law provides no guidance regarding this question.	
2.5.4.	Should fees paid to external consultants assisting the company to determine its R&D super deduction be eligible, and to what extent?	No	

C.	**Contracted Expenditure**		
2.6.	**Subcontracting expenses**		
2.6.1.	What if R&D activity is outsourced? *Currently in France, payments to R&D service suppliers, public or private, accredited by the French Ministry of research and located in the EU or the EEA, qualify as eligible expenses.*	Outsourced R&D activity is, in principle, eligible.	Arts. 205/1 et seq. BITC
2.6.2.	Should there be a territorial limit to exclude payments to subcontractors outside the EEA (which cannot invoke the freedom to provide services).	No	
2.6.3.	Should there be other limits? *Under current French law for instance, R&D costs invoiced by accredited private subcontractors can be retained within the limit of three times the total amount of all the other R&D eligible expenses incurred by the company; and such expenses can be retained by the company subcontracting R&D works within a yearly limit of EUR 12 or 10 million and EUR 2 million when the parties (i.e. ordering company and R&D supplier) are related companies.*	For the innovation deduction, R&D activity outsourced to related parties is not eligible.	Arts. 205/1 et seq. BITC
B.	**Reimbursed expenditure**		
2.7.	**Treatment of public subsidies**		
2.7.1.	Should governmental and other State agencies subsidies/grants related to R&D eligible projects be deducted from eligible expenses of the year during which these expenses are incurred?	No	Administrative Commentary to the ITC, No. 68/53.

Section III
Croatia

		Answers and comments	Technical source (when necessary)
1.	'Research and Development' – Definition		
1.1.	As indicated in Section I (*supra*), should 'research and development' be excluded if there is no particular application or use in view for the economy or the internal market?	No. Research and development is costly and lengthy business, with unpredictable results (especially basic and applied research) what leads to huge risks for the business. At the time when companies' decisions about undertaking of the R&D and financial issues of the projects on the strategical management positions are made, and, later, while R&D process is performed, business is not certain about particular application of the process. It would not be fair to make decisions on the application of the R&D results using information unknown and unforeseeable at the time of the business decision or R&D process. Moreover, if some R&D project fails, it is still activity or R&D which should be recognised for the tax incentive due to the efforts undertaken in good faith by the entrepreneurs. Research and development activities increase the general level of the knowledge and lead to further improvements of the expertise, whether they are recognised immediately or afterwards. For example, the results of the projects which failed can be used in some other project (some most profitable products where the results of the failure of the initial projects). Likewise, the project which was halted, due to the insufficient funds or collapse of the market, still represents the R&D activity.	

		It would be contrary to the aim of the R&D incentive to exclude basic research which is characterised as '[...] experimental or theoretical work undertaken primarily to acquire new knowledge of the underlying foundation of phenomena and observable facts, without any particular application or use in view', (Frascati manual, OECD 2002, Recital 64). Since the aim of the R&D incentive is to encourage entrepreneurs to invest into R&D activities, it should cover all reasonable expenses without any link with the outcome of the R&D. Unsuccessful investment in R&D results in the profit loss as any other unsuccessful business project recognised by the corporate income tax. Therefore, if entrepreneurs are encouraged to undertake this risky move, they must not be punished twice for the possible failure (from the competitors and from the tax administration). The problems might occur while determining the R&D cost in general, as well as exact type of R&D activity for particular cost (basic, applied or experimental development). The Directive or Annex to the Directive might be useful for such standardisation, but further explanations would be facilitative for the entrepreneurs and tax administrations. Therefore, the guidelines with the examples in different fields of industry at the EU level might be suggested (as one presented in Table 4.2., p. 81 of the Frascati Manual 2002).	
1.2.	Should the level of novelty be new 'to the world', 'to the internal market (EU)', 'to the market', or 'to the firm'?	If previous definition is accepted (1.1.) then 'to the firm' would be more convenient since the competitiveness of every firm contributes to the competitiveness of the whole market (by urging competitiveness of the competitors of the firm). For example, if some product is new to the firm and not to the market, but it is competitive on the market, other competitors will try to find another, new product to the market (worldwide or European).	

1.3.	Should R&D be limited to the industrial sector, or also include the service industry (banking and insurance, but also humanities)?	No. This might trigger the question of the State Aid. R&D in service sector also raise the competitiveness of the whole market and employs highly-qualified residents of the Member States (e.g. IT).	
1.3.1.	In the latter case, which criteria help to identify the presence of R&D in services activities?		
1.3.1.1.	Links with public research laboratories;	No. Business projects (projects of the taxpayers) can be entirely rendered within the business community. The goal of this incentive is to foster taxpayers' R&D.	
1.3.1.2.	Involvement of staff with PhDs or PhD students;	Not necessarily. As stated in Frascati 2002 (rec. 32 and 33) a wide variety of personnel is involved in the R&D projects and their roles and responsibilities are not directly linked to the position within the project. Though involvement of the PhD staff and PhD students is important, this requirement might be unrealisable for the small and medium entrepreneurs. Additionally, this requirement needs further clarification: e.g. number of staff with PhDs or PhD students in correlation to the total staff involved or the total value of the project, which, again, might be unfeasible for the SMEs (or, if divided in several categories, too complicated).	
1.3.1.3.	Publication of research findings in scientific journals;	Business projects are not necessarily linked with the public announcements.	
1.3.1.4.	Organisation of scientific conferences;	Business projects are not necessarily linked with the public announcements.	
1.3.1.5.	Involvement in scientific reviews;		
1.3.1.6.	Others?	Unpredictability and technical improvement of the project.	

2.	'COSTS' (FOR RESEARCH AND DEVELOPMENT) – DEFINITION		
A.	**Capital expenditure**		
2.1.	**Depreciation allowances**	All depreciation allowance that is recognised by the accounting standards.	
<u>a.</u>	<u>*General Principles*</u>	**<u>Draft Art. 9-3</u>** provides: *'In addition to the amounts which are deductible as costs for research and development in accordance with paragraph 2, the taxpayer may also deduct, per tax year, an extra 50% of such costs, with the exception of the cost related to movable tangible fixed assets, that it incurred during that year. To the extent that costs for research and development reach beyond EUR 20,000,000, the taxpayer may deduct 25% of the exceeding amount.'* In addition, the Explanatory Memorandum (**para. 8**) provides: *'R&D costs will be fully expensed in the year incurred (with the exception of immovable property).'* **<u>Draft Art. 10</u>** (Other deductible items) provides: *'A deduction shall be made in respect of the depreciation of fixed assets referred to in Articles 30 to 40.* [...]' **<u>Draft Art. 12</u>** (Non-deductible items) provides: *'By way of derogation from Articles 9 and 10, the following items shall be non-deductible:* [...] *(i) acquisition or construction costs or cost connected with the improvement of fixed assets which are deductible under Articles 10 and 18, except for the cost related to research and development. The costs referred to in point (a) of Article 33(1) and points (a) and (b) of Article 33(2) shall not be treated as costs related to research and development;* [...]' – **<u>For additional context, see Annex</u>**. *<u>Based on your national tax background:</u>*	
2.1.1.	Do you share our understanding that depreciation allowances have to be distinguished depending on the assets concerned, whether they are movable or immovable?	Movable property is often important and necessary part of the R&D process (e.g. specially equipped vehicles, microscopes, other apparatus for the laboratories). Different projects require different assets. It would be discriminatory if some of the assets, though valuable and essential for some projects are not recognised for the tax incentive. If there is a doubt about necessity of some assets for R&D projects and possible tax avoidance triggered by its usage, it would be more fair and practical to specify them (for example, 'except vehicles for the personal use').	

2.1.2.	Do you share our understanding that depreciation allowances are not available for movable fixed assets, because they are fully expensed in the year incurred, and not eligible to the super-deduction?	If some asset is used in R&D process and its expense is a part of the R&D project, it should be eligible to the super-deduction. Other expenses that are not depreciable but expensed in the year when they incurred (e.g. salaries) are also eligible for the tax incentive so the criteria for the non-recognition of these items is not quite evident. Due to the fact that the idea of this incentive is to promote research and development which leads to the improvement in the competitiveness on the market, all expenses should be treated equally for the incentive. Property which is paid/bought by the business is already expensed so the depreciation is often accrued (postponed cost) for the accounting reporting. R&D projects include only this depreciated amounts of the total costs of the assets. If super-deduction includes only depreciation of the assets that are depreciated in long-term then the costs of the assets that are fully expensed in the year incurred, would never be the part of the super-deduction. For R&D projects which involve majority of such assets, it would be discriminatory. For example, one asset is fully expensed in the year incurred and its value is recognised cost whilst the other asset is depreciated in two years and its increased value is eligible to the super-deduction in these two years. If one project consists predominantly of the first assets and the other of the later, and if both values of the assets are substantial, the differences might be significant, in spite of the fact that both projects represent R&D.	
2.1.3.	Do you share our understanding that depreciation allowances remain available for immovable [property], because it cannot be fully expensed in the year incurred, and is eligible to the super-deduction?	Yes, though the rationale for availability is that all expenses (costs and depreciation of the assets) that are proved as part of R&D project should be treated in the same way for the super-deduction.	

2.1.4.	What if an asset is used both for research and non-research purposes (such as manufacturing)?	It should be included in super-deduction in accordance with the usage within R&D project.	
2.1.5.	If eligible, which criteria for proportional eligibility if asset used both for R&D and manufacturing purposes (e.g. an equipment used both to manufacture prototypes and serial products)?	Working hours or some other *pro rata* key. This must be documented and explained in details from the taxpayer.	
2.1.6.	What if the asset is 'indirectly' used for R&D purposes?	See 2.1.5.	
2.1.7.	What do you think of the following definition: 'Is considered directly used for R&D purposes an asset permitting, in and of itself, to carry out research programs of the business'?	Further clarification of the issue is required.	
2.1.8.	Is the production of the following assets an R&D activity? (i) production of prototypes; (ii) construction of a pilot plant/or pilot facilities.	Ad (i) Yes. Ad (ii) Yes. These costs are inevitable as the final phase where the results of R&D should be revised. All expenses which occur after this phase should not be recognised for the tax incentive.	
2.1.9.	Would you characterise the following assets as, potentially, directly used for R&D activities: (i) Handling devices; (ii) Calculation tools; (iii) Computers; (iv) Machines used to manufacture components of a prototype; (v) Telephones, small office appliances, office furniture?	For all: yes, if properly documented and clarified as necessary for R&D project.	
<u>*b.*</u>	<u>*Specific Rules*</u>		
(i)	*Intangible Assets*	<u>**Draft Art. 33.1(e)**</u> provides: '*Without prejudice to paragraph 2 and Articles 37 and 38, fixed assets shall be depreciated individually over their useful lives on a straight-line basis. The useful life of a fixed asset shall be determined as follows:* [...] *(e) fixed intangible assets: the period for which the asset enjoys legal protection or for which the right has been granted or, where that period cannot be determined, 15 years*'.	

		The problem is that not all intangible items (e.g. intellectual property, brand names), meet the definition of an intangible asset. If an item does meet the definition of an intangible asset, expenditure to acquire it or generate it internally should be recognised as an expense when it is incurred. Therefore, *based on your national tax background*:	
2.1.10.	Should we use the European Union Accounting Rule 6 defining intangible asset (i.e. identifiability, control over a resource, and existence of future economic benefits or service potential)?	Yes	
2.1.11.	If not, what should be the definition of intangible assets?	N/A	
2.1.12.	Are intangible fixed assets (including intellectual property (IP)) costs fully expensed in the year incurred and included in the CCTB super-deduction?	No; according to the Croatian Profits Tax Act, intangible fixed assets are fully expensed in the four or two year period.	
	The inclusion of mere intellectual property costs is not advisable: it may create a bias in favour of patented research compared to that stemming from unpatented technology.		
2.1.13.	Will in practice this provision be limited to patents costs acquired with a view to carry on new experimental research and development?	Yes	
2.1.14.	What if these patents are (also) used in the manufacturing process?	Divided *pro rata*, if possible. If such allocation is impossible to document or prove, it should not be included in super-deduction at all.	
2.1.15.	Should plant variety rights be treated in the same manner as patents?	Further research and consideration is needed; probably – no.	
2.1.16.	What about outlays incurred to acquire licences or know-how?	If licence or know-how is used in R&D project and make compulsory part of R&D process, it should be recognised as outlay for the super-deduction.	
(ii)	*Immovable [property]*		
	In any case, not covered by exclusion in Art. 9-3		
	In Austria, building costs and financing expenses related to R&D activity may be taken into account.		

2.1.17.	Should the concept of 'immovable property' (Recital No. 8) be preferred to the one of 'immovable fixed asset' (as opposed to Art. 9.3 CCTB)?	See 2.1.1.	
2.1.18.	Would building costs and financing expenses related to the acquisition of immovable [property] be eligible to the super-deduction?	It depends on the nature of the property. If some facilities must be prepared for the new project, these building costs should be eligible. Contrary, other investments are usually incentivised by other legal acts (e.g. Law on investment incentives).	
2.1.19.	What is your understanding of Art. 12(i): 1st meaning: that costs related to acquisition or construction of new commercial or second-hand commercial or industrial immovable [property] is excluded from the super-deduction? Or 2nd meaning: that costs related to acquisition or construction of new commercial or second-hand commercial or industrial immovable [property] is not fully deductible the year incurred but should be depreciated and such depreciation allowances are eligible to the super-deduction?	2nd meaning.	
(iii)	*Lease payments*		
2.1.20.	What if equipment is used according to the terms of a leasing-type transaction?	Eligible but only for these equipment strictly dedicated to R&D activity.	
2.1.21.	Are leasing instalments eligible for super-deduction under current wording of Art. 9-3?	Yes, except for the leasing instalments related to movable tangible fixed assets.	
2.1.22.	Should they be?	Yes, all payments for the assets used in R&D should be eligible for super-deduction.	

(iv)	*Alternative readings*		
2.1.23.	Please feel free to add any alternative readings you may have of relevant CCTB provisions and that has not yet been discussed.		
B.	**Current expenditure**		
2.2.	**R&D staff cost**		
a.	*What is meant by R&D staff?*		
2.2.1.	Should eligibility be limited to staff directly-involved in R&D?	No.	
2.2.2.	In case the staff participates both in R&D and non R&D activities, should the text allow for proportional eligibility based on time spent (or other criteria)?	Yes.	
2.2.3.	How can researchers or scientists be defined? Should the text use black letter criteria (list diplomas (PhDs), qualifications...) or a more open definition?	Every person who is fully or partially included in R&D project and whose engagement can be documented and proved.	
2.2.4.	Are research technicians R&D staff?	Yes. R&D processes are impossible to be rendered without them.	
2.2.5.	What about other employees (not 'official researchers') which still have contributed to a patented invention?	Yes, they should be included due to their contribution. R&D projects depend on different supports and personnel who provides the continuity of the processes.	
2.2.6.	What about the managers of the business (e.g. running a research program)?	Yes	
2.2.7.	What about other staff (secretariat, cleaning, etc.)? Can, in the alternative, their compensation be taken into account, proportionally, as other operating R&D expenses (cf. I-3 below)?	Compensation for other staff should be taken into account as much as they are involved in the concrete project(s) what have to be documented and proved in details. In addition to the project plans and documentation, the employment contracts and internal organisation acts can be used for the determination of the exact roles and responsibilities of the staff dedicated to R&D.	

		For example, in laboratories, cleaning personnel have to be specialised and educated in aim to handle with specific equipment. Their involvement in different R&D projects might be calculated in accordance with the time spent on cleaning particular rooms, facilities, etc.	
b.	*What is meant by R&D staff cost?*		
2.2.8.	Wages, bonuses, benefits in kind?	Wages and benefits in kind should be involved but bonuses are subjective and more doubtful.	
2.2.9.	Social security contributions (compulsory and/or non-compulsory)?	Yes, if they are not already used as allowance for the PIT.	
2.2.10.	Employer's contribution to participation of employees in profits of the enterprise by means of profit-sharing plan, employee share-ownership?	No. The taxation of this remunerations are taxed with PIT with great dissimilarities among Member States so the unique approach to them is almost impossible.	
2.2.11.	Can a Member State provide that compensation paid to holders of PhD will count more (e.g. double) for a limited period of time (in order to promote hiring of PhD holders)?	Yes, if they really contribute to the R&D project, which has to be documented and explained.	
2.3.	**Standardisation expenses**		
	Based on your national tax background:		
2.3.1.	Should expenses related to the establishment of technical standards concerning products of the business be eligible for the super-deduction (e.g. expenses incurred on participation of employees in official meetings of standardisation bodies)?	In general: no. Yes, if it is proven as important for the commercialisation of the project results.	

2.3.2.	If yes, should it still be the case even if these employees are not scientists or research technicians?	Yes, if they are involved in R&D process and these costs (e.g. particular meetings) are directly linked with the outcome of the project. This can be proved with the minutes providing conclusions from the meeting or with other official documents.	
2.3.3.	How should these expenses be assessed (e.g. as portion of employee compensation related to the time spent in connection with such meetings)?	Yes (together with the travelling costs, accommodation, etc.).	
2.3.4.	Should expenses related to technical monitoring/ technological watch be taken into account?	Yes, if connected to R&D project.	
2.4.	**Patent related expenses**		
2.4.1.	Are expenses linked to patents eligible? Please define NB: *under current French tax law, expenses linked to the filing, the maintenance and the defence of patents incurred in France or in another State (IP consultant's fees, translation costs taxes...) are eligible to the R&D tax credit; insurance costs linked to patents are eligible within a threshold of EUR 60,000. However, under the Frascati criterion, R&D would typically not include administrative and legal work connected with patents, routine tests or data collection.*	Yes. In Croatia, eligible expenses include the amortisation of the costs incurred to acquire patents used in research, as well as license fees paid to use technology in qualified research. Amortisation is prescribed by the Corporate income tax Act.	
2.5.	**Other operating expenses related to R&D**		
2.5.1.	Should such category be identified?	Yes.	
2.5.2.	Is a detailed list possible of expenses advisable?	It would be advisable to present list with the possible expenses but only as an example, due to the vast variety of R&D projects in different industries. Moreover, possible rigid interpretations of tax authorities may occur if this list is to be defined as final and detailed.	

2.5.3.	Is it appropriate to assess these expenses notionally by reference to other precisely defined eligible expenses (e.g. 15% of immovable [property] depreciation allowances, and/or 50% of eligible staff expenses)?	Yes, though, it would be also appropriate to offer to the taxpayers possibility to provide detailed and precise list of the other operating expenses that incurred during R&D project and are necessary for research, being reasonably and consistently allocated directly to the research. Due to the development of IT and sophisticated programmes for record keeping, this would not create additional costs for the business. If taxpayers find it reasonable, in accordance with their appraisal of the cost effectiveness of such compliance, the exact calculations should be accepted as an alternative.	
2.5.4.	Should fees paid to external consultants assisting the company to determine its R&D super deduction be eligible, and to what extent?	Yes. The establishment and proper proving of the eligible expenses are important for the legal tax certainty of the entrepreneurs, many of whom do not have employees who are tax or accountant experts qualified to prepare all documentation needed for the tax authorities.	
C.	**Contracted Expenditure**		
2.6.	**Subcontracting expenses**		
2.6.1.	What if R&D activity is outsourced? *Currently in France, payments to R&D service suppliers, public or private, accredited by the French Ministry of research and located in the EU or the EEA, qualify as eligible expenses.*	It should be eligible for super-deduction if undertaken as an integral part of a research project.	
2.6.2.	Should there be a territorial limit to exclude payments to subcontractors outside the EEA (which cannot invoke the freedom to provide services).	No. If we want to encourage R&D activity of entrepreneurs established in the Member states and some of them need to subcontractor services which is not available (or it is more expensive) in the EU, there is no need to punish them with the heavier taxation in comparison to the entrepreneurs who have opportunity to use services rendered by the EU businesses.	

2.6.3.	Should there be other limits? *Under current French law for instance, R&D costs invoiced by accredited private subcontractors can be retained within the limit of three times the total amount of all the other R&D eligible expenses incurred by the company; and such expenses can be retained by the company subcontracting R&D works within a yearly limit of EUR 12 or 10 million and EUR 2 million when the parties (i.e. ordering company and R&D supplier) are related companies.*	Yes. If taxpayers from the EU wants to apply super-deduction to its R&D activities, their direct activity to the particular project must be at least presented as 30% of overall project. Different projects require various services that are not all possible to be conducted with the same taxpayer, but some substantial level of the work done within the company must be retained. Special consideration should be given to the use of the cost-sharing agreements of the multinational corporations.	
B.	**Reimbursed expenditure**		
2.7.	**Treatment of public subsidies**		
2.7.1.	Should governmental and other State agencies subsidies/grants related to R&D eligible projects be deducted from eligible expenses of the year during which these expenses are incurred?	Yes. If included in eligible expenses, this would represent double incentive for the same project of the same taxpayer.	

Section IV
Finland

		Answers and comments	Technical source (when necessary)
1.	'Research and Development' – Definition		
1.1.	As indicated in Section I (*supra*), should 'research and development' be excluded if there is no particular application or use in view for the economy or the internal market?	No. It is required that R&D activity is carried on for the benefit of (own) business but no other conditions regarding the intended or realised application is set.	3 § R&D Tax Incentive Act
1.2.	Should the level of novelty be new 'to the world', 'to the internal market (EU)', 'to the market', or 'to the firm'?	It is required that the company sets up a new R&D project but no other novelty requirements apart from the ones that may stem from the definition of R&D itself. Generally, the sufficient level of novelty should be new to the firm.	Tax administration guidelines
1.3.	Should R&D be limited to the industrial sector, or also include the service industry (banking and insurance, but also humanities)?	R&D is not limited in terms of field of business or science. However, R&D should be carried on for the purpose of benefitting business.	Stated in the preparatory works of the R&D super deduction
1.3.1.	In the latter case, which criteria help to identify the presence of R&D in services activities?	R&D is not limited in terms of field of business or science. However, R&D should be carried on for the purpose of benefitting business.	Stated in the preparatory works of the R&D super deduction
1.3.1.1.	Links with public research laboratories;		
1.3.1.2.	Involvement of staff with PhDs or PhD students;		
1.3.1.3.	Publication of research findings in scientific journals;		
1.3.1.4.	Organisation of scientific conferences;		
1.3.1.5.	Involvement in scientific reviews;		
1.3.1.6.	Others?		

2.	'COSTS' (FOR RESEARCH AND DEVELOPMENT) – DEFINITION		
A.	**Capital expenditure**	Not included.	
2.1.	**Depreciation allowances**	Not included.	
<u>a.</u>	<u>*General Principles*</u>	**<u>Draft Art. 9-3</u>** provides: *'In addition to the amounts which are deductible as costs for research and development in accordance with paragraph 2, the taxpayer may also deduct, per tax year, an extra 50% of such costs, with the exception of the cost related to movable tangible fixed assets, that it incurred during that year. To the extent that costs for research and development reach beyond EUR 20 000 000, the taxpayer may deduct 25% of the exceeding amount.'* In addition, the Explanatory Memorandum (**para. 8**) provides: *'R&D costs will be fully expensed in the year incurred (with the exception of immovable property).'* **<u>Draft Art. 10</u>** (Other deductible items) provides: *'A deduction shall be made in respect of the depreciation of fixed assets referred to in Articles 30 to 40. [...]'* **<u>Draft Art. 12</u>** (Non-deductible items) provides: *'By way of derogation from Articles 9 and 10, the following items shall be non-deductible:* [...] *(i) acquisition or construction costs or cost connected with the improvement of fixed assets which are deductible under Articles 10 and 18, except for the cost related to research and development. The costs referred to in point (a) of Article 33(1) and points (a) and (b) of Article 33(2) shall not be treated as costs related to research and development;* [...]' – **<u>For additional context, see Annex</u>**. *Based on your national tax background:*	
2.1.1.	Do you share our understanding that depreciation allowances have to be distinguished depending on the assets concerned, whether they are movable or immovable?	Yes.	Please note that the Finnish R&D Deduction did not apply to other expenditure than staff costs
2.1.2.	Do you share our understanding that depreciation allowances are not available for movable fixed assets, because they are fully expensed in the year incurred, and not eligible to the super-deduction?	Yes, provided that movable fixed assets are fully expensed. Full-expensing may not be available for all types of movable assets.	

2.1.3.	Do you share our understanding that depreciation allowances remain available for immovable [property], because it cannot be fully expensed in the year incurred, and is eligible to the super-deduction?	Yes.	
2.1.4.	What if an asset is used both for research and non-research purposes (such as manufacturing)?	Proportionate approach could be applied.	
2.1.5.	If eligible, which criteria for proportional eligibility if asset used both for R&D and manufacturing purposes (e.g. an equipment used both to manufacture prototypes and serial products)?	Should be flexible and allow the most appropriate method.	
2.1.6.	What if the asset is 'indirectly' used for R&D purposes?	Should not qualify.	
2.1.7.	What do you think of the following definition: 'Is considered directly used for R&D purposes an asset permitting, in and of itself, to carry out research programs of the business'?	No view on this.	
2.1.8.	Is the production of the following assets an R&D activity? (i) production of prototypes; (ii) construction of a pilot plant / or pilot facilities	The production activities would likely go beyond R&D activities which typically restrict to research, planning and documentation but not sure on this.	
2.1.9.	Would you characterise the following assets as, potentially, directly used for R&D activities: (i) Handling devices; (ii) Calculation tools; (iii) Computers; (iv) Machines used to manufacture components of a prototype; (v) Telephones, small office appliances, office furniture?	Case-by-case analysis is probably needed.	

b.	*Specific Rules*		
(i)	*Intangible Assets*	**Draft Art. 33.1(e)** provides: *'Without prejudice to paragraph 2 and Articles 37 and 38, fixed assets shall be depreciated individually over their useful lives on a straight-line basis. The useful life of a fixed asset shall be determined as follows:* [...] *(e) fixed intangible assets: the period for which the asset enjoys legal protection or for which the right has been granted or, where that period cannot be determined, 15 years.'* The problem is that not all intangible items (e.g. intellectual property, brand names), meet the definition of an intangible asset. If an item does meet the definition of an intangible asset, expenditure to acquire it or generate it internally should be recognised as an expense when it is incurred. Therefore, *based on your national tax background*:	
2.1.10.	Should we use the European Union Accounting Rule 6 defining intangible asset (i.e. identifiability, control over a resource, and existence of future economic benefits or service potential)?	Likely yes.	Please note that the Finnish R&D Deduction did not apply to other expenditure than staff costs
2.1.11.	If not, what should be the definition of intangible assets?	N.A.	
2.1.12.	Are intangible fixed assets (including intellectual property (IP)) costs fully expensed in the year incurred and included in the CCTB super-deduction?	No.	
	The inclusion of mere intellectual property costs is not advisable: it may create a bias in favour of patented research compared to that stemming from unpatented technology.		
2.1.13.	Will in practice this provision be limited to patents costs acquired with a view to carry on new experimental research and development?	No view on this.	
2.1.14.	What if these patents are (also) used in the manufacturing process?	No view on this.	
2.1.15.	Should plant variety rights be treated in the same manner as patents?	No view on this.	

2.1.16.	What about outlays incurred to acquire licences or know-how?	No view on this.	
(ii)	*Immovable [property]*	No view on this.	
	In any case, not covered by exclusion in Art. 9-3		
	In Austria, building costs and financing expenses related to R&D activity may be taken into account.		
2.1.17.	Should the concept of 'immovable property' (Recital No. 8) be preferred to the one of 'immovable fixed asset' (as opposed to Art. 9.3 CCTB)?	No view on this.	
2.1.18.	Would building costs and financing expenses related to the acquisition of immovable [property] be eligible to the super-deduction?	No view on this.	
2.1.19.	What is your understanding of Art. 12(i): 1st meaning: that costs related to acquisition or construction of new commercial or second-hand commercial or industrial immovable [property] is excluded from the super-deduction? Or 2nd meaning: that costs related to acquisition or construction of new commercial or second-hand commercial or industrial immovable [property] is not fully deductible the year incurred but should be depreciated and such depreciation allowances are eligible to the super-deduction?	No view on this.	
(iii)	*Lease payments*		
2.1.20.	What if equipment is used according to the terms of a leasing-type transaction?	No view on this.	

2.1.21.	Are leasing instalments eligible for super-deduction under current wording of Art. 9-3?	No view on this.	
2.1.22.	Should they be?	No view on this.	
(iv)	*Alternative readings*		
2.1.23.	Please feel free to add any alternative readings you may have of relevant CCTB provisions and that has not yet been discussed.	N.A.	
B.	**Current expenditure**		
2.2.	**R&D staff cost**		
a.	*What is meant by R&D staff?*		
2.2.1.	Should eligibility be limited to staff directly-involved in R&D?	Yes.	3 § R&D Tax Incentive Act
2.2.2.	In case the staff participates both in R&D and non R&D activities, should the text allow for proportional eligibility based on time spent (or other criteria)?	Yes, based on time spent.	Tax administration guidelines
2.2.3.	How can researchers or scientists be defined? Should the text use black letter criteria (list diplomas (PhDs), qualifications…) or a more open definition?	Not necessary, the R&D staff may extend beyond researchers and scientists. R&D staff should evaluated based on their activities.	Tax administration guidelines
2.2.4.	Are research technicians R&D staff?	Yes, provided that their activities qualify as R&D	Tax administration guidelines
2.2.5.	What about other employees (not 'official researchers') which still have contributed to a patented invention?	Yes, provided that their activities qualify as R&D	Tax administration guidelines
2.2.6.	What about the managers of the business (e.g. running a research program)?	Yes, provided that their activities qualify as R&D and relate to the R&D project. General management activities of a company (e.g. by the CEO) cannot be allocated to an R&D project.	Tax administration guidelines
2.2.7.	What about other staff (secretariat, cleaning, etc.)? Can, in the alternative, their compensation be taken into account, proportionally, as other operating R&D expenses (cf. I-3 below)?	Yes, provided that their activities qualify as R&D. Administrative activities directly and strictly related to R&D (project) should at least qualify.	Tax administration guidelines

b.	*What is meant by R&D staff cost?*		
2.2.8.	Wages, bonuses, benefits in kind?	All types of employment compensation subject to prepayment procedure unless expressly excluded. Wages, bonuses and benefits in kind qualify. Payments to individual pension schemes are excluded.	3 § R&D Tax Incentive Act
2.2.9.	Social security contributions (compulsory and/or non-compulsory)?	No.	
2.2.10.	Employer's contribution to participation of employees in profits of the enterprise by means of profit-sharing plan, employee share-ownership?	Limitations may apply. This should be verified in more detail. E.g. employer subsidised emission of shares is excluded.	
2.2.11.	Can a Member State provide that compensation paid to holders of PhD will count more (e.g. double) for a limited period of time (in order to promote hiring of PhD holders)?	No.	
2.3.	**Standardisation expenses**		
	Based on your national tax background:		
2.3.1.	Should expenses related to the establishment of technical standards concerning products of the business be eligible for the super-deduction (e.g. expenses incurred on participation of employees in official meetings of standardisation bodies)?	Not likely to qualify.	Personal view
2.3.2.	If yes, should it still be the case even if these employees are not scientists or research technicians?	N.A.	
2.3.3.	How should these expenses be assessed (e.g. as portion of employee compensation related to the time spent in connection with such meetings)?	N.A.	

2.3.4.	Should expenses related to technical monitoring/ technological watch be taken into account?	Not likely to qualify.	
2.4.	**Patent related expenses**		
2.4.1.	Are expenses linked to patents eligible? Please define NB: *under current French tax law, expenses linked to the filing, the maintenance and the defence of patents incurred in France or in another State (IP consultant's fees, translation costs taxes...) are eligible to the R&D tax credit; insurance costs linked to patents are eligible within a threshold of EUR 60,000. However, under the Frascati criterion, R&D would typically not include administrative and legal work connected with patents, routine tests or data collection.*		
2.5.	**Other operating expenses related to R&D**		
2.5.1.	Should such category be identified?	No.	
2.5.2.	Is a detailed list possible of expenses advisable?	N.A.	
2.5.3.	Is it appropriate to assess these expenses notionally by reference to other precisely defined eligible expenses (e.g. 15% of immovable [property] depreciation allowances, and/or 50% of eligible staff expenses)?	N.A.	
2.5.4.	Should fees paid to external consultants assisting the company to determine its R&D super deduction be eligible, and to what extent?		

C.	**Contracted Expenditure**		
2.6.	**Subcontracting expenses**		
2.6.1.	What if R&D activity is outsourced? *Currently in France, payments to R&D service suppliers, public or private, accredited by the French Ministry of research and located in the EU or the EEA, qualify as eligible expenses.*	Only R&D costs of own employees qualify.	1 § R&D Tax Incentive Act
2.6.2.	Should there be a territorial limit to exclude payments to subcontractors outside the EEA (which cannot invoke the freedom to provide services).	N.A.	
2.6.3.	Should there be other limits? *Under current French law for instance, R&D costs invoiced by accredited private subcontractors can be retained within the limit of three times the total amount of all the other R&D eligible expenses incurred by the company; and such expenses can be retained by the company subcontracting R&D works within a yearly limit of EUR 12 or 10 million and EUR 2 million when the parties (i.e. ordering company and R&D supplier) are related companies.*	N.A.	
B.	**Reimbursed expenditure**		
2.7.	**Treatment of public subsidies**		
2.7.1.	Should governmental and other State agencies subsidies/grants related to R&D eligible projects be deducted from eligible expenses of the year during which these expenses are incurred?	Yes.	4 § R&D Tax Incentive Act. EU state aid rules require deduction/monitoring of cascading state aids

Section V
France

		Answers and comments	Technical source (when necessary)
1.	'Research and Development' – Definition		
1.1.	As indicated in Section I (*supra*), should 'research and development' be excluded if there is no particular application or use in view for the economy or the internal market?	The French current regulations include the same R&D definition including fundamental/basic, applied and experimental development activities. My personal opinion is that fundamental R&D should be encouraged in a similar way as applied research and experimental development as they are all likely to lead to economic growth. While more risky, basic research leads to highly valuable innovations and technological breakthroughs. Companies also engage in R&D activities if they expect a reasonable economic benefit.	
1.2.	Should the level of novelty be new 'to the world', 'to the internal market (EU)', 'to the market', or 'to the firm'?	Under French regulations, the novelty is appreciated based on the state of the art of scientific and/or technological accessible knowledge at the start of the R&D project. This criterion appears relevant to the CCTB. The availability of a product on any given market is not a relevant criteria for R&D since commercial constraints also impact the market. Expanding the novelty criteria to the level of the firm would extend beyond R&D to include other innovations.	
1.3.	Should R&D be limited to the industrial sector, or also include the service industry (banking and insurance, but also humanities)?	All business sectors, including humanities, may undertake R&D activities valuable for the society and the economy. Objective and efficient criteria for qualifying expenses and activities may be defined without reference to any particular sector.	

1.3.1.	In the latter case, which criteria help to identify the presence of R&D in services activities?		
1.3.1.1.	Links with public research laboratories;		
1.3.1.2.	Involvement of staff with PhDs or PhD students;		
1.3.1.3.	Publication of research findings in scientific journals;		
1.3.1.4.	Organisation of scientific conferences;		
1.3.1.5.	Involvement in scientific reviews;		
1.3.1.6.	Others?		
2.	'Costs' (For Research and Development) – Definition		
A.	**Capital expenditure**		
2.1.	**Depreciation allowances**		
<u>a.</u>	<u>*General Principles*</u>	**<u>Draft Art. 9-3</u>** provides: *'In addition to the amounts which are deductible as costs for research and development in accordance with paragraph 2, the taxpayer may also deduct, per tax year, an extra 50% of such costs, with the exception of the cost related to movable tangible fixed assets, that it incurred during that year. To the extent that costs for research and development reach beyond EUR 20,000,000, the taxpayer may deduct 25% of the exceeding amount.'* In addition, the Explanatory Memorandum (**para. 8**) provides: *'R&D costs will be fully expensed in the year incurred (with the exception of immovable property)'*. **<u>Draft Art. 10</u>** (Other deductible items) provides: *'A deduction shall be made in respect of the depreciation of fixed assets referred to in Articles 30 to 40.* [...]'. **<u>Draft Art. 12</u>** (Non-deductible items) provides: *'By way of derogation from Articles 9 and 10, the following items shall be non-deductible:* [...] *(i) acquisition or construction costs or cost connected with the improvement of fixed assets which are deductible under Articles 10 and 18, except for the cost related to research and development. The costs referred to in point (a) of Article 33(1) and points (a) and (b) of Article 33(2) shall not be treated as costs related to research and development;* [...]" – **<u>For additional context, see Annex</u>**. *Based on your national tax background:*	
2.1.1.	Do you share our understanding that depreciation allowances have to be distinguished depending on the assets concerned, whether they are movable or immovable?	My understanding is that movable fixed assets which qualify as R&D related are fully expensed during the year, and are therefore not subject to depreciation/amortisation.	

2.1.2.	Do you share our understanding that depreciation allowances are not available for movable fixed assets, because they are fully expensed in the year incurred, and not eligible to the super-deduction?		
2.1.3.	Do you share our understanding that depreciation allowances remain available for immovable [property], because it cannot be fully expensed in the year incurred, and is eligible to the super-deduction?		
2.1.4.	What if an asset is used both for research and non-research purposes (such as manufacturing)?	According to French regulations, such an asset may still qualify as eligible expense. Additionally, the asset has to be either created or acquired as 'new'. The eligibility of second-hand assets should be clarified in the CCTB.	
2.1.5.	If eligible, which criteria for proportional eligibility if asset used both for R&D and manufacturing purposes (e.g. an equipment used both to manufacture prototypes and serial products)?	Under French regulations, the criterion is the time spent on each activity.	
2.1.6.	What if the asset is 'indirectly' used for R&D purposes?	Under French regulations, such asset would not qualify to the tax credit. Including indirect assets in the CCTB may lead to uncertainty.	
2.1.7.	What do you think of the following definition: 'Is considered directly used for R&D purposes an asset permitting, in and of itself, to carry out research programs of the business'?	It is an accurate definition of the 'direct usage of an asset'. The term business may be replaced by company or taxpayer for clarification purposes.	
2.1.8.	Is the production of the following assets an R&D activity? (i) production of prototypes; (ii) construction of a pilot plant/or pilot facilities.	Under French regulations, yes.	

2.1.9.	Would you characterise the following assets as, potentially, directly used for R&D activities: (i) Handling devices; (ii) Calculation tools; (iii) Computers; (iv) Machines used to manufacture components of a prototype; (v) Telephones, small office appliances, office furniture?	Under French regulations, all such assets qualify except (v) Telephones, small office appliances, office furniture.	
b.	*Specific Rules*		
(i)	*Intangible Assets*	**Draft Art. 33.1(e)** provides: *'Without prejudice to paragraph 2 and Articles 37 and 38, fixed assets shall be depreciated individually over their useful lives on a straight-line basis. The useful life of a fixed asset shall be determined as follows:* [...] *(e) fixed intangible assets: the period for which the asset enjoys legal protection or for which the right has been granted or, where that period cannot be determined, 15 years.'* The problem is that not all intangible items (e.g. intellectual property, brand names), meet the definition of an intangible asset. If an item does meet the definition of an intangible asset, expenditure to acquire it or generate it internally should be recognised as an expense when it is incurred. Therefore, *based on your national tax background*:	
2.1.10.	Should we use the European Union Accounting Rule 6 defining intangible asset (i.e. identifiability, control over a resource, and existence of future economic benefits or service potential)?	Following a common set of accounting rules appears necessary.	
2.1.11.	If not, what should be the definition of intangible assets?		
2.1.12.	Are intangible fixed assets (including intellectual property (IP)) costs fully expensed in the year incurred and included in the CCTB super-deduction?	Intangible fixed assets are capitalised and amortised accordingly. Only non capitalized intangible items would be fully expensed in the year incurred. Only qualifying assets or costs would benefit from the super-deduction, which, in the case of intangibles, would mainly be accounted for as assets (other IP rights such as brands would most likely not qualify as R&D expenses).	

	The inclusion of mere intellectual property costs is not advisable: it may create a bias in favour of patented research compared to that stemming from unpatented technology.		
2.1.13.	Will in practice this provision be limited to patents costs acquired with a view to carry on new experimental research and development?	Most likely, yes.	
2.1.14.	What if these patents are (also) used in the manufacturing process?	Under French regulations, patent costs qualify only to the extent used in the R&D activity. The split is based on the most relevant usage criteria for the case at hand.	
2.1.15.	Should plant variety rights be treated in the same manner as patents?	Under French regulations, they are.	
2.1.16.	What about outlays incurred to acquire licences or know-how?	Licences for IP rights that are capitalised should be treated in the same manner as patents. Know-how can't be capitalised and acquisition costs are expensed in the year of acquisition.	
(ii)	*Immovable [property]*		
	In any case, not covered by exclusion in Art. 9-3		
	In Austria, building costs and financing expenses related to R&D activity may be taken into account.		
2.1.17.	Should the concept of 'immovable property' (Recital No. 8) be preferred to the one of 'immovable fixed asset' (as opposed to Art. 9.3 CCTB)?	The use of immovable property is confusing and should be replaced by immovable fixed assets.	
2.1.18.	Would building costs and financing expenses related to the acquisition of immovable [property] be eligible to the super-deduction?	They should be taken into account only to the extent that they are capitalised and depreciated.	

2.1.19.	What is your understanding of Art. 12(i): <u>1st meaning</u>: that costs related to acquisition or construction of new commercial or second-hand commercial or industrial immovable [property] is excluded from the super-deduction? Or <u>2nd meaning</u>: that costs related to acquisition or construction of new commercial or second-hand commercial or industrial immovable [property] is not fully deductible the year incurred but should be depreciated and such depreciation allowances are eligible to the super-deduction?	I understand that Art. 12(i) only concerns costs of improvement of fixed assets. Such costs are not tax deductible (whether as expense or depreciation), unless they qualify as R&D expenses (in which case they follow the normal depreciation and super-deduction regime).	
(iii)	*Lease payments*		
2.1.20.	What if equipment is used according to the terms of a leasing-type transaction?	Under French regulations, assets acquired under a leasing agreement represent a depreciable asset.	
2.1.21.	Are leasing instalments eligible for super-deduction under current wording of Art. 9-3?	My interpretation is yes, unless the asset is a movable tangible fixed assets. This point should nevertheless be clarified.	
2.1.22.	Should they be?	Yes, leasing is a financing tool that does not impact the R&D purpose or usage of the underlying asset.	
(iv)	*Alternative readings*		
2.1.23.	Please feel free to add any alternative readings you may have of relevant CCTB provisions and that has not yet been discussed.		
B.	**Current expenditure**		
2.2.	**R&D staff cost**		
<u>a.</u>	<u>*What is meant by R&D staff?*</u>		
2.2.1.	Should eligibility be limited to staff directly-involved in R&D?	Yes, taking into consideration indirect staff may become a source of uncertainty and potential abuses.	

2.2.2.	In case the staff participates both in R&D and non R&D activities, should the text allow for proportional eligibility based on time spent (or other criteria)?	Yes, time spent appears as the most appropriate criteria.	
2.2.3.	How can researchers or scientists be defined? Should the text use black letter criteria (list diplomas (PhDs), qualifications…) or a more open definition?	Under French regulations, researchers include scientists (staff with at least a master degree or equivalent) and engineers (staff with an engineer diploma). A staff member can be assimilated to an engineer if recognised as such by the employing company (i.e. working directly and exclusively in the research activities and having acquired competencies equivalent to an engineer).	
2.2.4.	Are research technicians R&D staff?	Under French regulations, yes. – Research technicians are staff who provide indispensable support to the actual researchers. They have in particular the following activities: – preparation of substances, material and appliances for experimentation; – assist researchers during the experimentations or actually perform the experimentations; – maintain and control the functioning of the appliances and equipment required.	
2.2.5.	What about other employees (not 'official researchers') which still have contributed to a patented invention?	All remuneration granted to employees on behalf of their invention may qualify as R&D expenses. Staff made available by another company may also qualify as researcher.	
2.2.6.	What about the managers of the business (e.g. running a research program)?	Business managers may be assimilated to researchers if they personally and actively participate to the research program.	
2.2.7.	What about other staff (secretariat, cleaning, etc.)? Can, in the alternative, their compensation be taken into account, proportionally, as other operating R&D expenses (cf. I-3 below)?	Under French regulations they are formally excluded. They are taken into consideration based on a fixed amount of indirect costs (see answers below).	

b.	*What is meant by R&D staff cost?*		
2.2.8.	Wages, bonuses, benefits in kind?	Under French regulations, all remuneration including wages, bonuses, benefits in kind and remuneration for an invention is included.	
2.2.9.	Social security contributions (compulsory and/or non-compulsory)?	Under French regulations, only compulsory contributions are eligible.	
2.2.10.	Employer's contribution to participation of employees in profits of the enterprise by means of profit-sharing plan, employee share-ownership?	Under French regulations, they are included.	
2.2.11.	Can a Member State provide that compensation paid to holders of PhD will count more (e.g. double) for a limited period of time (in order to promote hiring of PhD holders)?	Compensation paid to PhD holders in France can be taken into account for double for the first 2 years if it is the first employment of the PhD holder, if the contract is for indefinite period, and if the number of research staff does not decrease from the preceding year. Under the CCTB, this should nevertheless be harmonised and not be subject to a national decision.	
2.3.	**Standardisation expenses**		
	Based on your national tax background:		
2.3.1.	Should expenses related to the establishment of technical standards concerning products of the business be eligible for the super-deduction (e.g. expenses incurred on participation of employees in official meetings of standardisation bodies)?	Under French regulations, such expenses are eligible.	
2.3.2.	If yes, should it still be the case even if these employees are not scientists or research technicians?	Under French regulations, they only must be employees of the company and not external consultants.	

2.3.3.	How should these expenses be assessed (e.g. as portion of employee compensation related to the time spent in connection with such meetings)?	Under French regulations, 50% of the salaries and social charges are taken into account (based on time spent) plus 15% of such salaries for administrative expenses.	
2.3.4.	Should expenses related to technical monitoring/ technological watch be taken into account?	Technology watch is eligible under French regulations up to EUR 60,000.	
2.4.	**Patent related expenses**		
2.4.1.	Are expenses linked to patents eligible? Please define NB: *under current French tax law, expenses linked to the filing, the maintenance and the defence of patents incurred in France or in another State (IP consultant's fees, translation costs taxes...) are eligible to the R&D tax credit; insurance costs linked to patents are eligible within a threshold of EUR 60,000. However, under the Frascati criterion, R&D would typically not include administrative and legal work connected with patents, routine tests or data collection.*	Under current French tax law, expenses linked to the filing, the maintenance and the defence of patents incurred in France or in another State (IP consultant's fees, translation costs taxes...) are eligible to the R&D tax credit; insurance costs linked to patents are eligible within a threshold of EUR 60,000. However, under the Frascati criterion, R&D would typically **not** include administrative and legal work connected with patents, routine tests or data collection.	
2.5.	**Other operating expenses related to R&D**		
2.5.1.	Should such category be identified?	They should be either defined or estimated according to a pre determined calculation.	
2.5.2.	Is a detailed list possible of expenses advisable?	A description of the assets used and other operating expenses should be either defined or listed comprehensively if they are taken into account based on actual values rather than estimation.	
2.5.3.	Is it appropriate to assess these expenses notionally by reference to other precisely defined eligible expenses (e.g. 15% of immovable (property) depreciation allowances, and/or 50% of eligible staff expenses)?	Yes, it seems more appropriate than a list of expenses which may lead to uncertainty. French regulations evaluate general and administrative expenses to 75% of the amortisation of assets directly affected to the research and 50% of the research staff expenses.	

2.5.4.	Should fees paid to external consultants assisting the company to determine its R&D super deduction be eligible, and to what extent?	They are taken into consideration under French law to decrease the amount of the tax credit. If the remuneration is a proportion of the tax credit obtained, it comes fully at a reduction of the tax basis for the credit. Otherwise, the amount is deductible after reduction of the higher between 5% of the tax basis before this reduction or EUR 15,000. In my opinion, such expense is of a tax nature rather than an R&D nature and should be excluded from the incentive scheme.	
C.	**Contracted Expenditure**		
2.6.	**Subcontracting expenses**		
2.6.1.	What if R&D activity is outsourced? *Currently in France, payments to R&D service suppliers, public or private, accredited by the French Ministry of research and located in the EU or the EEA, qualify as eligible expenses.*	Based on French regulations payments to R&D service suppliers, public or private accredited the French Ministry of research, and located in the EU or EEA, qualify as eligible expenses.	
2.6.2.	Should there be a territorial limit to exclude payments to subcontractors outside the EEA (which cannot invoke the freedom to provide services).	Yes, this is useful to protect the economic purposes of the incentive.	
2.6.3.	Should there be other limits? *Under current French law for instance, R&D costs invoiced by accredited private subcontractors can be retained within the limit of three times the total amount of all the other R&D eligible expenses incurred by the company; and such expenses can be retained by the company subcontracting R&D works within a yearly limit of EUR 12 or 10 million and EUR 2 million when the parties (i.e. ordering company and R&D supplier) are related companies.*	Under current French law, R&D costs invoiced by accredited private subcontractors can be retained within the limit of three times the total amount of all the other R&D eligible expenses incurred by the company; and such expenses can be retained by the company subcontracting R&D works within a yearly limit of EUR 12 or 10 million and EUR 2 million when the parties (i.e. ordering company and R&D supplier) are related companies. The super deduction should be excluded if the subcontractor or the company itself benefits from another incentive scheme under its national law or the CCTB.	

B.	**Reimbursed expenditure**		
2.7.	**Treatment of public subsidies**		
2.7.1.	Should governmental and other State agencies subsidies/grants related to R&D eligible projects be deducted from eligible expenses of the year during which these expenses are incurred?	Yes, this would otherwise constitute a double incentive and may create a distortion of competition.	

SECTION VI
Germany

The entry into force of the Act on Tax Incentives for Research and Development of 14 December 2019[148] for the first time established tax incentives for R&D in Germany. It is largely based on the Federal Government's draft bill of 23 May 2019, which is the basis for the following information. Deviations of the Act on Tax Incentives for Research and Development of 14 December 2019 from the draft bill are identified in the footnotes.

Previously, Germany tried to strengthen research activities especially through direct financial support, such as subsidies. So, according to statistics of the competent ministry in 2015 the State approximately spent EUR 25 billion on R&D whereby roughly 90% of this amount was distributed to universities and other public respectively non-profit organisations, only EUR 2 billion were distributed among companies of the private sector. The government realised that the application procedure for such support is way too complex for small and medium-sized enterprises and therefore wants to slightly change the strategy now. Considering the private sector, companies in 2015 approximately spent EUR 60 billion on R&D, according to different sources which obviously follow a different definition of R&D the amount is EUR 150 billion (2013). This could, on the one hand justify efforts to keep R&D activities in Germany, or, on the other hand bear significant risks for the budget if R&D incentives would cover all sizes of companies. Despite SMEs by far forming the major part of the German economy, their share of R&D costs of companies is approximately 20 % and only slightly increased over the past two decades.

In 2019, the Federal Ministry of Finance published a draft law on (tax) incentives for research and development, which has (with some minor changes) been transposed into a government bill. The aim is to strengthen Germany as a business location, in particular to improve its attractiveness

148. Gesetz zur steuerlichen Förderung von Forschung und Entwicklung ofvom 14 Decemberzember 2019, Bundesgesetzblatt 2019 pp. 2763.

in the field of R&D. The Federal Ministry of Finance intends to achieve this by introducing tax incentives for research and development by implementing a separate law (not by amending the existing tax law) which shall apply equally to all taxable enterprises regardless of their size or business purpose. Unlike earlier initiatives, this draft law does neither refer to R&D costs in general nor provide for a super-deduction but grants a refund of staff costs.

From a German *constitutional law perspective* R&D tax incentives and the definition of R&D have to be in line with the principle of equality, especially the ability to pay principle. Thus, any unequal treatment of comparable taxpayers has to be justified. A reason for justification may be the aim to strengthen research activities within Germany and/or by German enterprises. Against this background the incentive has to be effective as to this aim: On one hand, the deduction shall not be too limited as to the eligible costs, because otherwise the incentive will not raise motivation to start new research. On the other hand, windfall effects must be minimised. This in mind, the argument mentioned above (problems of application proceedings) could be one aspect to justify the limitation of R&D incentives to small and medium sized enterprises.

		Answers and comments	**Technical source (when necessary)**
1.	'RESEARCH AND DEVELOPMENT' – DEFINITION		
1.1.	As indicated in Section I (*supra*), should 'research and development' be excluded if there is no particular application or use in view for the economy or the internal market?	The closer R&D comes to the improvement of existing technology, the less does it qualify as really innovative: If a product or process is essentially established and if the primary aim of further activity is market development, or if this activity is intended to make the production system function smoothly, these activities can no longer be attributed to R&D. Moreover, basic research without direct commercial application in particular is included in the definition of R&D (Sec. 2 para. 1 draft law government[149]).	Sec. 2 para. 2 of the Act on Tax Incentives for Research and Development
1.2.	Should the level of novelty be new 'to the world', 'to the internal market (EU)', 'to the market', or 'to the firm'?	The draft law does not contain any statement on that issue.	

149. Editorial note: According to the law on tax incentives for research and development, 'basic research' and 'experimental development' are also among the favoured research and development projects. However, the term 'applied research' (draft law of the Federal Government) has been replaced by the term 'industrial research' (Sec. 2 para. 1).

1.3.	Should R&D be limited to the industrial sector, or also include the service industry (banking and insurance, but also humanities)?	The draft law of the BMF[150] contains a definition that states that industrial as well as experimental research shall be covered (Sec. 2 para. 1).[151] Industrial research is defined as planned research or critical investigation aimed at the discovery of new knowledge and skills with the aim of developing new products, processes or services or bringing about substantial improvements in existing products, processes or services. Experimental development means the acquisition, combination, design and exploitation of existing scientific, technical, economic and other relevant knowledge and skills in order to develop new or improved products, processes or services. Experimental development shall not include routine or periodic changes to existing products, production lines, production processes, services or other ongoing operational processes, even if such changes constitute improvements. In general, the R&D activity to which the grant relates is determined by the following five criteria: The R&D activity must - aim to gain new knowledge (be innovative), - be based on original, non-obvious concepts and hypotheses (to be creative), - be uncertain about the outcome, - follow a plan and be budgeted (systematic), - lead to results that can be reproduced (transferable/reproducible). To sum up, the R&D definition covers all kinds of business and not only the industrial sector.	Annex 1 to Sec. 2 para. 1 draft law BMF; Explanatory memorandum of Sec. 2 paras. 1–3 draft law BMF
1.3.1.	In the latter case, which criteria help to identify the presence of R&D in services activities?	There is no specific provision.	

150. *Bundesministerium der Finanzen* (Federal Ministry of Finance).

151. Editorial note: According to both the law on tax incentives for research and development and the BMF's draft law, basic research, industrial research and experimental.development are among the favoured research and development projects. In contrast to the Act on Tax Incentives for Research and Development, the BMF's draft bill contains an annex to Sec. 2 para. 1, in which the terms 'basic research', 'industrial research' and 'experimental development' are defined.

1.3.1.1.	Links with public research laboratories;	There is no specific provision.	
1.3.1.2.	Involvement of staff with PhDs or PhD students;	There is no specific provision.	
1.3.1.3.	Publication of research findings in scientific journals;	There is no specific provision.	
1.3.1.4.	Organisation of scientific conferences;	There is no specific provision.	
1.3.1.5.	Involvement in scientific reviews;	There is no specific provision.	
1.3.1.6.	Others?		
2.	'COSTS' (FOR RESEARCH AND DEVELOPMENT) – DEFINITION		
A.	**Capital expenditure**		
2.1.	**Depreciation allowances**		
a.	*General Principles*	**Draft Art. 9-3** provides: *'In addition to the amounts which are deductible as costs for research and development in accordance with paragraph 2, the taxpayer may also deduct, per tax year, an extra 50% of such costs, with the exception of the cost related to movable tangible fixed assets, that it incurred during that year. To the extent that costs for research and development reach beyond EUR 20 000 000, the taxpayer may deduct 25% of the exceeding amount.'* In addition, the Explanatory Memorandum (**para. 8**) provides: *'R&D costs will be fully expensed in the year incurred (with the exception of immovable property).'* **Draft Art. 10** (Other deductible items) provides: *'A deduction shall be made in respect of the depreciation of fixed assets referred to in Articles 30 to 40. […]'* **Draft Art. 12** (Non-deductible items) provides: *'By way of derogation from Articles 9 and 10, the following items shall be non-deductible:* […] *(i) acquisition or construction costs or cost connected with the improvement of fixed assets which are deductible under Articles 10 and 18, except for the cost related to research and development. The costs referred to in point (a) of Article 33(1) and points (a) and (b) of Article 33(2) shall not be treated as costs related to research and development;* […]' – **For additional context, see Annex**. *Based on your national tax background:*	
2.1.1.	Do you share our understanding that depreciation allowances have to be distinguished depending on the assets concerned, whether they are movable or immovable?	The draft law introduces a tax research allowance, which is neither based on the tax base of the income determination nor on the tax to be assessed. Eligible expenses are only employee's wages and salaries,[152] so that the distinction between movable and immovable goods is irrelevant.	Sec. 3 para. 1 draft law

152. Editorial note: According to Sec. 3 para. 1 sent. 1 of the Act on Tax Incentives for Research and Development, eligible expenses also include 'the employer's expenses for securing the employee's future in accordance with section 3 no. 62 of the Income Tax Act'. This half-sentence is missing in the Federal Government's draft.

2.1.2.	Do you share our understanding that depreciation allowances are not available for movable fixed assets, because they are fully expensed in the year incurred, and not eligible to the super-deduction?	See above.	Sec. 3 para. 1 draft law
2.1.3.	Do you share our understanding that depreciation allowances remain available for immovable [property], because it cannot be fully expensed in the year incurred, and is eligible to the super-deduction?	See above.	Sec. 3 para. 1 draft law
2.1.4.	What if an asset is used both for research and non-research purposes (such as manufacturing)?	See above.	Sec. 3 para. 1 draft law
2.1.5.	If eligible, which criteria for proportional eligibility if asset used both for R&D and manufacturing purposes (e.g. an equipment used both to manufacture prototypes and serial products)?	See above.	Sec. 3 para. 1 draft law
2.1.6.	What if the asset is 'indirectly' used for R&D purposes?	See above.	Sec. 3 para. 1 draft law
2.1.7.	What do you think of the following definition: 'Is considered directly used for R&D purposes an asset permitting, in and of itself, to carry out research programs of the business'?		
2.1.8.	Is the production of the following assets an R&D activity? (i) production of prototypes; (ii) construction of a pilot plant / or pilot facilities	See above.	Sec. 3 para. 1 draft law

2.1.9.	Would you characterise the following assets as, potentially, directly used for R&D activities: (i) Handling devices; (ii) Calculation tools; (iii) Computers; (iv) Machines used to manufacture components of a prototype; (v) Telephones, small office appliances, office furniture?	See above.	Sec. 3 para. 1 draft law
b.	*Specific Rules*		
(i)	*Intangible Assets*	**Draft Art. 33.1(e)** provides: '*Without prejudice to paragraph 2 and Articles 37 and 38, fixed assets shall be depreciated individually over their useful lives on a straight-line basis. The useful life of a fixed asset shall be determined as follows: [...] (e) fixed intangible assets: the period for which the asset enjoys legal protection or for which the right has been granted or, where that period cannot be determined, 15 years.*' The problem is that not all intangible items (e.g. intellectual property, brand names), meet the definition of an intangible asset. If an item does meet the definition of an intangible asset, expenditure to acquire it or generate it internally should be recognised as an expense when it is incurred. Therefore, *based on your national tax background*:	
2.1.10.	Should we use the European Union Accounting Rule 6 defining intangible asset (i.e. identifiability, control over a resource, and existence of future economic benefits or service potential)?	Eligible expenses are only employee's wages and salaries,[153] so this question doesn't even arise.	
2.1.11.	If not, what should be the definition of intangible assets?	See above	
2.1.12.	Are intangible fixed assets (including intellectual property (IP)) costs fully expensed in the year incurred and included in the CCTB super-deduction?	See above.	

153. Editorial note: According to Sec. 3 para. 1 sent. 1 of the Act on Tax Incentives for Research and Development, eligible expenses also include 'the employer's expenses for securing the employee's future in accordance with section 3 no. 62 of the Income Tax Act'. This half-sentence is missing in the Federal Government's draft.

	The inclusion of mere intellectual property costs is not advisable: it may create a bias in favour of patented research compared to that stemming from unpatented technology.		
2.1.13.	Will in practice this provision be limited to patents costs acquired with a view to carry on new experimental research and development?	See above	Sec. 3 para. 1 draft law
2.1.14.	What if these patents are (also) used in the manufacturing process?	See above.	Sec. 3 para. 1 draft law
2.1.15.	Should plant variety rights be treated in the same manner as patents?	See above	Sec. 3 para. 1 draft law
2.1.16.	What about outlays incurred to acquire licences or know-how?	See above.	Sec. 3 para. 1 draft law
(ii)	*Immovable [property]*		
	In any case, not covered by exclusion in Art. 9-3		
	In Austria, building costs and financing expenses related to R&D activity may be taken into account.		
2.1.17.	Should the concept of 'immovable property' (Recital No. 8) be preferred to the one of 'immovable fixed asset' (as opposed to Art. 9.3 CCTB)?	Eligible expenses are only employee's wages and salaries.[154]	
2.1.18.	Would building costs and financing expenses related to the acquisition of immovable [property] be eligible to the super-deduction?	See above.	Sec. 3 para. 1 draft law

154. Editorial note: According to Sec. 3 para. 1 sent. 1 of the Act on Tax Incentives for Research and Development, eligible expenses also include 'the employer's expenses for securing the employee's future in accordance with section 3 no. 62 of the Income Tax Act'. This half-sentence is missing in the Federal Government's draft.

2.1.19.	What is your understanding of Art. 12(i): 1st meaning: that costs related to acquisition or construction of new commercial or second-hand commercial or industrial immovable [property] is excluded from the super-deduction? Or 2nd meaning: that costs related to acquisition or construction of new commercial or second-hand commercial or industrial immovable [property] is not fully deductible the year incurred but should be depreciated and such depreciation allowances are eligible to the super-deduction?	See above.	
(iii)	*Lease payments*		
2.1.20.	What if equipment is used according to the terms of a leasing-type transaction?	See above.	Sec. 3 para. 1 draft law
2.1.21.	Are leasing instalments eligible for super-deduction under current wording of Art. 9-3?	See above.	Sec. 3 para. 1 draft law
2.1.22.	Should they be?		
(iv)	*Alternative readings*		
2.1.23.	Please feel free to add any alternative readings you may have of relevant CCTB provisions and that has not yet been discussed.		

B.	**Current expenditure**		
2.2.	**R&D staff cost**		
a.	*What is meant by R&D staff?*	Draft law does not distinguish between different kinds of employees. It only states that employee's wages and salaries are eligible insofar and so long as they work for the R&D project.	Sec. 3 para. 1 draft law[155]
2.2.1.	Should eligibility be limited to staff directly-involved in R&D?		
2.2.2.	In case the staff participates both in R&D and non R&D activities, should the text allow for proportional eligibility based on time spent (or other criteria)?	Yes, in those cases the division scales shall be verified and substantiated by means of suitable documentation.	Explanatory memorandum of Sec. 3 para. 1 draft law BMF
2.2.3.	How can researchers or scientists be defined? Should the text use black letter criteria (list diplomas (PhDs), qualifications...) or a more open definition?	The draft law doesn't include a definition of researchers and scientists as all persons (regardless of their profession) are included who 'work in a (eligible) project'. Therefore, it is not sufficient to be formally part of a R&D department.	Explanatory memorandum of Sec. 3 para. 1 draft law BMF
2.2.4.	Are research technicians R&D staff?	See above.	
2.2.5.	What about other employees (not 'official researchers') which still have contributed to a patented invention?	These persons are also included under the conditions mentioned above.	
2.2.6.	What about the managers of the business (e.g. running a research program)?	These persons are also included under the conditions mentioned above.	
2.2.7.	What about other staff (secretariat, cleaning, etc.)? Can, in the alternative, their compensation be taken into account, proportionally, as other operating R&D expenses (cf. I-3 below)?	These persons are also included under the conditions mentioned above. But consider: According to the explanatory memorandum of Section. 3 para. 1 draft law BMF (pp. 18–19) wages paid to employees who work for a R&D project but do not carry out research themselves, are not eligible expenses (e.g. personnel expenses for cleaning staff, office clerks or managers who do not conduct research themselves).	

155. Editorial note: According to Sec. 3 para. 1 sent. 1 of the Act on Tax Incentives for Research and Development, eligible expenses also include 'the employer's expenses for securing the employee's future in accordance with section 3 no. 62 of the Income Tax Act'. This half-sentence is missing in the Federal Government's draft.

b.	What is meant by R&D staff cost?		
2.2.8.	Wages, bonuses, benefits in kind?	Eligible costs are the gross wages and salaries of the employees of the company employed in R&D projects, which are subject to income tax. The draft insofar refers to Section 19 Income Tax Act (EStG) which is an operand also used for the calculation of the source tax on wages. Thus, the legislator tried to facilitate application of the new law. If a company employs workers whose wages are not subject to taxation in Germany, the company's wage costs are not included in the eligible tax base. An exception is made for those expenses which are exempt from taxation in Germany due to a DTT between Germany and other EU Member States, EEA Member States or Switzerland (Sec. 3 para.-2 of the Act on Tax Incentives for Research and Development). Another exception is made for individual entrepreneurs and members of a partnership (Sec. 3 para. 3 of the Act on Tax Incentives for Research and Development).	Sec. 3 para. 1 draft law[156] Explanatory memorandum of Sec. 3 draft law BMF
2.2.9.	Social security contributions (compulsory and/or non-compulsory)?	Employer contributions to pension insurance, health and long-term care insurance are not included with their actual costs in under this draft.[157] Instead, the draft states that gross wages and salaries are multiplied with the factor 1.2 to determine the assessment base. The factor of 1.2 reflects the average security contributions in Germany, which is 20 % of the wage costs.	Sec. 3 para. 3 draft law government and explanatory memorandum

156. Editorial note: According to Sec. 3 para. 1 sent. 1 of the Act on Tax Incentives for Research and Development, eligible expenses also include 'the employer's expenses for securing the employee's future in accordance with section 3 no. 62 of the Income Tax Act'. This half-sentence is missing in the Federal Government's draft.

157. Editorial note: According to Sec. 3 para. 1 sent. 1 of the Act on Tax Incentives for Research and Development, eligible expenses also include 'the employer's expenses for securing the employee's future in accordance with section 3 no. 62 of the Income Tax Act'.

2.2.10.	Employer's contribution to participation of employees in profits of the enterprise by means of profit-sharing plan, employee share-ownership?	See above.	
2.2.11.	Can a Member State provide that compensation paid to holders of PhD will count more (e.g. double) for a limited period of time (in order to promote hiring of PhD holders)?	No such provision will be included.	
2.3.	**Standardisation expenses**		
	Based on your national tax background:		
2.3.1.	Should expenses related to the establishment of technical standards concerning products of the business be eligible for the super-deduction (e.g. expenses incurred on participation of employees in official meetings of standardisation bodies)?	No super-deduction approach in the draft law.	
2.3.2.	If yes, should it still be the case even if these employees are not scientists or research technicians?		
2.3.3.	How should these expenses be assessed (e.g. as portion of employee compensation related to the time spent in connection with such meetings)?	Probably similar to the wages of other employees who do not work exclusively for the R&D project.	
2.3.4.	Should expenses related to technical monitoring/ technological watch be taken into account?	Experimental development may include the development of commercially viable prototypes and pilot projects where this is necessarily the final commercial product and its production alone would be too expensive for demonstration and validation purposes. Experimental development does not include routine or periodic changes to existing products, production lines, production processes, services or other operational processes, even if these changes represent improvements.	Annex to Sec. 2 para. 1. draft law BMF

2.4.	**Patent related expenses**		
2.4.1.	Are expenses linked to patents eligible? Please define NB: *under current French tax law, expenses linked to the filing, the maintenance and the defence of patents incurred in France or in another State (IP consultant's fees, translation costs taxes...) are eligible to the R&D tax credit; insurance costs linked to patents are eligible within a threshold of EUR 60,000. However, under the Frascati criterion, R&D would typically not include administrative and legal work connected with patents, routine tests or data collection.*	Not sure, however, the distinction should in principle be made according to the criteria of the Frascati Manual in order to establish international comparability and to be able to fall back on existing case law.	Explanatory memorandum of Sec. 2 draft law government
2.5.	**Other operating expenses related to R&D**		
2.5.1.	Should such category be identified?		
2.5.2.	Is a detailed list possible of expenses advisable?	The eligible expenses are in accordance with Section. 19 Income Tax Act (EStG) and are exhaustively listed. Therefore a separate listing would have no further benefit.	
2.5.3.	Is it appropriate to assess these expenses notionally by reference to other precisely defined eligible expenses (e.g. 15% of immovable [property] depreciation allowances, and/or 50% of eligible staff expenses)?	The eligible expenses are in accordance with Section. 19 Income Tax Act (EStG) and are exhaustively listed. Therefore, no such notional assessment is foreseen.	
2.5.4.	Should fees paid to external consultants assisting the company to determine its R&D super deduction be eligible, and to what extent?	No, since these fees are not part of wages and salaries of the company's employees belonging to the taxable income of the employee according to Section 19 Income Tax Act (EStG)	

C.	**Contracted Expenditure**		
2.6.	**Subcontracting expenses**		
2.6.1.	What if R&D activity is outsourced? *Currently in France, payments to R&D service suppliers, public or private, accredited by the French Ministry of research and located in the EU or the EEA, qualify as eligible expenses.*	Beneficiary R&D projects may be organised as 1. projects of a single company, 2. cooperation projects between at least two companies which are independent of each other in terms of company law 3. cooperation projects between businesses in cooperation with one or more institutions for research and dissemination of knowledge.	Sec. 2 para. 4 draft law BMF[158]
2.6.2.	Should there be a territorial limit to exclude payments to subcontractors outside the EEA (which cannot invoke the freedom to provide services).		
2.6.3.	Should there be other limits? *Under current French law for instance, R&D costs invoiced by accredited private subcontractors can be retained within the limit of three times the total amount of all the other R&D eligible expenses incurred by the company; and such expenses can be retained by the company subcontracting R&D works within a yearly limit of EUR 12 or 10 million and EUR 2 million when the parties (i.e. ordering company and R&D supplier) are related companies.*	The research allowance is calculated as a percentage of eligible expenditure. The research allowance amounts to 25 per cent of the eligible expenditure according to Section. 3, up to a maximum of 25 percent of EUR 2 million. The maximum research allowance to be determined for an eligible company is thus EUR 500,000 per financial year. If a R&D project is carried out as a cooperation project between at least two companies which are independent of each other in terms of company law or between businesses in cooperation with one or more institutions for research and dissemination of knowledge, each cooperation partner may claim the assessment basis of EUR 2 million, insofar as the cooperation partner in question is entitled to claim under Section 1 and the cooperation partners entitled to claim are not affiliated companies.	Sec. 4 para. 1,[159] Sec. 3 paras. 5–7[160] draft law BMF

158. Editorial note: Sec. 2 para. 4 of the Act on Tax Incentives for Research and Development deviates partially from Sec. 2 para. 4 of the draft. Moreover, Sec. 2 para. 5 has also been included in the Act. According to para. 5, additional requirements must be met, if research and development projects are commissioned. These are only eligible if the contractor has its registered office in a member state of the European Union or in another state to which the Agreement on the European Economic Area (EEA Agreement) applies and which, on the basis of a contractual obligation, provides administrative assistance in accordance with the EU Administrative Assistance Act to an extent that is necessary for the verification of the eligibility requirements.
159. Editorial note: Sec. 4 para. 1 of the draft deviates in part from Sec. 4 para. 1 of the Act on Tax Incentives for Research and Development, but the research allowance amounts to 25% in both cases.
160. Editorial note: Sec. 3 paras. 6–7 of the draft is identical to Sec. 3. paras. 6–7 of the Act on Tax Incentives for Research and Development.

B.	**Reimbursed expenditure**		
2.7.	**Treatment of public subsidies**		
2.7.1.	Should governmental and other State agencies subsidies/grants related to R&D eligible projects be deducted from eligible expenses of the year during which these expenses are incurred?	The research allowance may, in principle, be granted in addition to other State aid. However, granting research allowances in addition to other grants or other aids is limited by the fact that the same expenditure is double-funded. This means that wage expenses may not be included in the basis of assessment under this Act if they have already been included in the basis of assessment under other grants or other state aids.	Sec. 7 paras. 1[161] and 2[162] draft law government and explanatory memorandum Sec. 7 draft law

161. Editorial note: Sec. 7 para. 1 Draft Law Government corresponds to Sec. 7 para. 1 of the Act on Tax Incentives for Research and Development.
162. Editorial note: Sec. 7 para. 2 of the draft differs in part from Sec. 7 para. 2 of the Act on Tax Incentives for Research and Development. Under the Act in force, eligible expenses may not be included in the assessment basis pursuant to Sec. 3 para. 5 if they were or are subsidised within the framework of other subsidies or state aid. This exclusion of cumulation shall also apply if the other subsidies originate from Union funds.

Section VII
Greece

		Answers and comments	Technical source (when necessary)
1.	'Research and Development' – Definition	There are 40 definitions relating to all areas of R&D, under Article 2 of the Law 4310/2014. Under Article 1 of the joint Ministerial Decision 100335/21.6.2019, signed by the Minister for Education and Research and the Minister for the Economy, as amended, there is a provision for the definition of 'Activities of scientific and technological research', with further definitions of 'basic research', 'applied research' and 'experimental development'.	Article 2 of the Greek Law 4429/2016 provides for the establishment of the Hellenic Foundation for Research and Innovation
1.1.	As indicated in Section I (*supra*), should 'research and development' be excluded if there is no particular application or use in view for the economy or the internal market?	No, 'R&D should not be excluded if there is no practical application or use in view for the economy or the internal market. Such distinction doesn't exist in the domestic law.	
1.2.	Should the level of novelty be new 'to the world', 'to the internal market (EU)', 'to the market', or 'to the firm'?	According to the domestic law, the level of novelty is defined as being new to the world, with no further specialisation concerning the internal market or the EU (Art. 2 of the Joint Ministerial Decision 109343/2017, signed by the Minister for Education and Research, Minister for the Economy, as amended.	
1.3.	Should R&D be limited to the industrial sector, or also include the service industry (banking and insurance, but also humanities)?	According to Article 4 of the Law 4310/2014, R&D may apply on the industry sector but may include other sectors as well, with no restrictive specifications. Further specifications are provided under Article 2 of the Joint Ministerial Decision 109343/2017, signed by the Minister for Education and Research, Minister for the Economy, as amended.	
1.3.1.	In the latter case, which criteria help to identify the presence of R&D in services activities?		

1.3.1.1.	Links with public research laboratories;	Yes. According to Article 3 para. 2 of the Law 4310/2014, there is a specification of the national research centers and institutions that are included in the scope of the law.	
1.3.1.2.	Involvement of staff with PhDs or PhD students;	Yes, according to Article 18 of the Law 4310/2014, the staff (researchers) of the research centers and institutions should be scientists with high scientific experience and training, holders of a PhD. Under Articles 1, 2, 3 of the joint Ministerial Decision 109343/2017, signed by the Minister for Education and Research, Minister for the Economy, as amended by the Joint Ministerial Decision 100335/21.6.2019, signed by the Minister for Education and Research and the joint Ministerial Decision 100335/21.6.2019, signed by the Minister for the Economy and the Minister of Development and Investments, there is a provision for the research staff involved with no further specification for PhD researchers or PhD candidates and students.	
1.3.1.3.	Publication of research findings in scientific journals;	Although there is no specification under domestic law, the answer is yes based mainly on Article 3 (provision of scientific and technological research expenses) of the Joint Ministerial Decision 109343/2017, signed by the Minister for Education and Research, Minister for the Economy, as amended.	
1.3.1.4.	Organisation of scientific conferences;	Although there is no specification under domestic law, the answer is yes based mainly on Article 3 (provision of scientific and technological research expenses) of the Joint Ministerial Decision 109343/2017, signed by the Minister for Education and Research, Minister for the Economy, as amended.	

1.3.1.5.	Involvement in scientific reviews;	Although there is no specification under domestic law, the answer is yes based mainly on Article 3 (provision of scientific and technological research expenses) of the Joint Ministerial Decision 109343/2017, signed by the Minister for Education and Research, Minister for the Economy, as amended.	
1.3.1.6.	Others?	Although there is no specification under domestic law, other activities might be the scientific collaboration and dialogue with researchers from different Member States on similar research objectives, exchange of best practices and participation in scientific events and congresses.	
2.	'COSTS' (FOR RESEARCH AND DEVELOPMENT) – DEFINITION		It should be noted that with the provisions of Article 12 of Law 4965/2022 (A΄ 162), for the requested amount of scientific and technological research expenses exceeding the amount of sixty thousand (60,000) euros, the submission of an audit report by a sworn auditor – accountant or audit firm for the realisation of the expenses and their amount is mandatory. This amendment applies to the requests for certification of scientific and technological research expenses, which concern the fiscal year 2022 and thereafter.
A.	**Capital expenditure**		
2.1.	**Depreciation allowances**		
<u>a.</u>	<u>*General Principles*</u>	**<u>Draft Art. 9-3</u>** provides: '*In addition to the amounts which are deductible as costs for research and development in accordance with paragraph 2, the taxpayer may also deduct, per tax year, an extra 50% of such costs, with the exception of the cost related to movable tangible fixed assets, that it incurred during that year. To the extent that costs for research and development reach beyond EUR 20,000,000, the taxpayer may deduct 25% of the exceeding amount.*' In addition, the Explanatory Memorandum (**para. 8**) provides: "*R&D costs will be fully expensed in the year incurred (with the exception of immovable property).*' **<u>Draft Art. 10</u>** (Other deductible items) provides: '*A deduction shall be made in respect of the depreciation of fixed assets referred to in Articles 30 to 40.* [...]'	

		<u>Draft Art. 12</u> (Non-deductible items) provides: *'By way of derogation from Articles 9 and 10, the following items shall be non-deductible:* [...] *(i) acquisition or construction costs or cost connected with the improvement of fixed assets which are deductible under Articles 10 and 18, except for the cost related to research and development. The costs referred to in point (a) of Article 33(1) and points (a) and (b) of Article 33(2) shall not be treated as costs related to research and development;* [...]' – **<u>For additional context, see Annex</u>**. *Based on your national tax background:*	
2.1.1.	Do you share our understanding that depreciation allowances have to be distinguished depending on the assets concerned, whether they are movable or immovable?	Yes, depreciation allowances have to be distinguished depending on the assets concerned. In Greece, there is no such a distinction, nevertheless we believe that it should be done.	
2.1.2.	Do you share our understanding that depreciation allowances are not available for movable fixed assets, because they are fully expensed in the year incurred, and not eligible to the super-deduction?	Yes, we share the same understanding.	
2.1.3.	Do you share our understanding that depreciation allowances remain available for immovable [property], because it cannot be fully expensed in the year incurred, and is eligible to the super-deduction?	Yes. Immovable property is eligible to the 'super-deduction'. According to Greek law (Art. 22A, Law 4172/2013 and Joint Ministerial Decisions 109343/2017, and 100335/2019 (as amended by Ministerial Decision 79230/2021, Art. 3) depreciation of costs of purchase, construction or repair, maintenance, renovation of buildings and according to their part, after apportionment, exclusively related to scientific and technological research activities.	
2.1.4.	What if an asset is used both for research and non-research purposes (such as manufacturing)?	According to Greek law, if an asset is used for both purposes, it is eligible only to the extent, that the specific item is used for scientific purposes.	

2.1.5.	If eligible, which criteria for proportional eligibility if asset used both for R&D and manufacturing purposes (e.g. an equipment used both to manufacture prototypes and serial products)?	We believe that time could be a criterion for proportional eligibility, i.e. the asset can be eligible only for the time period, during which it is used for scientific purposes and to manufacture prototypes and not for the line production.	
2.1.6.	What if the asset is 'indirectly' used for R&D purposes?	Even if the asset is used 'indirectly' for R&D purposes, yet we believe that it should be eligible for the super-deduction.	
2.1.7.	What do you think of the following definition: 'Is considered directly used for R&D purposes an asset permitting, in and of itself, to carry out research programs of the business'?	This definition is clear and thorough. It is ok.	
2.1.8.	Is the production of the following assets an R&D activity? (i) production of prototypes; (ii) construction of a pilot plant/or pilot facilities.	We believe that the production of prototypes is an R&D activity, as well as the construction of a pilot plan/or pilot facilities. According to Greek Law, an R&D activity includes the construction and operation of pilot projects in an experimental phase in order to gain experience and combine construction studies and other data for the creation of new product specifications, the design of special equipment and structures as well as for the preparation of operating instructions and manuals of procedures and methods. (Art. 2 of Ministerial Decision 109343/2017, as amended by Ministerial Decisions 100335/2019 and 79230/2021)	
2.1.9.	Would you characterise the following assets as, potentially, directly used for R&D activities: (i) Handling devices; (ii) Calculation tools; (iii) Computers; (iv) Machines used to manufacture components of a prototype; (v) Telephones, small office appliances, office furniture?	(i) Handling device: Yes. (ii) Calculation tools: Yes. (iii) Computers: Yes. (iv) Machines used to manufacture components of a prototype: Yes. (v) Telephones, small office appliances: No.	

b.	*Specific Rules*		
(i)	*Intangible Assets*	**Draft Art. 33.1(e)** provides: *'Without prejudice to paragraph 2 and Articles 37 and 38, fixed assets shall be depreciated individually over their useful lives on a straight-line basis. The useful life of a fixed asset shall be determined as follows: [...] (e) fixed intangible assets: the period for which the asset enjoys legal protection or for which the right has been granted or, where that period cannot be determined, 15 years.'* The problem is that not all intangible items (e.g. intellectual property, brand names), meet the definition of an intangible asset. If an item does meet the definition of an intangible asset, expenditure to acquire it or generate it internally should be recognised as an expense when it is incurred. Therefore, *based on your national tax background*:	
2.1.10.	Should we use the European Union Accounting Rule 6 defining intangible asset (i.e. identifiability, control over a resource, and existence of future economic benefits or service potential)?	Yes, we should use the European Union Accounting Rule 6 defining intangible asset.	In Greece, Law 4308/2014 (article defines the intangible assets as follows: Intangible asset: It is a customisable and non-monetary asset, without material substance. An intangible asset is customisable in either of the following two cases: a) It is separable, i.e. it can be separated or separated from the entity and sold, transferred, leased, or exchanged, either by itself or together with a related contract, asset or liability, b) It arises from contractual or other legal rights, regardless of whether the rights are transferable, or separable from the entity, or from other rights and obligations.
2.1.11.	If not, what should be the definition of intangible assets?		
2.1.12.	Are intangible fixed assets (including intellectual property (IP)) costs fully expensed in the year incurred and included in the CCTB super-deduction?	Since the intangible fixed assets may be fully expensed in the year incurred, we believe that they should not be eligible for the super deduction.	Greek Ministerial Decision 109343/2017 (as amended by Ministerial Decisions 100335/2019 and 79230/2021), Articles 3 and 22 A of Law 4172/2013 provides that expenses for the purchase of a patent in Greece and abroad and Expenses for the issuance of a patent in Greece and abroad are included in the costs for a 100% deduction.

	The inclusion of mere intellectual property costs is not advisable: it may create a bias in favour of patented research compared to that stemming from unpatented technology.		
2.1.13.	Will in practice this provision be limited to patents costs acquired with a view to carry on new experimental research and development?	This may turn out to be a strong possibility, according to the application of the law and the interpretation of the law by the national legal orders.	
2.1.14.	What if these patents are (also) used in the manufacturing process?	They will be included in the 'super-deduction' only to the extent that the cost is related to the creation of the patent and not for the massive production.	
2.1.15.	Should plant variety rights be treated in the same manner as patents?	Yes, they should be treated in the same way as patents.	
2.1.16.	What about outlays incurred to acquire licences or know-how?	Yes, they should be treated in the same way as patents.	
(ii)	*Immovable [property]*		
	In any case, not covered by exclusion in Art. 9-3		
	In Austria, building costs and financing expenses related to R&D activity may be taken into account.		
2.1.17.	Should the concept of 'immovable property' (Recital No. 8) be preferred to the one of 'immovable fixed asset' (as opposed to Art. 9.3 CCTB)?	Yes, the concept 'immovable property' should be preferred.	
2.1.18.	Would building costs and financing expenses related to the acquisition of immovable [property] be eligible to the super-deduction?	Yes, according to Article 3 para. A of the Ministerial Decision 109343/2017 (as amended by Ministerial Decisions 100335/2019 and 79230/2021), building costs and financing expenses related to the acquisition of immovable property should be eligible for super-deduction.	

2.1.19.	What is your understanding of Art. 12(i): 1st meaning: that costs related to acquisition or construction of new commercial or second-hand commercial or industrial immovable [property] is excluded from the super-deduction? Or 2nd meaning: that costs related to acquisition or construction of new commercial or second-hand commercial or industrial immovable [property] is not fully deductible the year incurred but should be depreciated and such depreciation allowances are eligible to the super-deduction?	We understand it as the 2nd meaning.	
(iii)	*Lease payments*		
2.1.20.	What if equipment is used according to the terms of a leasing-type transaction?	Yes, it is eligible (Art. 3 of the Ministerial Decision 109343/2017 (as amended by Ministerial Decisions 100335/2019 and 79230/2021).	Article 3(b) of the Ministerial Decision 100335/2019 (as amended by Ministerial Decision 79230/2021), as combined with Article 22A of Law 4172/2013, provides that 'depreciation of purchase or leasing costs of laboratory infrastructure equipment and instruments for the period of time they are used for research purposes, such as devices, tools, scientific instruments, devices and their accessories (laboratory or semi-industrial scale) as well as semi-industrial (demonstration) facilities) tests, are eligible for a deduction of 100%. The costs of this category may include any additional costs of transporting and installing the equipment as well as training the staff in its use'.

2.1.21.	Are leasing instalments eligible for super-deduction under current wording of Art. 9-3?	Yes, according to our interpretation, this article includes leasing instalments as well.	
2.1.22.	Should they be?	Yes, we believe they should be.	
(iv)	*Alternative readings*		
2.1.23.	Please feel free to add any alternative readings you may have of relevant CCTB provisions and that has not yet been discussed.		
B.	**Current expenditure**		
2.2.	**R&D staff cost**		
a.	*What is meant by R&D staff?*	According to the Greek Law 4310/2014 (Art. 18) and the ministerial decision 109343/2017 (as amended by Ministerial Decisions 100335/2019 and 79230/2021).) Article 3 para. d, R&D staff means every researcher or other person (technicians, administrative staff), (all kinds of personnel, including scientists, post – graduate students, technicians, and administrative staff) who work individually or in groups in order to produce, or improve knowledge, produce products, or procedures.	
2.2.1.	Should eligibility be limited to staff directly-involved in R&D?	No, it may also include other staff, even indirectly involved, as long as the tasks focus on R&D purposes.	Greek law provides that: Remuneration of each level of staff (employees with a dependent employment contract, open-ended or fixed-term contract or project lease), employed in the execution of the scientific and technological research project during the period of its implementation and in proportion to the time of his employment, such as specialised scientists, postgraduate students, technicians and auxiliary administrative staff is eligible to be calculated as current expenditure . It is pointed out that the costs of the technical-administrative staff of the company cannot exceed 20% of the total payroll costs of the approved research team of the project [Art. 3 para. 1(e) of the Ministerial Decision 109343/2017 (as amended by Ministerial Decisions 100335/2019 and 79230/2021). and Art. 22A of law 4172/2013]

2.2.2.	In case the staff participates both in R&D and non R&D activities, should the text allow for proportional eligibility based on time spent (or other criteria)?	Yes, it should allow for proportional eligibility, based on time spent, as stated in a clear relevant provision in Article 3 para. d of the Joint Greek Ministerial Decision 109343/2017 (as amended by Ministerial Decisions 100335/2019 and 79230/2021)..	
2.2.3.	How can researchers or scientists be defined? Should the text use black letter criteria (list diplomas (PhDs), qualifications...) or a more open definition?	According to the Greek Law 4310/2014, researchers or scientists are defined using specific criteria (black letter criteria).	
2.2.4.	Are research technicians R&D staff?	Yes, according to Greek law, research technicians are R&D staff.	
2.2.5.	What about other employees (not 'official researchers') which still have contributed to a patented invention?	According to Greek law, other employees are R&D staff. (Art. 3 para. 1. Joint Greek Ministerial Decision 109343/2017 (as amended by Ministerial Decisions 100335/2019 and 79230/2021).	Remuneration of each level of staff (employees with a dependent employment contract, open-ended or fixed-term contract or project lease), who are employed in the execution of the scientific and technological research project during the period of its implementation and in proportion to the time of their employment, such as specialized scientists, post-graduate students, technicians and auxiliary administrative staff. The expenses of the technical-administrative staff of the company may not exceed 20% of the total payroll expenses of the approved research team of the project (see above 2.2.1)
2.2.6.	What about the managers of the business (e.g. running a research program)?	Yes, they are considered to be R&D staff, as long as there is a scientific purpose.	
2.2.7.	What about other staff (secretariat, cleaning, etc.)? Can, in the alternative, their compensation be taken into account, proportionally, as other operating R&D expenses (cf. I-3 below)?	According to the Greek legislation, administrative employees, who contribute to the running of the project, are included, but other type of staff, like cleaning services, are not.	

b.	*What is meant by R&D staff cost?*	In Greece R&D staff cost means:	
2.2.8.	Wages, bonuses, benefits in kind?	The wages are R&D cost staff. The bonuses and benefits are excluded according to Article 3 para. 3b of the Joint Greek Ministerial Decision 109343/2017 (as amended by Ministerial Decisions 100335/2019 and 79230/2021).	Article 3 para. 3 of the Joint Ministerial Decision 109343/2017 (as amended by Ministerial Decisions 100335/2019 and 79230/2021) provides as follows; In cases where staff are employed on the project for the whole of their contractual time or for a fixed percentage of the contractual employment time, the costs for staff fees can be calculated not on the basis of the hourly employment cost but as the product of the fixed percentage of his contractual time with the gross monthly employment costs. employment for twelve (12) and is a simplified cost option
2.2.9.	Social security contributions (compulsory and/or non-compulsory)?	Social security contributions in Greece, either compulsory or not, are included in the R&D staff costs.	
2.2.10.	Employer's contribution to participation of employees in profits of the enterprise by means of profit-sharing plan, employee share-ownership?	In Greece, employer's contribution to participation of employees in profits of the enterprise (shares, etc.) are not considered to be R&D cost.	
2.2.11.	Can a Member State provide that compensation paid to holders of PhD will count more (e.g. double) for a limited period of time (in order to promote hiring of PhD holders)?	Yes, it should be provided that compensation paid to holders of PhD will count more for a limited period of time, without such a provision to be interpreted as a legal discrimination.	
2.3.	**Standardisation expenses**		
	Based on your national tax background:		
2.3.1.	Should expenses related to the establishment of technical standards concerning products of the business be eligible for the super-deduction (e.g. expenses incurred on participation of employees in official meetings of standardisation bodies)?	Yes, expenses related to the establishment of technical standards concerning products of the business are eligible for the super-deduction (Art. 3 of Joint Greek Ministerial decision 109343/2017 (as amended by Ministerial Decisions 100335/2019 and 79230/2021).	

2.3.2.	If yes, should it still be the case even if these employees are not scientists or research technicians?	Yes, if they participate in some way in the R&D project.	
2.3.3.	How should these expenses be assessed (e.g. as portion of employee compensation related to the time spent in connection with such meetings)?	These expenses should be assessed according to the time spent in relation with such meetings.	
2.3.4.	Should expenses related to technical monitoring/ technological watch be taken into account?	Yes, as long as they are used for research purposes.	
2.4.	**Patent related expenses**		
2.4.1.	Are expenses linked to patents eligible? Please define NB: *under current French tax law, expenses linked to the filing, the maintenance and the defence of patents incurred in France or in another State (IP consultant's fees, translation costs taxes...) are eligible to the R&D tax credit; insurance costs linked to patents are eligible within a threshold of EUR 60,000.* *However, under the Frascati criterion, R&D would typically not include administrative and legal work connected with patents, routine tests or data collection.*	Yes, under Greek tax law, expenses linked to patents are eligible to the R&D tax credit.	
2.5.	**Other operating expenses related to R&D**		
2.5.1.	Should such category be identified?	Yes, a specific category of other operating expenses should be identified.	
2.5.2.	Is a detailed list possible of expenses advisable?	Even though Greek law has an exclusive list, we believe that it is not advisable, because there is rapid evolution in the R&D sector.	

2.5.3.	Is it appropriate to assess these expenses notionally by reference to other precisely defined eligible expenses (e.g. 15% of immovable [property] depreciation allowances, and/or 50% of eligible staff expenses)?	Yes, we should apply it proportionally.	
2.5.4.	Should fees paid to external consultants assisting the company to determine its R&D super deduction be eligible, and to what extent?	No, we believe that such fees should not be eligible for the super-deduction.	
C.	**Contracted Expenditure**		
2.6.	**Subcontracting expenses**		
2.6.1.	What if R&D activity is outsourced? *Currently in France, payments to R&D service suppliers, public or private, accredited by the French Ministry of research and located in the EU or the EEA, qualify as eligible expenses.*	Yes, according to the Greek legislation, such an activity is eligible for deduction up to 70% of the total budget of the research project.	Assignment by contract to external partners or bodies (private laboratories and companies, public research centers and laboratories, Universities), of a specific and clearly defined part of a scientific and technological research project. The eligible subcontracting costs (natural and legal persons) for the execution of part of the research project may not exceed 70% of the research project budget. Article 3 para. I of the of Joint Greek Ministerial decision 109343/2017 (as amended by Ministerial Decisions 100335/2019 and 79230/2021).
2.6.2.	Should there be a territorial limit to exclude payments to subcontractors outside the EEA (which cannot invoke the freedom to provide services).	Yes, according to our opinion, there should be a territorial limit in the EEE.	

2.6.3.	Should there be other limits? *Under current French law for instance, R&D costs invoiced by accredited private subcontractors can be retained within the limit of three times the total amount of all the other R&D eligible expenses incurred by the company; and such expenses can be retained by the company subcontracting R&D works within a yearly limit of EUR 12 or 10 million and EUR 2 million when the parties (i.e. ordering company and R&D supplier) are related companies.*	Yes, according to the Greek legislationn there is a limit up to a certain percentage (70% of the budget – Art. 3 para. I of the Joint Greek Ministerial Decision 109343/2017 (as amended by Ministerial Decisions 100335/2019 and 79230/2021	
B.	**Reimbursed expenditure**		
2.7.	**Treatment of public subsidies**		
2.7.1.	Should governmental and other State agencies subsidies/grants related to R&D eligible projects be deducted from eligible expenses of the year during which these expenses are incurred?	Yes, according to Greek law, the grants related to R&D eligible projects should be deducted from the expenses of the year during which these expenses are incurred.	

SECTION VIII
Hungary

		Answers and comments	Technical source (when necessary)
1.	'RESEARCH AND DEVELOPMENT' – DEFINITION	It should be stated previously that depending on the request of an applicant, the Hungarian Intellectual Property Office (HIPO), as a government body is a competent authority to define whether the R&D activities will be carried out within the taxpayer's operation or not. The National Tax and Customs Administration (NTCA), as the competent government body, carries out the tax audit measures on Corporate Tax. In connection with tax reliefs of R&D activities, NTCA according to its own regulatory, appoints HIPO as an expert and bases its decision on the opinion of HIPO. As a result of these regulations, the decision/expert report of the HIPO in the question of whether the company conducted R&D activity shall be considered as a binding classification by the National Tax and Customs Administration. Based upon the regulations of the R&D Act, the HIPO shall publish a Methodological Manual on the Classification Procedures (MMCP) (Subsection 3 Section 37 R&D Act). When HIPO applies MMCP, it takes into consideration Frascati Manual 2002 in the case of subjects which exclude the subjects of MMCP.	

		'R&D activities carried out within the taxpayer's operations' definition according to Point 32 Section 4 CTDT *'R&D activities carried out within the taxpayer's operations'* shall mean R&D activities carried out using the taxpayer's own assets and workers, at the taxpayer's risk and benefit, including where R&D activities are carried out by the taxpayer's workers using the taxpayer's own assets on behalf of others, as well as (joint) research and development activities carried out under research and development agreement.	Act LXXXI of 1996 on Corporate Tax and Dividend Tax (CTDT)
		As CTDT does not include a definition of 'R&D', thus the provision of R&D Act shall be applied according to the followings. *'Research and development' definition according to Point 11 Section 3 R&D Act* 'Research and development' includes basic research, applied research and experimental development.	Act LXXVI of 2014 on Scientific Research, Development and Innovation (R&D Act)
		'Basic research' definition according to Point 1 Section 3 R&D Act 'Basic research' means experimental or theoretical work aimed at new discoveries, carried out with the primary aim of obtaining new knowledge necessary for understanding phenomena, experiences, and observations, without envisaging its practical use or application; *'Applied research' definition according to Point 2 Section 3 R&D Act* 'Applied research' means planned research or targeted study aimed at obtaining new knowledge or expertise with the aim of developing new products, processes, technologies or services or contributing to the significant development of existing products, processes or services.	Frascati Manual 2002, 64

		'Experimented development' definition according to Point 2 Section 3 R&D Act 'Experimental development' means obtaining, aggregating, sharing, applying and utilising existing scientific, technological, business and other knowledge and expertise with the aim of creating or designing new, modified or improved products, processes or services. The following may qualify as experimental development: a) activities aimed at the conceptual definition, design and documentation of new products, processes and services; b) activities that include the creation of drafts, design drawings, plans and other forms of documentation not intended for commercial use; c) the making of prototypes not for commercial use; d) the development of commercially usable prototypes and experimental projects if the prototype itself is by necessity the commercial end product as well, and its manufacturing is too costly to be done for demonstration and certification purposes only; e) the experimental manufacturing and testing of products, processes and services, provided that they cannot be used for industrial or commercial purposes, or be modified for such use. Experimental development shall not include normal, periodical or routine changes carried out with regard to products, production lines, manufacturing processes, existing services or other ongoing operations even if such changes are considered development, or if they result in the improvement of the given product, process, operation or service.		

		2024 Modification The terms of 'applied **(industrial)** research' and 'experimental development' was amended with the following factors: applied (industrial mean the planned research or critical investigation aimed at the acquisition of new knowledge and skills for developing new products, processes or services or aimed at bringing about a significant improvement in existing products, processes or services, **including digital products, processes or services, in any area, technology, industry or sector (including, but not limited to, digital industries and technologies, such as super-computing, quantum technologies, block chain technologies, artificial intelligence, cyber security, big data and cloud technologies)**; **industrial research comprises the creation of components parts of complex systems, and may include the construction of prototypes in a laboratory environment or in an environment with simulated interfaces to existing systems as well as of pilot lines, when necessary for the industrial research and notably for generic technology validation.** The terms of 'experimental development' was modified and amended with the following factors: 'experimental development' shall mean acquiring, combining, shaping and using existing scientific, technological, business and other relevant knowledge and skills with the aim of developing new or improved products, processes or services, **meaning including digital products, processes or services, in particular:any area, technology, industry or sector (including, but not limited to, digital industries and technologies, such as for example super-computing, quantum technologies, block chain technologies, artificial intelligence, cyber security, big data and cloud or edge technologies);**	

		The ministerial statement of the Modification stressed that the interpretive provisions aim, on the one hand, to incorporate into legislation the definitions of terms commonly used among actors in research, development, and innovation, particularly by policymakers. On the other hand, they seek to harmonize the terminology used in EU and OECD documents with the interpretive provisions of the law. The modified definitions clearly shows that the terms of R&D including all activities regarding IT sector and digital economy, which fulfil the general requirements of R&D activities.	
1.1.	As indicated in Section I (*supra*), should 'research and development' be excluded if there is no particular application or use in view for the economy or the internal market?	Definitely not. According to the R&D definition, stated in the Point 11 Section 3 R&D Act, R&D definition includes **basic research**. Pursuant to the Point 1 Section 3 R&D Act, an activity can be considered as basic research **without** envisaging its practical use or application.	Frascati Manual 2002, 240 Frascati Manual 2015, 2.18
1.2.	Should the level of novelty be new 'to the world', 'to the internal market (EU)', 'to the market', or 'to the firm'?	To delimitate R&D activities and activities related to R&D, the key elements of R&D activities are the resolution of scientific or technological uncertainty and novelty according to the Point 84 Frascati Manual 2002. The MMCP recital the Frascati Manuals 2002 in connection with the main factor of the resolution of scientific or technological uncertainty and criteria of novelty. As it is referred into Point 84 Frascati Manual 2002, the resolution of scientific or technological uncertainty and novelty can be identified 'when the solution to a problem is not readily apparent to someone familiar with the basic stock of common knowledge and techniques for the area concerned'.	Frascati Manual 2002,84

		It complies with a viewpoint of the Point 13 Guidelines on the Meaning of Research and Development for Tax Purposes. Interestingly, the Curia of Hungary (the Hungarian Supreme Court) gave an interpretation of the level of the novelty in relation to innovation contribution. Due to the regulations of the Act XC of 2003 on the Research and Innovation Fund, companies were obliged to pay innovation contribution after the tax base of local business tax. It should be noticed that before 2012, the gross amount of the innovation contribution could have been deducted by the direct costs of R&D related to the business activities of the relevant company. As legal disputes had been incurred related to the relief of the innovation contribution, the interpretation of the level of the novelty can be found in this context in Hungarian case law. According to the interpretation of Curia of Hungary, novelty can be found if the level of the novelty is new to the Hungarian economy. It has to be account that the Act on Research and Innovation Fund announced and entered into force before the accession to the European Union of Hungary, thus – having regard to the general principles of R&D Act referring to EUROPE 2020 – this interpretation should be amended and stated that novelty shall be meant **a new to the internal market**.	Guidelines on the Meaning of Research and Development for Tax Purposes
1.3.	Should R&D be limited to the industrial sector, or also include the service industry (banking and insurance, but also humanities)?	There is no such a limitation based on the sectors of the economy in relation with R&D. Besides industrial sector R&D can be stated, in connection with any commercial or financial activities, or even in humanities, social sciences.	

		Additional Note Furthermore, pursuant to the Frascati Manual 2002, any other related scientific and technological activities should be excluded from R&D **except when carried out solely or primarily for the purposes of an R&D project**. Depending on the request of the applicant, HIPO observes the portion of the basic research/ the applied research and experimented development in the whole project and provides a binding report for the applicant.	Frascati Manual 2002, 69
1.3.1.	In the latter case, which criteria help to identify the presence of R&D in services activities?	Pursuant to Frascati Manual 2002, all the above-mentioned criteria mostly help to find the key factors of R&D activities. It is important to emphasise here that during the classification, all the circumstances shall be examined in details and in overall by aggregating all the facts related to the relevant project, thus the resolution on the presence of R&D activities shall be established by a conviction of an independent expert.	Frascati Manual 2002, 149-150 Frascati Manual 2015, 2.85
1.3.1.1.	Links with public research laboratories;	These factors may suggest that the activity can be considered as the carried out within the taxpayer's own scope of activities. However, R&D must be distinguished from many other scientific activities, such as general education and training, other related scientific and technical other industrial activities and ancillary administrative and management support activities. Activities that do not constitute R&D activities per se, but contribute directly to to the R&D project, or which are carried out solely to achieve the objective of the R&D activity, are part of the R&D activity and cannot be excluded from the scope of the R&D activity. In contrast, subtasks which do not constitute R & D per se and are not an integral part of the project, i.e. they are not necessarily necessary to achieve the project objective, nor can they be considered R&D.	
1.3.1.2.	Involvement of staff with PhDs or PhD students;		
1.3.1.3.	Publication of research findings in scientific journals;		
1.3.1.4.	Organisation of scientific conferences;		
1.3.1.5.	Involvement in scientific reviews;		

1.3.1.6.	Others?	As stated by the Court of Hungary, the Hungarian Tax and Customs Administration shall observe the whole procedure of R&D project and it should be compared with the relevant business activities and developed programs to define whether the R&D activities fall within the scope of business interest.	
2.	'Costs' (For Research and Development) – Definition	**The relevant regulation of CTDT on the costs for R&D are the followings.** **According to Point t) Subsection 1 Section 7 CTDT** [The following shall be deducted from the pre-tax profit:] 'taking into consideration of what is contained in Subsections (17)-(18), the direct costs of basic research, applied research and experimental development carried out within the taxpayer's own scope of activities (not including the value of research and experimental development services provided by a resident taxpayer, by the domestic branch of a nonresident entrepreneur or – pursuant to the Personal Income Tax Act – by a private entrepreneur directly or indirectly) claimed in the tax year in which it is incurred or, at the taxpayer's discretion, if these costs are shown under the capitalized value of experimental development (intellectual property) in the tax year in which depreciation is claimed, up to the amount claimed as depreciation; these costs (charges) may not be deducted from pre-tax profit and shown under the costs of development or operating costs (charges) in the amount of any support or assistance requested from the tax authority before the balance sheet date or received during the tax year for development purposes without any obligation of repayment, or – if applicable – in the amount of income included in the pre-tax profit for the tax year under the title of grant or support'.	

		According to Subsection 17 Section 7 CTDT 'In connection with basic research, applied research and experimental development performed jointly by a taxpayer and an institution of higher education, the Magyar Tudományos Akadémia (Hungarian Academy of Sciences), a research institution operated as a central budgetary agency or a research institution (research facility) established by either of them or jointly, as well as any research institution operating in a form of a business association under majority State ownership directly or indirectly, the taxpayer may claim ***three times the amount*** referred to in and calculated according to Subsection t) of Subsection (1) hereof up to ***maximum fifty million forints***, whose value calculated by the tax rate referred to in Section 19 for the purposes of the provisions governing state subsidies shall be treated as ***de minimis*** aid received for the tax year. These provisions shall also apply to any equivalent organization established in any Member State of the European Union or any State that is a party to the Agreement on the European Economic Area.' **According to Subsection 18 Section 7 CTDT** 'The provisions of Subsection t) of Subsection (1) may be applied in connection with research and experimental development services by the person to whom they were provided if the service provider declares of having provided the service without the involvement of research and experimental development services provided by a resident taxpayer or by the Hungarian branch of a nonresident entrepreneur, or by a private entrepreneur governed under the Act on Personal Income Tax.'	

		According to Subsection 22 Section 7 CTDT (As regards research and development services ordered from an affiliated company (other than a business establishment) for the purpose of the acquisition or production of an intangible asset embodying rights to royalties or notified intangible asset, or any purchased (received) intangible asset embodying rights to royalties or notified intangible asset, the taxpayer may take into consideration as a deductible item provided for in Subsections c), e) and s) of Subsection (1) a sum determined in proportion to: a) the direct costs of basic research, applied research and experimental development incurred in connection with the acquisition or development of such asset (including the costs accounted for by the taxpayer's business establishment, but excluding the direct costs of research and development services ordered from an affiliated company (other than a business establishment) and the cost of any purchased (received) intangible asset embodying rights to royalties or notified intangible asset), and b) the direct costs of basic research, applied research and experimental development incurred in connection with the acquisition or development of such asset (including the costs accounted for by the taxpayer's business establishment, the direct costs of research and development services ordered from an affiliated company and the cost of any purchased (received) intangible asset embodying rights to royalties or notified intangible asset), with the proviso that direct costs shall be taken into consideration at the fair market price prevailing at the time when determining said ratio in the tax year when the cost was actually incurred (irrespective of its accrual).	

		According to Point d) Subsection 1 Section 8 CTDT [Pre-tax profit shall be ***increased*** by the following:] 'amounts claimed as costs or expenditures, and deducted from the pre-tax profit, including the depreciation allowances of tangible assets and intangible assets, which ***are not related to the business operations or the gainful activity***, with particular regard to what is contained in Schedule No. 3' **According to Subsection 14 Section 17 CTDT** If the taxpayer opts to claim the tax allowance available on research and development activities as provided for in Chapter IX of Act CLVI of 2011 on the Amendment of Tax Laws and Other Related Regulations, 50 per cent of its tax loss resulting from the tax base reduction under Subsection t) of Subsection (1) of Section 7 shall be recognized as deferred loss. **According to Point 15 Part A) Schedule No. 3 CTDT** [For the purposes of Subsection d) of Subsection (1) of Section 8, the following, in particular, shall not qualify as costs or expenses incurred in the interest of business operations:] 'direct costs of research and development activities, if not connected to the taxpayer's business operations or gainful activity' **Additional Note** **According to Point e) Subsection 1** **Section 22/B CTDT** [***Tax credit*** shall be granted to taxpayers:] for investment projects concerning basic research, applied research and experimental development, if valued at 100 million forints or more at current prices;	

A.	Capital expenditure		
2.1.	Depreciation allowances	**The relevant regulation of CTDT and Accounting Act on depreciation allowances are the followings.** **According to Subparagraphs a) and g) Point 5 Schedule No. 1 CTDT** [Ordinary depreciation, as defined in the Accounting Act, (including lump-sum depreciation) may be claimed on:] a) intangible assets (excluding goodwill) and rights to immovables, g) tangible assets that are used **exclusively** for basic research, applied research and/or experimental development **According to Subsection 1 Section 52 Accounting Act:** According to the Subsection 1 Act C of 2000 on Accounting: The cost (original or production cost) of ***intangible assets*** and ***tangible*** assets less the residual value estimated for the end of the useful life of the asset shall be distributed over the number of years in which such assets are expected to be used (ordinary depreciation). **According to Subsection 1 Section 25 Accounting Act:** 'Assets other than tangible assets (such as concessions and similar rights with the exception of rights attached to immovables, ***intellectual property***, goodwill), advances and prepayments on intangible assets and value adjustments of intangible assets shall be shown under intangible assets.'	**Act C of 2000 on Accounting (Accounting Act)**

		According to Subsection 4 Section 25 Accounting Act: 'The capitalized value of experimental development shall consist of the sums paid to subcontractors as invoiced to achieve the purpose of the experimental development and the direct costs of own activities (Section 51) incurred in the course of experimental development procedures, which are likely to be recovered during future use of the results produced by such activities, and which are not included among other products that can be capitalized (such as intellectual property, tangible assets, inventories) as they exceed the – estimated – market value of the final product. The capitalized value of experimental development, when activated, may not exceed the amount that is likely to be recovered by future profits it is presumed to generate, after the deduction of further development-related expenses, estimated production costs, or the direct costs of sales when applicable.' **According to Subsection 5 Section 25 Accounting Act:** 'The direct costs of experimental development that is already in progress but is not concluded by the balance sheet date of the financial year may be shown as capitalized value of experimental development. In this case, the capitalized value of experimental development includes – apart from the extra costs of experimental development operations – the direct costs of products that are to be shown under inventories, tangible assets or intellectual property following the conclusion of such operations, by decreasing the capitalized value of experimental development. Costs of basic and applied research and the indirect costs and overhead of experimental development may not be capitalized.'	

<table>
<tr><td></td><td></td><td>According to Subsection 4 Section 52 Accounting Act:
Completed experimental development projects and the capitalized value of formation/restructuring shall be depreciated over a period of five years or less – at least five years, not exceeding ten years in the case of goodwill – if the useful economic lives thereof cannot be estimated.</td><td></td></tr>
<tr><td><u>a.</u></td><td><u>General Principles</u></td><td colspan="2"><u>Draft Art. 9-3</u> provides: 'In addition to the amounts which are deductible as costs for research and development in accordance with paragraph 2, the taxpayer may also deduct, per tax year, an extra 50% of such costs, with the exception of the cost related to movable tangible fixed assets, that it incurred during that year. To the extent that costs for research and development reach beyond EUR 20,000,000, the taxpayer may deduct 25% of the exceeding amount.'
In addition, the Explanatory Memorandum (para. 8) provides: 'R&D costs will be fully expensed in the year incurred (with the exception of immovable property)'.
<u>Draft Art. 10</u> (Other deductible items) provides: 'A deduction shall be made in respect of the depreciation of fixed assets referred to in Articles 30 to 40. […]'
<u>Draft Art. 12</u> (Non-deductible items) provides: 'By way of derogation from Articles 9 and 10, the following items shall be non-deductible:
[…] (i) acquisition or construction costs or cost connected with the improvement of fixed assets which are deductible under Articles 10 and 18, except for the cost related to research and development. The costs referred to in point (a) of Article 33(1) and points (a) and (b) of Article 33(2) shall not be treated as costs related to research and development;
[…]' – <u>For additional context, see Annex</u>.
Based on your national tax background:</td></tr>
<tr><td></td><td></td><td>Recital 'R&D activities carried out within the taxpayer's operations' definition according to Point 32 Section 4 CTDT
'R&D activities carried out within the taxpayer's operations' shall mean R&D activities carried out using the taxpayer's own assets and workers, at the taxpayer's risk and benefit, including where R&D activities are carried out by the taxpayer's workers using the taxpayer's own assets on behalf of others, as well as (joint) research and development activities carried out under research and development agreement.</td><td></td></tr>
</table>

2.1.1.	Do you share our understanding that depreciation allowances have to be distinguished depending on the assets concerned, whether they are movable or immovable?	**No, we do not.** The Hungarian regulation provides much wider and generous tax relief in this field as under the account of the assets of the research and experimented development activities, the depreciation allowance after immovable/movable tangible and intangible assets can be registered. In case that the use of the fixed asset is to be considered to be direct R&D purposes within the business interest of the company, there is no reason make the difference between movable and immovable fixed assets. On the other hand, if a cost is not incurred related to the business interest of the company, all the cost shall be considered as an item which increases the tax base.	
2.1.2.	Do you share our understanding that depreciation allowances are not available for movable fixed assets, because they are fully expensed in the year incurred, and not eligible to the super-deduction?	**No, we do not.** **According to Subsection 3 Section 1 CTDT:** 'Where costs and expenditures, as well as the reduction (increase) of pretax profit, or the claiming of tax exemption or tax relief are to be taken into account on the same grounds, but under different entitlements as prescribed by this Act, it may (shall) be claimed only once, unless any provision of the law expressly refers to the application of such on several occasions.' **According to Subsection 5 Section 1 CTDT:** 'This Act shall be interpreted according to and in accordance with the provisions of the Accounting Act. Any deviation from the provisions of the Accounting Act in order to receive a true and fair view shall not be permitted to result in lower tax liabilities.' The Hungarian regulation expressly provides a 'double deduction' or in certain circumstances even 'triple deduction' for movable fixed assets by allowing the deduction of pretax profit and even the tax base itself.	2011/26. Questions on Taxation

		According to the statement of the NTCA, without taking into consideration the fact that a movable fixed asset is being expensed, the tax base can be deducted at the option of the company with the direct costs of R&D or the depreciation allowance for the costs of the experimented development.	
2.1.3.	Do you share our understanding that depreciation allowances remain available for immovable [property], because it cannot be fully expensed in the year incurred, and is eligible to the super-deduction?	**Yes, definitely, but we have some limitation at this point. According to the Subsections 5–7 Section 52 accounting Act:** (5) 'No ordinary depreciation may be claimed relating to the cost (original cost) of land, plots of land (other than those used for mining or for the disposal of hazardous waste), forest, works of art, archeological findings, or of the assets that were not commissioned or validated.' (6) No ordinary depreciation may be claimed in connection with assets that do not depreciate when used, but rather, due to their unique characteristics and properties, appreciate over the years. (7) Ordinary depreciation shall apply relating to intangible and tangible assets already commissioned, validated and put into operation while such assets are used for their intended purpose. The rules of Accounting Act referred above, comply with the relevant articles of CCTB. If an immovable fixed asset is not to be considered as the object of the depreciation allowances, the deduction is not available at all.	
2.1.4.	What if an asset is used both for research and non-research purposes (such as manufacturing)?	The company shall determine the portion of the usage for research purposes. In itself, the circumstances that the asset is used for non-research purposes does not exclude the eligibility of the tax relief of R&D activities.	

		According to Frascati Manual 2002, to determine the R&D portion of the project, the company shall provide an appropriate method for rating. This calculation shall be based on objective circumstances, like the estimated area of the site, working hours, numbers of staff, etc., to be assigned to R&D activities. **Additional Note** Previously, the first element which should be examined is that whether the activities in which the asset is used shall be considered as activities within the business interest of the company or not. If the circumstance does not meet the requirements of the term of 'within the business', the costs shall increase the tax base. The situation is the same if the portion of the activities conducted beside the business interest of the company is dominant compared to the activities conducted within the business interest of the company.	Frascati Manual 2002, 385
2.1.5.	If eligible, which criteria for proportional eligibility if asset used both for R&D and manufacturing purposes (e.g. an equipment used both to manufacture prototypes and serial products)?	To claim the tax relief in connection with R&D purposes, the company shall distinguish the portion of use for R&D purposes from the portion of use for other activities, like manufacturing. As it mentioned under point 2.1.4, the calculation of the company shall be based on objective circumstances depends on the features of the asset, like the period of use for R&D purposes. The use for manufacturing purposes does not entitle the company to enjoy the tax benefits of R&D activities. To distinguish R&D activities see our answer under point 2.1.8.	
2.1.6.	What if the asset is 'indirectly' used for R&D purposes?	If an asset is used for indirect purposes of R&D, the acquisition value of the assets shall be taken account to as an indirect cost of R&D activities. However, the costs related to assets used for indirect R&D purposes shall be considered as the costs of R&D but tax relief of 'super-deduction' is not eligible.	

		According to the CTDT, tax base could be deducted exclusively with direct costs of basic research, applied research or experimented development or the costs of capitalised value of experimented development. The costs shall not be registered under the account of the capitalised value of experimented development, as well, thus indirect costs of R&D shall be taken account in accordance with the general rules and deduct the pre-tax profit once time.	
2.1.7.	What do you think of the following definition: 'Is considered directly used for R&D purposes an asset permitting, in and of itself, to carry out research programs of the business'?	In our perspective, the criteria of 'directly using for R&D purposes' and 'the research within the business interest or the gainful activity of the relevant company' are definitely different from each other, thus these two criteria shall be examined dividedly. According to the CTDT, any costs of the asset deducted from the pre-tax profit do not fall under the criteria of 'the research within the business interest or the gainful activity of the relevant company', it shall be considered as tax base increasing factor. If assets cannot be used, permitting in and of itself, to carry out R&D projects, it does not mean that the asset is not necessary for R&D purposes. For instance, in most cases, the management of hazardous waste materials is directly connected to R&D projects. There is no reason to exclude these costs from R&D costs which are directly related to it. On the other hand, since the practical use of the asset depends on the own discretion of the company, this definition, therefore, may provide an opportunity for abuse, unless all the circumstances of the use of the asset are examined in details, in all cases.	
2.1.8.	Is the production of the following assets an R&D activity? (i) production of prototypes; (ii) construction of a pilot plant/or pilot facilities	**Recital to the Subparagraphs c)-e) Point 7 Section 3 R&D Act:** [The following may qualify as experimental development:] c) the making of prototypes ***not for commercial use***;	

		d) the development of commercially usable prototypes and experimental projects if the prototype itself is ***by necessity the commercial end product as well***, and ***its manufacturing is too costly to be done for demonstration and certification purposes only***; e) the experimental manufacturing and testing of products, processes, and services, provided that ***they cannot be used for industrial or commercial purposes, or be modified*** for such use. […] Experimental development ***shall not include*** normal, periodical or routine changes carried out with regard to products, production lines, manufacturing processes, existing services or other ongoing operations even if such changes are considered development, or if they result in the improvement of the given product, process, operation or service.	
		The prototype is to be an original model which had been planned to include all the new technological features and performance of the new product. The boundary between R&D and commercial purposes depends on whether all the necessary modifying and test had been made or not. If it is done, there is no more need to modify the model, then any other activities related to the prototype is excluded from R&D activities because after that stage the model is ready to serve commercial purposes. Distinguishing between R&D and manufacturing purposes in case pilot plants or pilot facilities is much more difficult. To consider the costs of these facilities as costs of R&D activities, the purpose of developing new techniques and procedures by collecting technical and other kind of data and gaining experiences for the purpose of the studying hypothesis, planning new end products or special facilities and structures for new procedures, creating new specification for new end products, set up new operating instructions or handling manuals for new procedures.	Frascati Manuals 2015,2.55

		This stage of development is finished when the production for commercial purposes (or the use for own business purposes) is beginning. If they are carried out for the preparation, execution, and maintenance of production standardisation (e.g. jigs, machine tools) or to promote the sale of products (e.g. offers, leaflets, catalogues of spare parts), they should be excluded from R&D. There is a thin boundary between R&D activities and manufacturing when the company begins to produce the goods of serial zero. The additional costs of serial zero which is usually produced after the setting up of the prototype could be considered as indirect costs of R&D activities, thus the claim for tax relief is not eligible for the company.	Frascati Manual 2002,85 Frascati Manaul 2015,2.21
2.1.9.	Would you characterise the following assets as, potentially, directly used for R&D activities: (i) Handling devices; (ii) Calculation tools; (iii) Computers; (iv) Machines used to manufacture components of a prototype; (v) Telephones, small office appliances, office furniture?	There are no special rules for these assets to find the content of R&D activities, thus they should be classified by applying the rules of the general principles of accounting. As these assets are usually used for both R&D activities and for other purposes, so the company shall be cautious during the capitalisation and take special attention to the general principle of 'true and fair view'. According to Subsection 3 Section 15 Accounting Act: 'Assets shown in the books and contained in the financial report shall be such that they can be found and verified as in fact being in existence, tenable and verifiable. The measurement of such assets shall be carried out in accordance with the valuation principles prescribed in this Act, as well as with the relevant valuation procedures ("true and fair view" principle).' The operation costs and depreciation of fixed assets, like buildings, appliances, fixtures, and furnishing of offices which serve to the whole operation of the company are not measured as the direct costs of R&D activities, but the general costs of operation.	

		Should direct connection to the R&D project could be found and these assets are necessary to carry out the R&D project, the costs of these assets can be considered as other direct costs of R&D activities in that portion in which they are used for R&D activities. The calculation of this portion shall be strictly based on objective indicators and features.	
b.	*Specific Rules*		
(i)	*Intangible Assets*	**Draft Art. 33.1(e)** provides: '*Without prejudice to paragraph 2 and Articles 37 and 38, fixed assets shall be depreciated individually over their useful lives on a straight-line basis. The useful life of a fixed asset shall be determined as follows:* [...] *(e) fixed intangible assets: the period for which the asset enjoys legal protection or for which the right has been granted or, where that period cannot be determined, 15 years*'. The problem is that not all intangible items (e.g. intellectual property, brand names), meet the definition of an intangible asset. If an item does meet the definition of an intangible asset, expenditure to acquire it or generate it internally should be recognised as an expense when it is incurred. Therefore, *based on your national tax background*:	
		According to the Subsection 1 Section 25 Accounting Act: Assets other than tangible assets (such as concessions and similar rights with the exception of rights attached to immovables, **intellectual property**, goodwill), advances and prepayments on intangible assets and value adjustments of intangible assets shall be shown under **intangible assets**. **Recital to Subsections 4-5 Section 25 Accounting Act:** (4) The capitalized value of experimental development shall consist of the sums paid to subcontractors as invoiced to achieve the purpose of the experimental development and the direct costs of own activities (Section 51) incurred in the course of experimental development procedures, which are likely to be recovered during future use of the results produced by such activities, and which are not included among other products that can be capitalized (such as intellectual property, tangible assets, inventories) **as they exceed the – estimated – market value of the final product.**	

		The capitalized value of experimental development, when activated, may not exceed the amount that is likely to be recovered by future profits it is presumed to generate, after the deduction of further development-related expenses, estimated production costs, or the direct costs of sales when applicable. (5) The direct costs of experimental development that is **already in progress** but is not concluded by the balance sheet date of the financial year may be shown as capitalized value of experimental development. In this case, the capitalized value of experimental development includes – **apart from the extra costs of experimental development operations** – the direct costs of products that are to be shown under inventories, tangible assets or intellectual property following the conclusion of such operations, by decreasing the capitalized value of experimental development. **Costs of basic and applied research and the indirect costs and overhead of experimental development may not be capitalised.** **According to the Subsection 6-7 Section 25 Accounting Act:** (6) Under intangible assets, concessions and similar rights shall include those acquired rights which are not related to real estate property. This includes, in particular, lease rights, rights of use, trusteeship, rights of use of intellectual property, licenses, furthermore, concessions, gaming rights, and other rights which are not related to real estate property. (7) The following shall be shown under **intellectual property**: a) industrial property rights (such as, in particular, patents, utility models, designs rights, know-how, trademarks, geographical indications and trade names); b) copyrighted works and neighboring rights (such as, in particular, software products and engineering plans);	

		c) **assets without legal protection but monopolised through secrecy**; irrespective of whether or not used.	
2.1.10.	Should we use the European Union Accounting Rule 6 defining intangible asset (i.e. identifiability, control over a resource, and existence of future economic benefits or service potential)?	The aspect of Hungarian accounting regulation differs from the definition of the intangible assets of the EU Accounting Rule 6. In our approach, it does not mean a problem in connection with interpretation in practice because the appliance of the definition of the intangible assets in related to the CTDT is possible in a much wider field than the scope of the definition of the CCTB. **Recital to Subparagraphs a) and g) Point 5 Schedule No. 1 CTDT** The ordinary depreciation, as defined in the Accounting Act, (including lump-sum depreciation) may be claimed on intangible assets (excluding goodwill) and rights to immovable. Therefore, such an incoherence related to the intellectual properties is not found in the Hungarian regulations, thus we agree with your understanding to apply the definition of intangible assets of EU Accounting Rule 6 much more rather than Art. 33.1-e CCTB.	
2.1.11.	If not, what should be the definition of intangible assets?	See the above-mentioned at (i.) intangible assets.	
2.1.12.	Are intangible fixed assets (including intellectual property (IP)) costs fully expensed in the year incurred and included in the CCTB super-deduction?	Not exactly. If the value of the acquisition is not higher than HUF 100 000 (approx. EUR 400 in 2024), it can be fully expensed in the year incurred. In opposite, the measured depreciation of the intangible fixed assets can be taken account in the year incurred as direct costs of R&D, thus 'super-deduction' is eligible in this way.	

	The inclusion of mere intellectual property costs is not advisable: it may create a bias in favour of patented research compared to that stemming from unpatented technology.	This proposal is agreeable.	
2.1.13.	Will in practice this provision be limited to patents costs acquired with a view to carry on new experimental research and development?	Since we do not have any experience in connection with a situation like this, it is hard to study your question. In a lack of these confusing legal environment, we may assess that such a result of this measurement could not be reached.	
2.1.14.	What if these patents are (also) used in the manufacturing process?	The costs could be taken into account in that portion in which the patents are used for R&D purposes only that case if it is even possible in regard to the specific features of it. The calculation shall be based on objective circumstances.	
2.1.15.	Should plant variety rights be treated in the same manner as patents?	According to the above-mentioned rules of the Hungarian regulation, there is no difference between the treatments of these two kinds of intangible asset in the aspect of CTDT.	
2.1.16.	What about outlays incurred to acquire licences or know-how?	Since these costs shall be considered as intangible fixed assets, the tax base can be deducted with the expenses which are directly related to R&D purposes which is within the business interest of the company.	
(ii)	*Immovable [property]*		
	In any case, not covered by exclusion in Art. 9-3		
	In Austria, building costs and financing expenses related to R&D activity may be taken into account.		
2.1.17.	Should the concept of '*immovable property*' (Recital No. 8) be preferred to the one of '*immovable fixed asset*' (as opposed to Art. 9.3 CCTB)?	In our approach, the depreciation of buildings shall be taken account of direct costs of R&D activities comprising in that portion in which R&D content can be found. That is the reason why 'immovable property' (Recital No. 8) should be referred to 'immovable fixed assets'.	

2.1.18.	Would building costs and financing expenses related to the acquisition of immovable [property] be eligible to the super-deduction?	However these two terminus do not comply with each other, the depreciation in that year incurred and the use of this asset is related to R&D purposes directly, can be calculated as costs of R&D activities.	
2.1.19.	What is your understanding of Art. 12(i): 1st meaning: that costs related to acquisition or construction of new commercial or second-hand commercial or industrial immovable [property] is excluded from the super-deduction? Or 2nd meaning: that costs related to acquisition or construction of new commercial or second-hand commercial or industrial immovable [property] is not fully deductible the year incurred but should be depreciated and such depreciation allowances are eligible to the super-deduction?	The costs of the buildings as fixed tangible assets shall be measured as the followings. **According to Subsection 1 Section 47 Accounting Act:** The cost (purchase, manufacturing) of an asset shall mean the expenditure required for the acquisition, creation, installation of the asset incurred before commissioning or delivery thereof to the warehouse, and which may be attached to the asset in question. The cost (original cost) includes the purchase price reduced by any discounts and increased by any premium, the costs and charges paid to intermediaries, or for the delivery, loading, foundation, installation and commissioning services supplied in connection with the purchase, commissioning and delivery of the asset to the warehouse (if any or all of these activities are performed by the company, the capitalized value of direct costs as defined Section 51), any commission, as well as the taxes and similar levies, and customs charges. **According to Subsection 1 Section 47 Accounting Act:** The following shall ***comprise a part of the cost*** (original cost) referred to in Subsection (1): a) in connection with the acquisition or manufacturing of the asset: aa) *the fee for any bank guarantee paid before the loan or credit is received and prescribed as a prerequisite for the credit or loan,* ab) ***service and handling charges, lending commissions and commitment fees and commissions related to the loan or credit as contracted,*** ac) the fee for notarisation of the contract of a credit or loan,	

		ad) ***the interest charged for the period until the asset is commissioned or delivered to the warehouse***; b) insurance premiums directly related to an asset applicable for the period until the asset is commissioned or delivered to the warehouse; furthermore; c) * the positive or negative spread resulting from the conversion of a foreign currency liability – for which there is no cover in the foreign currency account – that is directly connected to a tangible or intangible asset and has been recognised for the period up to the time when the asset is put into operation; and d) the fees and direct costs of planning and design, preparations and enforcement of a project, and the fees and direct costs of training in connection with new technologies. e) in connection with the acquisition of natural gas, electricity and drinking water, the statutory fees and charges prescribed by specific other legislation, invoiced upon the supply of natural gas, electricity or drinking water to end-users (consumers) by providers of universal natural gas services, natural gas suppliers, providers of universal electricity services, electricity suppliers or drinking water suppliers. Partially, it is possible to comprise financial costs as a part of costs of the assets. In any other cases, the financial costs cannot be eligible to 'super-deduction' because it shall be registered within the expenses on financial transactions. In our viewpoint, the 2nd meaning of Art. 12(i) can be accepted.	
(iii)	*Lease payments*	**According to Point 13 Subsection 8 Section 3 Accounting Act:** *'Financial leasing'* shall mean an arrangement made under a financial leasing agreement provided for in the Act on Credit Institutions and Financial Enterprises, including if made between a parent company and its subsidiary.	

		According to Point 89 Section 6 Act CCXXXVII of 2013 on Credit Institutions and Financial Enterprises: *'Financial leasing'* shall mean an operation where the lessee acquires title of use on movable tangible property or real estate property owned by the lessor, or a right held by the lessor for a specified period of time, upon which the lessee: a) shall bear all risks stemming from the passing of risk, b) becomes entitled to collect proceeds, c) shall bear direct costs (including maintenance and depreciation costs or amortisation charges), d) ***gains entitlement for acquiring title of ownership*** – or to assign such entitlement to another party – of the leased property following expiration of the lease period as stipulated in the contract and upon payment of principal and interests in full and payment of the residual value described in the contract. If the lessee decides not to exercise this right, the possession of the leased property shall revert to the lessor. Parties shall stipulate the principal – which equals the contract price of the leased tangible property or leased right – and the interest amount of lease payments and the due dates of such payments **According to Subsections 3-4 Section 23 Accounting Act:** (3) Assets *received within the framework of financial leasing* shall be shown under assets, as well as payments on accounts for the improvement and renovation of leased (borrowed) assets, as well as the value of assets acquired or constructed under concession arrangements. (4) Assets shall be listed under fixed assets or current assets on the basis of their purpose and use.	

2.1.20.	What if equipment is used according to the terms of a leasing-type transaction?	According to the mentioned provisions of the Accounting Act, it shall be registered as the tangible fixed assets, thus it can be treated the same way as other fixed assets depend on its own features.	
2.1.21.	Are leasing instalments eligible for super-deduction under current wording of Art. 9-3?	As leasing installments shall be considered as a kind of tangible fixed assets, these assets fall under the provision of exemption, thus super-deduction is not eligible.	
2.1.22.	Should they be?	Yes, they should be. See 2.1.20.	
(iv)	*Alternative readings*		
2.1.23.	Please feel free to add any alternative readings you may have of relevant CCTB provisions and that has not yet been discussed.		
B.	**Current expenditure**		
2.2.	**R&D staff cost**	**Recital 'R&D activities carried out within the taxpayer's operations' definition according to Point 32 Section 4 CTDT** *'R&D activities carried out within the taxpayer's operations'* shall mean R&D activities carried out using the taxpayer's ***own assets and workers***, at the taxpayer's risk and benefit, including where R&D activities are ***carried out by the taxpayer's workers*** using the taxpayer's own assets on behalf of others, as well as (joint) research and development activities carried out under research and development agreement.	
a.	*What is meant by R&D staff?*	In our approach, R&D staff includes all the employees and contracted contributors who are directly engaged in R&D activities within the business interest of the company or a gainful activity. It also means that the key in this field is also the direct contributions conducted by individuals which shall be fall under the own scope of the activities of the taxpayer company.	

		The classification based on the qualification, such as academic background, special knowledge or technical skills, may not be taken into account in the viewpoint of the application of the tax relief. The costs of the employment of the workers who provide all the conditions for carrying out R&D activities shall be considered as the direct costs of R&D activities and shall be treated in the same way as the costs of the employment of academic staff. Should a contracted contributor take part in the R&D project, the situation is the same. Determining the key element of R&D staff, the necessity of the contribution for R&D project on the side of the relevant individuals should be found, thus the direct engagement of individuals in R&D activities could be stated if his/her exercise is necessary to carry out the project.	
2.2.1.	Should eligibility be limited to staff directly-involved in R&D?	Yes, definitely. According to the MMCP, the wages and the taxes and contributions after the wages of the employee who are engaged in the relevant R&D project shall be considered as direct costs of R&D activity. All people are directly employed in R&D job should be assigned to R&D staff and those too, who provide direct services such as R&D managers, administrators and members of the office personnel, according to the Frascati Manual. If there is no direct relationship between the job of the staff and R&D activities, then tax relief is not provided, as well. Amendment Note If the job of the employee is not related to a certain R&D project, the costs of the wages and the taxes and contributions after the wages shall be taken into account as indirect costs of the R&D activities, thus 'super-deduction' is not eligible.	294 Frascati Manual 2002

2.2.2.	In case the staff participates both in R&D and non R&D activities, should the text allow for proportional eligibility based on time spent (or other criteria)?	Yes, definitely. According to the practice in the field of accounting, the measurement of the participating in R&D activities is exclusively based on the records of working hours in Hungary. It is important that in the case of division by working time, the working time justified by a person appointed for that purpose can be such a basis.	
2.2.3.	How can researchers or scientists be defined? Should the text use black letter criteria (list diplomas (PhDs), qualifications…) or a more open definition?	**According to Point 15 Section 3 R&D Act:** 'Researcher/developer means a natural person who is involved in creating or developing new knowledge, intellectual creations, products, services, processes, methods or systems or in managing projects with such aims.' There is no definition for 'scientist' according to the R&D Act or CTDT. If it is necessary for tax purposes, a more open definition might be declared according to Frascati Manual.	
		Amendment Note The company which is taken into account as research organisation considered as conduct business activities may enjoy tax benefits of social security contribution tax after its employee if the employee as a researcher/developer possess PhD diploma/higher academic grant or take part in doctoral studies or being a doctoral candidate. According to CTDT, in case of claiming tax benefits of social security contribution tax, the tax base shall not be reduced by the amount of it. **According to Point 16 Section 4 R&D Act:** 'Research organisation means an institution, organisational unit or enterprise carrying out research and development activities as its core or main activity or in connection with its core or main activity.'	Act CLVI of 2011 on the Amendment of Tax Laws and other Related Regulations

		According to MMCP: Those service projects are considered to be an R&D that are resulting in new knowledge or using the given knowledge to evolve new application. Those activities that support R&D indirectly are not considered to be a R&D activity, only contributes to establishing the conditions of the research. The transportation, warehousing, cleaning, repairing, maintenance and security activities, and the central financial and the personnel management activities which are not able to be activated in books are such activities. Only the direct costs of R&D activity can be taken into account as a deducting item when calculating corporate tax, in the case of this costs relates to R&D activities carried out within the taxpayer's operations. Direct costs include any costs related to any R&D activity, in case of which it can determined clearly at the time the cost incurred which division is connected to the producing – and the service activity or all activities connected to the R&D activity, in case of which it can be clearly determine the extent of the linkage to the activities with certain indicators, and characteristics. Wages and contributions of the researchers directly connect to the R&D activity.	
2.2.4.	Are research technicians R&D staff?	Yes, definitely, in the portion of the time of direct contribution to R&D activities.	
2.2.5.	What about other employees (not 'official researchers') which still have contributed to a patented invention?	Yes, definitely, in the portion of the time of direct contribution to R&D activities.	

2.2.6.	What about the managers of the business (e.g. running a research program)?	However, there is no problem in connection with the in the case of the full-time employment related to directly to R&D activities, there are several kinds of employment in which the working hours engaged in other activities shall be marked. For instance, managers and coordinators spend only a certain part of their working hours related directly to R&D. Only these working hours related directly to R&D activities can be taken account. As sales costs, administrative costs that cannot be directly attributed to production and other general costs, cannot be included in direct costs of R&D activities as well. For example, costs such as project coordinators' contact with the sales department cannot be taken into account as tax relief.	
2.2.7.	What about other staff (secretariat, cleaning, etc.)? Can, in the alternative, their compensation be taken into account, proportionally, as other operating R&D expenses (cf. I-3 below)?	No, 'super-deduction' is not eligible, because these costs have to be considered (maximum) indirect costs of R&D. Other auxiliary staff includes skilled workers and auxiliary workers, secretarial and office staff are involved in the R&D project or directly connected to such a project. The wage costs of those people who provide indirect services (security guard, maintenance, co-workers of the library, calculator center and central office) should be ranked in other current expenses.	
b.	*What is meant by R&D staff cost?*	**According to Subsection 1-4, Section 79 of Accounting Act** (1) Staff costs shall include the amounts accounted for as wages and salaries to employees or as labor charges to cooperative members, the amount withdrawn as consideration for the personal involvement of the owner (member) as a natural person, as well as other employee benefits and contributions on wages and salaries.	

(2) ***Wages and salaries*** shall include all payments related to the financial year as remuneration to employees, workers and members in accordance with the relevant legislation, including the amount withdrawn as consideration for the personal involvement of the owner (member) as a natural person, the sums paid for work – and accounted as such – to persons in any form of employment relationship for the financial year (including any premiums and bonuses and extra monthly salaries paid and accounted for the financial year) all constituents of which can be considered as wages according to statistical accounts, regardless of whether or not personal income tax is due on such payments, and whether or not they form a base for contributions on wages and salaries.
(3) ***Other employee benefits*** shall include the amounts paid to natural persons, and not accounted for as wage costs or contract fees, including any non-deductible value added tax thereof and the amount of personal income tax payable (paid) by the company on such payments.
(4) Contributions on wages and salaries shall include social contribution tax, healthcare contributions, vocational training contributions, and all other costs payable as taxes, which are established on the basis of staff costs or by the number of employees, irrespective of their designation.

According to the Point 3 Subsection 7 Section 3 of the Accounting Act

'Other employee benefits' shall mean payments made to and sums credited to natural persons by the payer, other than wages and salaries or contract fees, whether required by law or based on the payer's own decision. Included in this category are, in particular: royalties, rental allowances, home building assistance (including interests and handling charges),

		meal allowances, commuting allowances, anniversary premiums, reimbursements for employee commitments, income supplement to miners, awards, ***other benefits in kind***, income supplement to incapacitated employees, ***sick leave compensation, employer's contribution for sick-pay and sick-pay supplement***, insurance premiums paid by the employer for the employee's accident, life and pension insurance policies, employer's membership contribution paid to voluntary funds, membership supplement paid by employer to private pension funds, employer's share of and contribution to personal income tax payments, welfare and cultural expenses, severance pay, employer's contribution to early retirement pension benefits or benefits provided before the legal age limit in lieu of early retirement pension benefits, furthermore, payments to employees and workers such as per diem, separation allowances, costs reimbursed on the basis of the relevant legislation, personal basic salary paid following discharge from military or civil service, invention fees, patent licensing fees or purchase costs, innovation fees, and participation fees paid in connection with these, also royalties and fees paid for other copyrighted products to non-employees and participation fees paid in connection with such, payments to seasonal agricultural workers, benefits provided in kind and entertainment costs, and all other payments classified by statistical regulations as other work-related income and social expense. According to MMCP, costs of the employment of R&D staff, including wages, other employee benefits or compulsory payments could be a part of the category of R&D staff cost, if the expenses and the job of the staff itself are directly engaged in a certain R&D project.	

		There is a thin boundary between R&D costs and non-R&D expenses in special cases like the compensation of a researcher, when the expenses on the side of the employer, because of its own features, cannot be connected a certain project, but the whole job description of the researcher is related to R&D activities.	
2.2.8.	Wages, bonuses, benefits in kind?	Yes, definitely.	
2.2.9.	Social security contributions (compulsory and/or non-compulsory)?	Yes, definitely.	
2.2.10.	Employer's contribution to participation of employees in profits of the enterprise by means of profit-sharing plan, employee share-ownership?	**According to Subsection 2 Section 40 Accounting Act:** In addition to the conditions set out in Subsection (1), an increase of subscribed capital shall be implemented by the transfer of funds from the own funds available in addition to the subscribed capital even if free or discounted employees' stocks or employees' business shares are issued. **According to Subsection 1 Section 3:236 Act V of 2013 on the Civil Code:** Limited companies may issue employee shares and provide them to full-time and part-time employees free of charge or at a reduced price, below the share's nominal value. **Amended Note** **According to Subsection 1 Section 77/A Act CXVII of 1995 on Personal Income Tax:** In connection with any valuable consideration obtained by a private individual in the form of securities, income shall mean the fair market value of the security prevailing at the time of acquisition of the security, less the verified cost (value) of the security and any incremental costs associated with it. [...] **According to Point d) Subsection 2 Section 77/A Act CXVII of 1995 on Personal Income Tax:** The valuable consideration obtained by a private individual in the form of securities *shall not be treated as income* if the private individual [...]	

		d) obtained the security through an increase in the subscribed share capital from the ***equity capital*** as part of an employee stock ownership plan; [...] These kinds of benefits are excluded from wages and other employee benefits and should be registered under equity, thus tax relief cannot be calculated after them. It should be noted that personal income tax benefit can be applied to the income related to the value of a securities obtained through an employee stock ownership program.	
2.2.11.	Can a Member State provide that compensation paid to holders of PhD will count more (e.g. double) for a limited period of time (in order to promote hiring of PhD holders)?	It is possible by this means. The Hungarian government provides a tax benefit in connection with social security contribution tax for the companies which employ PhD holders,PhD candidates or even persons who attend to doctoral school. The minimum amount of the compensation is based on the provisions of the Labour Act, but it is possible to provide more than the minimum standard. The above-mentioned measurement of Hungarian government has the same goals: to promote hiring of PhD holders and other academic staff. According to CTDT, in case of claiming tax benefits of social security contribution tax, the tax base shall not be reduced by the amount of it, thus this kind of tax benefit shall not be tripled in this way.	Act CLVI of 2011 on the Amendment of Tax Laws and other Related Regulations
2.3.	**Standardisation expenses**	In our approach, in connection with the expenses of standardisation procedures, the *ex-ante commercial or manufacturing purposes* might be found and the relationship with R&D activities seems to be weakened.	

		Since only the direct costs of R&D activities can be eligible for 'super-deduction' and the expenses of the standardization procedures shall not be taken into account as the direct costs of R&D, these expenses can be registered by the application of the general rules (Deduction may be calculated once, in the year incurred).	
	Based on your national tax background:		
2.3.1.	Should expenses related to the establishment of technical standards concerning products of the business be eligible for the super-deduction (e.g. expenses incurred on participation of employees in official meetings of standardisation bodies)?	No, definitely.	
2.3.2.	If yes, should it still be the case even if these employees are not scientists or research technicians?	No, definitely.	
2.3.3.	How should these expenses be assessed (e.g. as portion of employee compensation related to the time spent in connection with such meetings)?	No, definitely.	
2.3.4.	Should expenses related to technical monitoring/ technological watch be taken into account?	No, definitely.	
2.4.	**Patent related expenses**	Hungary provides a wide-range tax allowance regarding patent related expenses, which is not covered with terms of R&D activites' super-deduction in our approach. It is essential to see that the tax base of CIT can be deducted under three different bases regarding patent: 1. the profit from the sale of intangible assets embodying rights to royalties (other than notified intangible assets); 2. capital gains from the sale of a notified intangible asset; 3. 50 per cent of the (pre-tax) profit made off royalties.	

		The research and development services ordered from an affiliated company (other than a business establishment) for the purpose of the acquisition or production of an intangible asset embodying rights to royalties or notified intangible asset, or any purchased (received) intangible asset embodying rights to royalties or notified intangible asset the taxpayer may take into consideration as a deductible item a sum determined in proportion to: a) the direct costs of basic research, applied research and experimental development incurred in connection with the acquisition or development of such asset (*excluding the direct costs of research and development services ordered from an affiliated company (other than a business establishment) and the cost of any purchased (received) intangible asset embodying rights to royalties or notified intangible asset*); and b) the direct costs of basic research, applied research and experimental development incurred in connection with the acquisition or development of such asset (*including the costs accounted for by the taxpayer's business establishment, the direct costs of research and development services ordered from an affiliated company and the cost of any purchased (received) intangible asset embodying rights to royalties or notified intangible asset*). The direct costs shall be taken into consideration at the fair market price prevailing at the time when determining said ratio in the tax year when the cost was actually incurred (irrespective of its accrual).	

2.4.1.	Are expenses linked to patents eligible? Please define NB: *under current French tax law, expenses linked to the filing, the maintenance and the defence of patents incurred in France or in another State (IP consultant's fees, translation costs taxes...) are eligible to the R&D tax credit; insurance costs linked to patents are eligible within a threshold of EUR 60,000. However, under the Frascati criterion, R&D would typically not include administrative and legal work connected with patents, routine tests or data collection.*	No. The situation is similar to the approach in related to the standardisation expenses where the connection to R&D direct activities is being weakened. The 'super-deduction' is available for direct costs of R&D activities, thus the expenses linked to patents is not eligible.	
2.5.	**Other operating expenses related to R&D**		
2.5.1.	Should such category be identified?	No, it is not necessary. The definition of R&D activities and the term of business interest is enough to determine the direct costs of R&D activities in practice.	
2.5.2.	Is a detailed list possible of expenses advisable?	Yes, such a list may make easier to measure the content of R&D in certain activities. In MMCP, a non-exclusive list is stated to orientate the companies in this field, e.g. the costs of expert related directly to R&D can be registered.	
2.5.3.	Is it appropriate to assess these expenses notionally by reference to other precisely defined eligible expenses (e.g. 15% of immovable (property) depreciation allowances, and/or 50% of eligible staff expenses)?	No, it is not appropriate. In our approach, all the current costs related to directly to R&D activities can be taken into account in connection with tax relief. The proportion of R&D content is the main issues which shall be measured by the company on the basis of objective circumstances. In the case of lack of these objective circumstances, i.e. direct connection with a certain R&D project, the costs shall be considered maximum indirect costs of R&D, thus 'super-deduction' is not eligible.	

2.5.4.	Should fees paid to external consultants assisting the company to determine its R&D super deduction be eligible, and to what extent?	See point 2.5.3. On the other hand, the HIPO is the competent authority which is entitled to issue an expert report on the R&D content of a project. As the procedure of the HIPO is always related to a certain project, thus the expenses of procedures, i.e. compulsory administrative fees, are considered as direct costs of R&D project unless the R&D content is not found as a result of the procedure of HIPO.	
C.	**Contracted Expenditure**	**According to Point t) Subsection 1 Section 7 CTDT** [The following shall be deducted from the pre-tax profit:] 'taking into consideration of what is contained in Subsections (17)-(18), the direct costs of basic research, applied research and experimental development carried out within the taxpayer's own scope of activities (***not including*** **the value of research and experimental development services provided by a *resident* taxpayer, by the domestic branch of a *nonresident* entrepreneur or – pursuant to the Personal Income Tax Act – by a private entrepreneur directly or indirectly**) claimed in the tax year in which it is incurred [...] **According to Subsection 17 Section 7 CTDT** 'In connection with basic research, applied research and experimental development performed jointly by a taxpayer and an institution of higher education, the Magyar Tudományos Akadémia (Hungarian Academy of Sciences), a research institution operated as a central budgetary agency or a research institution (research facility) established by either of them or jointly, as well as any research institution operating in a form of a business association under majority State ownership directly or indirectly, the taxpayer may claim ***three times the amount*** referred to in and calculated according to Subsection t) of Subsection (1) hereof up to ***maximum fifty million forints***,	

whose value calculated by the tax rate referred to in Section 19 for the purposes of the provisions governing state subsidies shall be treated as ***de minimis aid*** received for the tax year. These provisions shall also apply to any equivalent organization established in any Member State of the European Union or any State that is a party to the Agreement on the European Economic Area.'

According to Subsection 18 Section 7 CTDT

'The provisions of Subsection t) of Subsection (1) may be applied in connection with research and experimental development services by the person to whom they were provided if the service provider declares of having provided the service without the involvement of research and experimental development services provided by a resident taxpayer or by the Hungarian branch of a nonresident entrepreneur, or by a private entrepreneur governed under the Act on Personal Income Tax.'

'Research and development agreement' definition according to Point 23€ Section 4 CTDT

'Research and development agreement' shall mean the research and development agreement defined in the Act on Scientific Research, Development and Innovations.

'Research and development agreement' definition according to Point 14 Section 3 R&D Act

'Research and development agreement' means: an agreement concluded between two or more enterprises or enterprises and research organisations (hereinafter in this entry: parties), regarding:

a) joint research and development regarding the product, process or service named in the agreement and the joint exploitation of the results of such research and development;

		b) the joint exploitation of the results of joint research and development carried out based on a prior agreement concluded between the same parties regarding the product, process or service named in the agreement; c) joint research and development regarding the product, process or service named in the agreement, without any joint exploitation of the results; d) paid-for research and development regarding the product, process or service named in the agreement and the joint exploitation of the results of such research and development; e) the joint exploitation of the results of paid-for research and development carried out based on a prior agreement concluded between the same parties regarding the product, process or service named in the agreement; f) paid-for research and development regarding the product, process or service named in the agreement, without any joint exploitation of the results. **'Research and development agreement' definition according to Point 16 Section 3 R&D Act** 'Research organisation' means an institution, organisational unit or enterprise carrying out research and development activities as its core or main activity or in connection with its core or main activity.	
2.6.	**Subcontracting expenses**	**The (sub)contracted R&D** are activities performed by one party and financed by another funding party, where the funding party does not itself engage in research and development activities. Joint R&D projects generally qualify as R&D activities carried out within the company's own scope of activity if the results are jointly utilised by the parties. However, it is not a requirement that the funding party refrains from conducting R&D activities itself (as in the case of contracted research and development), whereby it simply pays the invoiced costs.	

		For the applicability of the super-deduction, it is essential that the R&D activity is connected to the economic activity of the funding party. If no such connection exists, these costs are considered to fall outside the company's scope of interest and must therefore be treated as a tax base increasing item.	
2.6.1.	What if R&D activity is outsourced? *Currently in France, payments to R&D service suppliers, public or private, accredited by the French Ministry of research and located in the EU or the EEA, qualify as eligible expenses.*	'Super-deduction' is only eligible related to the subcontracting expenses, if the subcontractor is not obliged to be CTDT payer. (According to this regulation the subcontractor cannot deduct its own tax base, thus the 'super-deduction' cannot be doubled related to the relevant contract.) This is the situation when the subcontractor has not got residency in Hungary or the subcontractor is to be considered as a research institution operated as a central budgetary agency or by an institution of higher education which is itself operated as a central budgetary agency. In connection with subcontracting expenses, the company (purchaser to whom the R&D service provided) possess the statement of the subcontractor (R&D provider) that the subcontractor did not take R&D service of an organization which had had a residency related to CTDT.	
2.6.2.	Should there be a territorial limit to exclude payments to subcontractors outside the EEA (which cannot invoke the freedom to provide services).	As there is no difference between a non-EEE-resident and EEE-resident (excluding which has residency in Hungary) subcontractors, there is no other territorial limit. In the aspect of CCTB or CCCTB, there should be a similar limitation to avoid the erosion of the tax base.	

2.6.3.	Should there be other limits? *Under current French law for instance, R&D costs invoiced by accredited private subcontractors can be retained within the limit of three times the total amount of all the other R&D eligible expenses incurred by the company; and such expenses can be retained by the company subcontracting R&D works within a yearly limit of EUR 12 or 10 million and EUR 2 million when the parties (i.e. ordering company and R&D supplier) are related companies.*	The outsourced R&D activities shall be in direct relationship with an own, certain R&D project of the company unless the costs are not eligible to 'super-deduction'. It is important that the outsourced R&D activities shall be directly connected to a certain R&D activities within the operation of the company. **Recital 'R&D activities carried out within the taxpayer's operations' definition means an R&D activity carried out using the taxpayer's own assets and workers, at the taxpayer's risk and benefit.** If a multinational joint company share the costs of joint R&D activities by an indicator established according to its own interest between its branches, the shared costs shall be not eligible to the deduction in itself. To take it into account as tax base deductive items, the costs shall be directly linked to the own R&D activities of the branch company. Generally, in case of subcontract between affiliated companies, the arm's length principle shall be taken into account. In our approach, other limitations are not necessary.	
B.	**Reimbursed expenditure**		
2.7.	**Treatment of public subsidies**		
2.7.1.	Should governmental and other State agencies subsidies/grants related to R&D eligible projects be deducted from eligible expenses of the year during which these expenses are incurred?	Definitely not. **According to 2nd Part of Point t) Subsection 1 Section 7 CTDT** 'These costs (charges) *may not be deducted from pre-tax profit and shown under the costs of development or operating costs (charges)* in the amount of any support or assistance requested from the tax authority before the balance sheet date or received during the tax year for development purposes without any obligation of repayment, or – if applicable – in the amount of income included in the pre-tax profit for the tax year under the title of grant or support.'	

Section IX
Ireland

		Answers and comments	Technical source (when necessary)
1.	'Research and Development' – Definition	Activities qualifying for the R&D tax credit must satisfy all of the following conditions. They must be: systematic, investigative or experimental activities, in a field of science or technology, encompassing one or more of the following categories of R&D: 1. Basic research; 2. Applied research; 3. Experimental development. In addition they must seek to achieve scientific or technological advancement, and involve the resolution of scientific or technological uncertainty.	All responses are based on section 766 *et al* Taxes Consolidation Act 1997 and associated guidance from the Revenue Commissioners
1.1.	As indicated in Section I (*supra*), should "research and development" be excluded if there is no particular application or use in view for the economy or the internal market?	Basic research means experimental or theoretical work undertaken primarily to acquire new scientific or technical knowledge without a specific practical application in view.	
1.2.	Should the level of novelty be new "to the world", "to the internal market (EU)", "to the market", or "to the firm"?	An advance in science or technology means an advance in the overall knowledge or capability in the field of science or technology (not an advance in the company's own state of knowledge or capability alone).	
1.3.	Should R&D be limited to the industrial sector, or also include the service industry (banking and insurance, but also humanities)?	The R&D tax credit is based upon qualifying activity, which can include research and development in the area of natural sciences (e.g. computer science, software development), engineering and technology, medical and agricultural science. It is not available for expenditure in the area of social sciences (economics, management, market research, marketing costs and other expenditure of the same kind).	

1.3.1.	In the latter case, which criteria help to identify the presence of R&D in services activities?	The tax credit is available in respect of expenditure incurred wholly and exclusively in the carrying on, by the company, of qualifying R&D activities. Within certain limits, and subject to a monetary cap, it is possible to claim R&D tax credits for R&D outsourced to third parties, such as universities in Ireland or another Member State of the EU or to other unconnected third parties. The outsourced activity must be qualifying R&D activity of the principal (i.e. the appointing company), not the agent (i.e. the sub-contractor). When documenting the scientific or technological advancement, scientific interest in the R&D, through scientific publications or conferences, is likely to be helpful evidence of such advancement.	
1.3.1.1.	Links with public research laboratories;		
1.3.1.2.	Involvement of staff with PhDs or PhD students;		
1.3.1.3.	Publication of research findings in scientific journals;		
1.3.1.4.	Organisation of scientific conferences;		
1.3.1.5.	Involvement in scientific reviews;		
1.3.1.6.	Others?		
2.	'COSTS' (FOR RESEARCH AND DEVELOPMENT) – DEFINITION	The tax credit is available in respect of expenditure incurred wholly and exclusively in the carrying on by the company of qualifying R&D activities. This statutory formulation excludes costs which are not wholly and exclusively incurred in the carrying on of the R&D activity, including indirect overheads such as recruitment fees, insurance, travel, equipment repairs or maintenance, shipping, business entertainment, telephone, bank charges and interest, do not qualify as relevant expenditure. However, overheads which are wholly and exclusively incurred directly in the carrying on of the qualifying R&D activity, for example power consumed in the R&D process, qualify for the credit. Certain employee costs, where they relate to R&D, may constitute qualifying expenditure.	

A.	**Capital expenditure**	Expenditure on buildings and capital expenditure on plant and machinery, where used for R&D, may, subject to conditions, qualify for an R&D tax credit.	
2.1.	**Depreciation allowances**	Expenditure on buildings and capital expenditure on plant and machinery may, subject to conditions, qualify for an R&D tax credit and for capital allowances (tax depreciation allowance).	
a.	*General Principles*	**Draft Art. 9-3** provides: '*In addition to the amounts which are deductible as costs for research and development in accordance with paragraph 2, the taxpayer may also deduct, per tax year, an extra 50% of such costs, with the exception of the cost related to movable tangible fixed assets, that it incurred during that year. To the extent that costs for research and development reach beyond EUR 20,000,000, the taxpayer may deduct 25% of the exceeding amount.*' In addition, the Explanatory Memorandum (**para. 8**) provides: '*R&D costs will be fully expensed in the year incurred (with the exception of immovable property).*' **Draft Art. 10** (Other deductible items) provides: '*A deduction shall be made in respect of the depreciation of fixed assets referred to in Articles 30 to 40.* [...]' **Draft Art. 12** (Non-deductible items) provides: '*By way of derogation from Articles 9 and 10, the following items shall be non-deductible:* [...] *(i) acquisition or construction costs or cost connected with the improvement of fixed assets which are deductible under Articles 10 and 18, except for the cost related to research and development. The costs referred to in point (a) of Article 33(1) and points (a) and (b) of Article 33(2) shall not be treated as costs related to research and development;* [...]' – **For additional context, see Annex**. *Based on your national tax background:*	
		The impact assessment of the CCCTB specifies that the allowance for R&D expenses is designed to at least maintain existing R&D tax incentives. This appears to indicate that harmonisation, via a CCCTB directive, would be at the level of the most member state most favourable to R&D. In relation to the CCTB proposal (step one), it is specified that R&D tax incentive will be enhanced and streamlined. The directive is subject to a legislative requirement for unanimity by Member States.	

2.1.1.	Do you share our understanding that depreciation allowances have to be distinguished depending on the assets concerned, whether they are movable or immovable?	Article 10: provides for depreciation of fixed assets as referred to in Articles 30 to 40. Article 38: provides that certain categories of fixed tangible assets will not be eligible for a depreciation allowance. These are fixed tangible assets which not subject to wear and tear and obsolescence, such as land, fine art, antiques, or jewellery, and financial assets. The explanatory memorandum of the current draft of the directive indicates that a distinction in relation to moveable and immovable assets will be maintained.	Proposal for Council Directive on a Common Corporate Tax Base (2016/0337)
2.1.2.	Do you share our understanding that depreciation allowances are not available for movable fixed assets, because they are fully expensed in the year incurred, and not eligible to the super-deduction?	Depreciation of fixed assets (defined, *inter alia*, as tangible and intangible assets) is provided for in the draft CCTB directive. Fixed tangible assets, and financial assets, are not eligible for a depreciation allowance (Article 38). The availability of an enhanced R&D deduction depends upon the identity of the taxpayer, rather than the nature of the R&D.	
2.1.3.	Do you share our understanding that depreciation allowances remain available for immovable [property], because it cannot be fully expensed in the year incurred, and is eligible to the super-deduction?	Article 10: provides for a depreciation allowance for certain fixed assets. Article 2: prohibits a deduction for costs related to fixed assets, except insofar as such costs qualify for R&D. Certain costs relating to immovable property (commercial, office and other buildings, as well as any other type of immovable property in use for the business, industrial buildings and structures) do not qualify for an expenses deduction as they are not treated as costs related to R&D (Article 12(i), Article 33(1) and (2)).	
2.1.4.	What if an asset is used both for research and non-research purposes (such as manufacturing)?	It is implicit in the definition of R&D that some attribution of the productivity of an asset for the purposes of R&D, and otherwise, will be necessary. This can be seen from Article 12(i) which envisages acquisition costs as being related to the cost of a fixed asset, but also partially related to R&D.	

		R&D is defined as meaning experimental or theoretical work undertaken primarily to acquire new knowledge of the underlying foundations of phenomena and observable facts, without any particular application or use in view (basic research); original investigation undertaken in order to acquire new knowledge but directed primarily towards a specific, practical aim or objective (applied research); systematic work, drawing on knowledge gained from research and practical experience and producing additional knowledge, which is directed to producing new products or processes or to improving existing products or processes (experimental development).	
2.1.5.	If eligible, which criteria for proportional eligibility if asset used both for R&D and manufacturing purposes (e.g. an equipment used both to manufacture prototypes and serial products)?	This is not clear.	
2.1.6.	What if the asset is 'indirectly' used for R&D purposes?	The concept of 'indirectly' seems to require further elaboration. A certain level of outsourcing is permitted.	
2.1.7.	What do you think of the following definition: 'Is considered directly used for R&D purposes an asset permitting, in and of itself, to carry out research programs of the business'?	This does not seem to advance matters. Clearly, an asset which, in and of itself, can be used for R&D purposes, could also be used for the same purpose, but which is not for the purpose of R&D. For example, software could be used to develop a new industrial process, but the same software could be used for existing industrial processes. There is nothing inherent in the nature of the asset which indicates that it is suitable solely for R&D.	
2.1.8.	Is the production of the following assets an R&D activity? (i) production of prototypes; (ii) construction of a pilot plant / or pilot facilities	These could come within the definition of applied or experimental research, but more facts would need to be known.	

2.1.9.	Would you characterise the following assets as, potentially, directly used for R&D activities: (i) Handling devices; (ii) Calculation tools; (iii) Computers; (iv) Machines used to manufacture components of a prototype; (v) Telephones, small office appliances, office furniture?	As noted above, it is not the inherent nature of the device, tool or machine which indicates R&D activity, but the use to which they are put. See definition of R&D activity, which is based on the activity, but without specifying the relevant tool to conduct that activity.	
<u>*b.*</u>	<u>*Specific Rules*</u>		
(i)	*Intangible Assets*	**<u>Draft Art. 33.1(e)</u>** provides: '*Without prejudice to paragraph 2 and Articles 37 and 38, fixed assets shall be depreciated individually over their useful lives on a straight-line basis. The useful life of a fixed asset shall be determined as follows:* [...] *(e) fixed intangible assets: the period for which the asset enjoys legal protection or for which the right has been granted or, where that period cannot be determined, 15 years.*' The problem is that not all intangible items (e.g. intellectual property, brand names), meet the definition of an intangible asset. If an item does meet the definition of an intangible asset, expenditure to acquire it or generate it internally should be recognised as an expense when it is incurred. Therefore, *<u>based on your national tax background</u>*:	
2.1.10.	Should we use the European Union Accounting Rule 6 defining intangible asset (i.e., identifiability, control over a resource, and existence of future economic benefits or service potential)?	Clearly, the use of a EU Accounting Rule would improve consistency in defining intangible assets. However, the accounting standard of control and ownership is aimed at identifying the health of a company, whereas the R&D allowance is aimed at incentivising expenditure on particular activities. Therefore, a different meaning of intangible assets for the purposes of R&D tax allowance could focus on the activity to which an asset is put, rather than ownership of the asset.	

2.1.11.	If not, what should be the definition of intangible assets?	Intangible assets are defined, for the purposes of claiming certain capital allowances under Irish law, as the acquisition of or the licence to use: patents and registered designs; trademarks, brands, brand names, domain names and services marks; copyright or related rights; know-how, generally related to manufacturing or processing, secret information concerning industrial, commercial or scientific experience whether protected or not; goodwill to the extent that it is directly attributable to specified intangible assets; computer software or a right to deal in or use such software; applications for grant or registration of patents, trademarks, copyrights, etc.	
2.1.12.	Are intangible fixed assets (including intellectual property (IP)) costs fully expensed in the year incurred and included in the CCTB super-deduction?	Only the costs of movable tangible fixed assets are excluded from the enhanced deduction under Article 9.	
	The inclusion of mere intellectual property costs is not advisable: it may create a bias in favour of patented research compared to that stemming from unpatented technology.		
2.1.13.	Will in practice this provision be limited to patents costs acquired with a view to carry on new experimental research and development?	Not clear.	
2.1.14.	What if these patents are (also) used in the manufacturing process?		
2.1.15.	Should plant variety rights be treated in the same manner as patents?	Not clear.	
2.1.16.	What about outlays incurred to acquire licences or know-how?		

(ii)	*Immovable [property]*		
	In any case, not covered by exclusion in Art. 9-3		
	In Austria, building costs and financing expenses related to R&D activity may be taken into account.		
2.1.17.	Should the concept of 'immovable property' (Recital No. 8) be preferred to the one of 'immovable fixed asset' (as opposed to Art. 9.3 CCTB)?	There needs to be consistency in usage in the various definitions.	
2.1.18.	Would building costs and financing expenses related to the acquisition of immovable [property] be eligible to the super-deduction?	Such costs do not appear to be specifically excluded, so their qualification will be considered in accordance with the general terms and conditions of R&D.	
2.1.19.	What is your understanding of Art. 12(i): 1st meaning: that costs related to acquisition or construction of new commercial or second-hand commercial or industrial immovable [property] is excluded from the super-deduction? Or 2nd meaning: that costs related to acquisition or construction of new commercial or second-hand commercial or industrial immovable [property] is not fully deductible the year incurred but should be depreciated and such depreciation allowances are eligible to the super-deduction?	Article 12 prohibits the deduction of expenditure. First, the deduction of costs of fixed assets, deductible under Articles 10 or 18 is not allowed. This is subject to an exception where such costs qualify for R&D. However, certain costs are not to be treated as costs of R&D, as listed in Article 33. This seems to be the first meaning, but the drafting is very unclear.	
(iii)	*Lease payments*		
2.1.20.	What if equipment is used according to the terms of a leasing-type transaction?	What about it?	

2.1.21.	Are leasing instalments eligible for super-deduction under current wording of Art. 9-3?	Such costs do not appear to be specifically excluded, so their qualification will be considered in accordance with the general terms and conditions of R&D.	
2.1.22.	Should they be?	Why not? The business decision as to whether to lease or purchase should not dictate R&D treatment.	
(iv)	*Alternative readings*		
2.1.23.	Please feel free to add any alternative readings you may have of relevant CCTB provisions and that has not yet been discussed.		
B.	**Current expenditure**		
2.2.	**R&D staff cost**		
a.	*What is meant by R&D staff?*	This is not defined. As the aim of the R&D allowance is to incentivise knowledge-based economy, staff and employee costs will have to be included in the allowance.	
2.2.1.	Should eligibility be limited to staff directly-involved in R&D?	Clearly, proportional eligibility is the only practical and feasible option.	
2.2.2.	In case the staff participates both in R&D and non R&D activities, should the text allow for proportional eligibility based on time spent (or other criteria)?	Time allocation for employees involved in both R&D and non-R&D activity is probably the most practical solution. This is the approach adopted under the current Irish legislation.	
2.2.3.	How can researchers or scientists be defined? Should the text use black letter criteria (list diplomas (PhDs), qualifications…) or a more open definition?	It should be open to the business to choose who to use in R&D. Specifying qualifications appears unduly restrictive.	
2.2.4.	Are research technicians R&D staff?	It depends upon their activity. Why should they be excluded if they are part of an R&D team?	
2.2.5.	What about other employees (not 'official researchers') which still have contributed to a patented invention?	As above. The current approach under Irish legislation is to look at the activity, not the qualifications.	
2.2.6.	What about the managers of the business (e.g. running a research program)?	This would need further elaboration.	

2.2.7.	What about other staff (secretariat, cleaning, etc.)? Can, in the alternative, their compensation be taken into account, proportionally, as other operating R&D expenses (cf. I-3 below)?	Under Irish law, these expenses would not qualify for R&D allowance, as they are not wholly and exclusively undertaken in connection with R&D activity.	
b.	*What is meant by R&D staff cost?*	All costs: wages, bonus, pension, incentive plans etc.	
2.2.8.	Wages, bonuses, benefits in kind?	See above.	
2.2.9.	Social security contributions (compulsory and/or non-compulsory)?	See above.	
2.2.10.	Employer's contribution to participation of employees in profits of the enterprise by means of profit-sharing plan, employee share-ownership?	See above.	
2.2.11.	Can a Member State provide that compensation paid to holders of PhD will count more (e.g. double) for a limited period of time (in order to promote hiring of PhD holders)?	Why? Surely businesses can decide whether they need employees who have completed a tertiary degree, or whether a graduate will be sufficient?	
2.3.	**Standardisation expenses**		
	Based on your national tax background:		
2.3.1.	Should expenses related to the establishment of technical standards concerning products of the business be eligible for the super-deduction (e.g. expenses incurred on participation of employees in official meetings of standardisation bodies)?	It is unlikely that such expenses would fit within the definition of qualifying expenditure. The problem is that, in general, such expenses would not achieve scientific or technological advancement, nor involve the resolution of scientific or technological uncertainty.	
2.3.2.	If yes, should it still be the case even if these employees are not scientists or research technicians?		

2.3.3.	How should these expenses be assessed (e.g. as portion of employee compensation related to the time spent in connection with such meetings)?		
2.3.4.	Should expenses related to technical monitoring/ technological watch be taken into account?	Routine testing and analysis for purposes of quality or quantity control does not constitute qualifying expenditure for the purposes of the R&D tax credit.	
2.4.	**Patent related expenses**		
2.4.1.	Are expenses linked to patents eligible? Please define NB: *under current French tax law, expenses linked to the filing, the maintenance and the defence of patents incurred in France or in another State (IP consultant's fees, translation costs taxes...) are eligible to the R&D tax credit; insurance costs linked to patents are eligible within a threshold of EUR 60,000. However, under the Frascati criterion, R&D would typically not include administrative and legal work connected with patents, routine tests or data collection.*	Legal and administrative work in connection with patent applications, records, litigation, or with the sale or purchase of patents are not qualifying expenditure for the purposes of the R&D tax credit.	
2.5.	**Other operating expenses related to R&D**		
2.5.1.	Should such category be identified?	Further detail is certainly necessary.	
2.5.2.	Is a detailed list possible of expenses advisable?	No. It would be impossible to have a complete list; a residual category would be required. Therefore a detailed list is not useful.	
2.5.3.	Is it appropriate to assess these expenses notionally by reference to other precisely defined eligible expenses (e.g. 15% of immovable [property] depreciation allowances, and/or 50% of eligible staff expenses)?		

2.5.4.	Should fees paid to external consultants assisting the company to determine its R&D super deduction be eligible, and to what extent?	No. This is not expenditure on R&D; it is expenditure on tax returns.	
C.	**Contracted Expenditure**		
2.6.	**Subcontracting expenses**		
2.6.1.	What if R&D activity is outsourced? *Currently in France, payments to R&D service suppliers, public or private, accredited by the French Ministry of research and located in the EU or the EEA, qualify as eligible expenses.*	See above on Irish situation in relation to outsourcing of R&D.	
2.6.2.	Should there be a territorial limit to exclude payments to subcontractors outside the EEA (which cannot invoke the freedom to provide services).	This is a pure policy decision, on which I do not have a legal view.	
2.6.3.	Should there be other limits? *Under current French law for instance, R&D costs invoiced by accredited private subcontractors can be retained within the limit of three times the total amount of all the other R&D eligible expenses incurred by the company; and such expenses can be retained by the company subcontracting R&D works within a yearly limit of EUR 12 or 10 million and EUR 2 million when the parties (i.e. ordering company and R&D supplier) are related companies.*		

B.	**Reimbursed expenditure**		
2.7.	**Treatment of public subsidies**		
2.7.1.	Should governmental and other State agencies subsidies/ grants related to R&D eligible projects be deducted from eligible expenses of the year during which these expenses are incurred?	From first principles, the R&D allowance is to incentivise expenditure on R&D. It is unclear why a state subsidy, in itself an incentive, should be further subsidised through the tax system.	

Section X
Italy

The answers given to this questionnaire are up to date with the Italian tax legislation in force as of tax year 2020.

		Answers and comments	Technical source (when necessary)
1.	'Research and Development' – Definition		
1.1.	As indicated in Section I (*supra*), should 'research and development' be excluded if there is no particular application or use in view for the economy or the internal market?	Research and development should include all the activities, irrespective of their application or use, due to the fact that it would be very difficult to determine a priori the result of such activities.	
1.2.	Should the level of novelty be new 'to the world', 'to the internal market (EU)', 'to the market', or 'to the firm'?	In the Italian tax system, the level of novelty is connected with the firm's previous R&D expenses, and in our view the application of this criterion is more efficient.	
1.3.	Should R&D be limited to the industrial sector, or also include the service industry (banking and insurance, but also humanities)?	In our opinion, there is no need to discriminate among sectors, also because this would lead to classification problems.	
1.3.1.	In the latter case, which criteria help to identify the presence of R&D in services activities?		
1.3.1.1.	Links with public research laboratories;	Yes.	
1.3.1.2.	Involvement of staff with PhDs or PhD students;	This is the criterion usually taken into account in the Italian legislation in order to apply special tax incentives on R&D and/or start-ups.	

1.3.1.3.	Publication of research findings in scientific journals;		
1.3.1.4.	Organisation of scientific conferences;		
1.3.1.5.	Involvement in scientific reviews;		
1.3.1.6.	Others?		
2.	'COSTS' (FOR RESEARCH AND DEVELOPMENT) – DEFINITION		
A.	**Capital expenditure**		
2.1.	**Depreciation allowances**		
a.	*General Principles*	**Draft Art. 9-3** provides: *'In addition to the amounts which are deductible as costs for research and development in accordance with paragraph 2, the taxpayer may also deduct, per tax year, an extra 50% of such costs, with the exception of the cost related to movable tangible fixed assets, that it incurred during that year. To the extent that costs for research and development reach beyond EUR 20,000,000, the taxpayer may deduct 25% of the exceeding amount.'* In addition, the Explanatory Memorandum (**para. 8**) provides: *"R&D costs will be fully expensed in the year incurred (with the exception of immovable property).'* **Draft Art. 10** (Other deductible items) provides: *'A deduction shall be made in respect of the depreciation of fixed assets referred to in Articles 30 to 40.* […]. **Draft Art. 12** (Non-deductible items) provides: *'By way of derogation from Articles 9 and 10, the following items shall be non-deductible:* […] *(i) acquisition or construction costs or cost connected with the improvement of fixed assets which are deductible under Articles 10 and 18, except for the cost related to research and development. The costs referred to in point (a) of Article 33(1) and points (a) and (b) of Article 33(2) shall not be treated as costs related to research and development;* […]' – **For additional context, see Annex**. *Based on your national tax background:*	
2.1.1.	Do you share our understanding that depreciation allowances have to be distinguished depending on the assets concerned, whether they are movable or immovable?	Yes.	
2.1.2.	Do you share our understanding that depreciation allowances are not available for movable fixed assets, because they are fully expensed in the year incurred, and not eligible to the super-deduction?	Yes.	

2.1.3.	Do you share our understanding that depreciation allowances remain available for immovable [property], because it cannot be fully expensed in the year incurred, and is eligible to the super-deduction?	Yes.	
2.1.4.	What if an asset is used both for research and non-research purposes (such as manufacturing)?	In our opinion, as for the general principles in the Italian corporate income tax legislation, the asset should be considered *pro quota* for the R&D activities (or, if not possible, the 50% should be taken into account).	
2.1.5.	If eligible, which criteria for proportional eligibility if asset used both for R&D and manufacturing purposes (e.g. an equipment used both to manufacture prototypes and serial products)?	In the Italian corporate income tax legislation, if not provided differently by the law, the determination of the criteria applicable is left to the taxpayer.	
2.1.6.	What if the asset is 'indirectly' used for R&D purposes?	In the Italian legislation, there is not explicit reference to indirect use of assets for R&D purposes, and in our opinion this could lead to a significant uncertainty on some assets.	
2.1.7.	What do you think of the following definition: 'Is considered directly used for R&D purposes an asset permitting, in and of itself, to carry out research programs of the business'?	In our opinion, this definition seems to fit the purpose, however more indication about 'in and of itself' should be needed.	
2.1.8.	Is the production of the following assets an R&D activity? (i) production of prototypes; (ii) construction of a pilot plant / or pilot facilities	Yes, they are both considered R&D activities.	
2.1.9.	Would you characterise the following assets as, potentially, directly used for R&D activities: (i) Handling devices; (ii) Calculation tools; (iii) Computers; (iv) Machines used to manufacture components of a prototype; (v) Telephones, small office appliances, office furniture?	In our legislation, there is not a pre-determination of the R&D expenses on the basis of the type of the asset (with some exceptions).	

b.	*Specific Rules*		
(i)	*Intangible Assets*	**Draft Art. 33.1(e)** provides: *'Without prejudice to paragraph 2 and Articles 37 and 38, fixed assets shall be depreciated individually over their useful lives on a straight-line basis. The useful life of a fixed asset shall be determined as follows:* [...] *(e) fixed intangible assets: the period for which the asset enjoys legal protection or for which the right has been granted or, where that period cannot be determined, 15 years.'* The problem is that not all intangible items (e.g. intellectual property, brand names), meet the definition of an intangible asset. If an item does meet the definition of an intangible asset, expenditure to acquire it or generate it internally should be recognised as an expense when it is incurred. Therefore, *based on your national tax background*:	
2.1.10.	Should we use the European Union Accounting Rule 6 defining intangible asset (i.e., identifiability, control over a resource, and existence of future economic benefits or service potential)?	In our opinion, this approach can lead to more certainty both for the taxpayers and the tax administrations.	
2.1.11.	If not, what should be the definition of intangible assets?	N/A.	
2.1.12.	Are intangible fixed assets (including intellectual property (IP)) costs fully expensed in the year incurred and included in the CCTB super-deduction?	In our opinion, they are not included in the super-deduction.	
	The inclusion of mere intellectual property costs is not advisable: it may create a bias in favour of patented research compared to that stemming from unpatented technology.		
2.1.13.	Will in practice this provision be limited to patents costs acquired with a view to carry on new experimental research and development?	It is the approach substantially adopted by the Italian legislator, and in our opinion it would be advisable.	
2.1.14.	What if these patents are (also) used in the manufacturing process?	In our opinion, the deduction should be limited to patents strictly connected to R&D activities.	
2.1.15.	Should plant variety rights be treated in the same manner as patents?		

2.1.16.	What about outlays incurred to acquire licences or know-how?		
(ii)	*Immovable [property]*		
	In any case, not covered by exclusion in Art. 9-3		
	In Austria, building costs and financing expenses related to R&D activity may be taken into account.		
2.1.17.	Should the concept of '*immovable property*' (Recital No. 8) be preferred to the one of '*immovable fixed asset*' (as opposed to Art. 9.3 CCTB)?	Yes, because it seems more precise in light of the aim of the legislation.	
2.1.18.	Would building costs and financing expenses related to the acquisition of immovable [property] be eligible to the super-deduction?	According to Art. 12(i), they would be deductible only in case they form part of the taxable value of the property because of the depreciation process.	
2.1.19.	What is your understanding of Art. 12(i): <u>1st meaning</u>: that costs related to acquisition or construction of new commercial or second-hand commercial or industrial immovable [property] is excluded from the super-deduction? Or <u>2nd meaning</u>: that costs related to acquisition or construction of new commercial or second-hand commercial or industrial immovable [property] is not fully deductible the year incurred but should be depreciated and such depreciation allowances are eligible to the super-deduction?	The second meaning seems preferable also because it would be more consistent with the general rules.	
(iii)	*Lease payments*		
2.1.20.	What if equipment is used according to the terms of a leasing-type transaction?	In principle, the super-deduction should be allowed irrespective of the legal form of the transactions.	

2.1.21.	Are leasing instalments eligible for super-deduction under current wording of Art. 9-3?	In our opinion, they can benefit of the super deduction.	
2.1.22.	Should they be?	In principle, they should not have a special regime and they should be subject to the same rules applicable to other costs.	
(iv)	*Alternative readings*		
2.1.23.	Please feel free to add any alternative readings you may have of relevant CCTB provisions and that has not yet been discussed.		
B.	**Current expenditure**		
2.2.	**R&D staff cost**		
a.	*What is meant by R&D staff?*	From an Italian tax law perspective, it should include all the human resources directly involved in the R&D activities.	
2.2.1.	Should eligibility be limited to staff directly-involved in R&D?	Yes.	
2.2.2.	In case the staff participates both in R&D and non R&D activities, should the text allow for proportional eligibility based on time spent (or other criteria)?	Yes.	
2.2.3.	How can researchers or scientists be defined? Should the text use black letter criteria (list diplomas (PhDs), qualifications…) or a more open definition?	In the Italian tax law, criteria like PhD or other degree are used for the application of some tax incentive, but for the R&D incentives, these criteria are not used since 2016.	
2.2.4.	Are research technicians R&D staff?	Yes.	
2.2.5.	What about other employees (not 'official researchers') which still have contributed to a patented invention?	They should be treated in the same way, unless a limitation based on qualification would apply.	
2.2.6.	What about the managers of the business (e.g. running a research program)?	They should be treated in the same way, unless a limitation based on qualification would apply.	

2.2.7.	What about other staff (secretariat, cleaning, etc.)? Can, in the alternative, their compensation be taken into account, proportionally, as other operating R&D expenses (cf. I-3 below)?	In our opinion, there should be a direct nexus with R&D activities, while takin into account a quota of the general costs of the enterprise would not be completely consistent with the aim of the provision.	
<u>*b.*</u>	<u>*What is meant by R&D staff cost?*</u>	Every consideration paid from the enterprise in connection to the staff's activity, irrespective of the name and/or the legal qualification of the payment.	
2.2.8.	Wages, bonuses, benefits in kind?	Yes.	
2.2.9.	Social security contributions (compulsory and/or non-compulsory)?	Yes.	
2.2.10.	Employer's contribution to participation of employees in profits of the enterprise by means of profit-sharing plan, employee share-ownership?	Yes.	
2.2.11.	Can a Member State provide that compensation paid to holders of PhD will count more (e.g. double) for a limited period of time (in order to promote hiring of PhD holders)?	It would be advisable, and a similar form of incentive has been applied (in few circumstances) in Italy (e.g. for the tax incentives of innovative start-ups).	
2.3.	**Standardisation expenses**		
	Based on your national tax background:		
2.3.1.	Should expenses related to the establishment of technical standards concerning products of the business be eligible for the super-deduction (e.g. expenses incurred on participation of employees in official meetings of standardisation bodies)?	To our knowledge, at the moment, there are not official guidelines. However, it would be advisable that such expenses are considered eligible for the super-deduction if they are included in the research of development stage.	
2.3.2.	If yes, should it still be the case even if these employees are not scientists or research technicians?	Yes.	

2.3.3.	How should these expenses be assessed (e.g., as portion of employee compensation related to the time spent in connection with such meetings)?	They would be assessed if and only if such expenses are separately identifiable and not if they form part of the general costs.	
2.3.4.	Should expenses related to technical monitoring/ technological watch be taken into account?	Only if connected with the research and/or development stage.	
2.4.	**Patent related expenses**		
2.4.1.	Are expenses linked to patents eligible? Please define NB: *under current French tax law, expenses linked to the filing, the maintenance and the defence of patents incurred in France or in another State (IP consultant's fees, translation costs taxes...) are eligible to the R&D tax credit; insurance costs linked to patents are eligible within a threshold of EUR 60,000. However, under the Frascati criterion, R&D would typically not include administrative and legal work connected with patents, routine tests or data collection.*	In the Italian tax legislation, patents can be eligible for tax incentives only if related to research and development. In our opinion it would be advisable that this criterion would apply.	
2.5.	**Other operating expenses related to R&D**		
2.5.1.	Should such category be identified?	In our opinion, at this stage such category can also be 'open'.	
2.5.2.	Is a detailed list possible of expenses advisable?	Yes, but in our opinion it is advisable in a further phase.	
2.5.3.	Is it appropriate to assess these expenses notionally by reference to other precisely defined eligible expenses (e.g. 15% of immovable [property] depreciation allowances, and/or 50% of eligible staff expenses)?	No, because such limits can be irrespective of the economic reality and inconsistent with the enterprise R&D activities.	

2.5.4.	Should fees paid to external consultants assisting the company to determine its R&D super deduction be eligible, and to what extent?	Yes, they should be fully deductible. In the Italian tax registration, they form part of the amount eligible for R&D tax incentives.	
C.	**Contracted Expenditure**		
2.6.	**Subcontracting expenses**		
2.6.1.	What if R&D activity is outsourced? *Currently in France, payments to R&D service suppliers, public or private, accredited by the French Ministry of research and located in the EU or the EEA, qualify as eligible expenses.*	They should be subject to the same tax regime. In the Italian tax law, such payments are eligible for tax incentives.	
2.6.2.	Should there be a territorial limit to exclude payments to subcontractors outside the EEA (which cannot invoke the freedom to provide services).	Yes, it would be advisable.	
2.6.3.	Should there be other limits? *Under current French law for instance, R&D costs invoiced by accredited private subcontractors can be retained within the limit of three times the total amount of all the other R&D eligible expenses incurred by the company; and such expenses can be retained by the company subcontracting R&D works within a yearly limit of EUR 12 or 10 million and EUR 2 million when the parties (i.e. ordering company and R&D supplier) are related companies.*	No.	

B.	**Reimbursed expenditure**		
2.7.	**Treatment of public subsidies**		
2.7.1.	Should governmental and other State agencies subsidies/grants related to R&D eligible projects be deducted from eligible expenses of the year during which these expenses are incurred?	Yes.	

SECTION XI
Latvia

Current Latvian corporate tax law is tax on distributed profit[163] and does not provide for any R&D tax incentive. According to the current law (Article 8: Expenditure not Related to Economic Activity) upon identifying the expenditure not related to economic activity it shall be assessed not only according to the legal form but also in conformity with economic essence of a transaction. All expenditure not directly related to economic activity of a taxpayer shall be included in the expenditure not related to economic activity and taxed as deemed distribution. In the study, 'super-deduction' as was introduced in 2013,[164] amended in 2014[165] and applicable for 2014-2017 tax years, is analysed. The tax law referred in the questionnaire is the law 'On enterprise income tax' (1995),which is *not* in force from 1 January 2018. Analysis provided is on former administrative and legislative practice. As stated by new Enterprise income tax law (2017), the R&D expenses are tax-deductible to the extent that they qualify as non-business-related expenses ('Expenses not Directly Related to Economic Activity' – *'Ar saimniecisku darbıbu nesaistıti izdevumi'*). We can assume that Latvian definition is close to the meaning of 'business related expenses' in Art. 9.1 CCCTB). However, the difference is that in the new model, there is no adjustments to taxable income, but 'non-business expenditures' are taxed as deemed profit distribution.

163. Enterprise income tax law (2017) available at https://likumi.lv/ta/en/en/id/292700-enterprise-income-tax-law (in English). Under the new CIT model, all undistributed corporate profits are exempt. This exemption covers both active (e.g. trading) and passive (e.g. dividends, interest, royalties) types of income. It also covers capital gains arising on the sale of all types of assets, including shares and securities, except for the sale of immovable property by non-residents. This tax regime is available to Latvian-resident companies and non-resident companies' permanent establishments (PEs) registered in Latvia.The taxation of corporate profits is postponed until those profits are distributed as dividends or deemed to be distributed.Profit distributions: – Dividends (including interim dividends); – Payments equal to dividends (i.e. profit share-outs by [a] cooperative societies, [b] sole traders, [c] partnerships, and [d] PEs); – Deemed dividends (i.e. part of earnings being added to share capital). Deemed distributions: – Non-business expenses; – Bad debts; – Excess interest payments; – Loans to related parties (with several exclusions); – Transfer pricing adjustments; – Surplus assets on liquidation; – Benefits a non-resident gives to employees of its PE.

164. Amendments to the Law 'On enterprise income tax', 6 November 2013, https://likumi.lv/ta/id/262325-grozijumi-likuma-par-uznemumu-ienakuma-nodokli- (in Latvian).

165. Technical amendments to the Law 'On enterprise income tax', 4 December 2014, including '(goods or services)' in the definition. Available at https://likumi.lv/ta/id/270873-grozijumi-likuma-par-uznemumu-ienakuma-nodokli- (in Latvian).

		Answers and comments	Technical source (when necessary)
1.	'RESEARCH AND DEVELOPMENT' – DEFINITION		
1.1.	As indicated in Section I (*supra*), should 'research and development' be excluded if there is no particular application or use in view for the economy or the internal market?	No. Personal opinion is that fundamental (basic) research should be included. However in the definition in Art. 1 term 'Research and development' includes creative work performed systematically to increase the volume of knowledge and to use such knowledge for the creation of new developments, provided that it corresponds to at least one of the following types of work: 1) industrial research – planned research or critical study with the aim of acquiring new knowledge and methods to be used for the development of new products (goods or services) or technologies or significant improvement of existing products or technologies; 2) experimental development – combination, modelling or use of scientific findings, technological, commercial or other important knowledge or skills in order to create new or significantly improved products (goods or services) or technologies, or activities with the aim of conceptually defining, planning and documenting new products (goods or services) or technologies. Thus scientific research also gives entitlement to the R&D super-deduction. The problem might occur while determining the R&D costs in general as well as exact type of activity. In Latvian practice research and development activities shall meet the following requirements: 1. the purpose of research and development is industrial research or experimental development, which also includes industrial research or experimental development in the service sector;	See also Cabinet of Ministers, 1 July 2014 Regulation No. 373 'Regulations for the application of research and development activities for enterprise income tax' (in force until 1 January 2018), https://likumi.lv/doc.php?id=267456

		2. the expected result of research and development is an element of innovation or the prevention of scientific or technological uncertainty; 3. the solution to the problem is not obvious to someone with specialist knowledge and experience in the field; 4. the element of innovation and scientific or technological uncertainty relate to the existing activity or activity of the taxable person, which he intends to initiate. Based on abovementioned Regulation of Cabinet of Ministers for the application of incentive as a new product or technology shall not be considered: 1. the development of a product or technology according to the order of a particular client, unless the product or technology significantly differs from the previously manufactured products; 2. improvement of organisational processes in the activities of the merchant; 3. replacement of an asset (purchase of new modules instead of used modules, extensions that do not result in specification upgrades, hardware and software updates); 4. daily, seasonal or cyclical changes and improvements; 5 aesthetic changes, changes in taste and perfume, and other enhancements for marketing purposes that do not change the function, use or technical properties; 6. other activities. Also,the Ministry of Economy worked out guidelines for determining R&D activities in the field of software and information systems The application of R&D investment discounts for the preparation and evaluation of research and development projects (see in Latvian https://www.em.gov.lv/files/es_fondi/ITvadl_Gala%20versija_30082016.pdf) in general following the Frascati *Manual.*	

1.2.	Should the level of novelty be new 'to the world', 'to the internal market (EU)', 'to the market', or 'to the firm'?	'To the firm' seems to be more convenient since abovementioned Regulations stated that the element of innovation (novelty) and scientific or technological uncertainty relate to the existing activity or activity of the taxable person, which he intends to initiate.	
1.3.	Should R&D be limited to the industrial sector, or also include the service industry (banking and insurance, but also humanities)?	No. R&D in the service sector also increase the competitiveness of the market.	
1.3.1.	In the latter case, which criteria help to identify the presence of R&D in services activities?		
1.3.1.1.	Links with public research laboratories;	Not necessarily, but for the definition of R&D costs, Latvia used also the amounts of remuneration for research services received from a scientific institution that is registered in the Register of Scientific Institutions of the Ministry of Education and Science, or equivalent scientific institutions that are a resident of a European Union Member State or such state of the European Economic Area with which Latvia has entered into a convention on the prevention of imposition of double taxation and tax evasion, provided that such convention is in force and the research services are directly related to the research and development work performed by the taxpayer (outsourced remuneration from research institutions)	
1.3.1.2.	Involvement of staff with PhDs or PhD students;	Based on definitions in the Law, personnel includes scientific staff (scientists who have acquired scientific qualification (a scientific doctoral degree) and professionals with an academic degree or a higher education diploma, who perform research activities in order to acquire new knowledge, products, processes, methods and systems, as well as project managers who are engaged in planning and management of scientific and technical aspects of research activities) and **research technical staff** (persons who have the necessary technical knowledge and experience in one or several areas and who participate in research activities by performing technical tasks under the guidance of the scientific staff.	Law On Enterprise Income Tax, Art. 1. part 30 and part 31 (https://likumi.lv/ta/en/en/id/34094-on-enterprise-income-tax) Law On Scientific Activity (https://likumi.lv/ta/en/en/id/107337-law-on-scientific-activity

		Engineers, technicians, laboratory assistants, technologists, and operators are included in the research technical staff). Definition in general follows definition in Latvian law on scientific activity. The Law On Scientific Activity grants right to perform scientific activity (creative activity that includes science, research and innovations) to any person, regardless of race, ethnicity, gender, language, age, political or religious conviction, social origin, or material, family or employment situation and other circumstances. Defines research attending staff – persons who perform assisting functions in the execution of scientific technical works (employees of planning, economic, financial, and scientific technical information structural units, employees of special and scientific technical libraries, patent service specialists, archivists, as well as qualified workers who ensure the assemblage, adjustment, maintenance and repair of the equipment and devices necessary for the performance of scientific activity. And research technical staff – persons who have the necessary technical knowledge and experience in one or several fields and who participate in scientific activity, under the guidance of scientists, by performing technical tasks. Engineers, technicians, laboratory assistants, technologists, and operators are included in research technical staff. For scientific institutions, at least five persons with a doctoral degree in science in a direction of research that conforms to the activities of the scientific institution are required by the law.	
1.3.1.3.	Publication of research findings in scientific journals;	No. Business projects are not necessarily linked to scientific publications, however, they are not to be excluded (because of results of experimental research as an example).	

1.3.1.4.	Organisation of scientific conferences;	No. Business projects are not necessarily linked to scientific conferences and public announcements, however, they are not to be excluded (because of result of experimental research).	
1.3.1.5.	Involvement in scientific reviews;	No.	
1.3.1.6.	Others?	Latvian law had also 'holding' limitation for incentive – 'The taxpayer was not entitled apply the tax relief laid down in this [6.[6]] Article if the intellectual property created as a result of research and development work is alienated within three taxation periods, counting from the taxation period in which the expenses comprise the last expenses related to the creation of such intellectual property.' If the tax relief has been applied to the expenses of the creation of the intellectual property violating 'holding period', the taxpayer shall adjust the enterprise income tax declaration in accordance with the procedures laid down in the Law On Taxes and Fees, excluding the taxable income corrections made for the purpose of tax relief. The remaining amount of the value of expenses by which the expenses were increased and by which the taxpayer does not have the right to adjust the declarations of the respective taxation periods shall be included in the taxable income of the taxation period during which the intellectual property has been alienated.	Law On enterprise income tax Art.6.[6].part 4 and part 5 (https://likumi.lv/ta/en/en/id/34094-on-enterprise-income-tax)
2.	'Costs' (For Research and Development) – Definition	General remark is that Latvian Law On the Annual Financial Statements and Consolidated Financial Statements defines research costs – the costs which are directly applicable to research measures, as well as such costs which have arisen in the project development stage of creation of a particular intangible investment object, if the undertaking cannot separate the research stage of such project from its development stage. (Art 1, p. 19)	Law On the Annual Financial Statements and Consolidated Financial Statements (https://likumi.lv/ta/en/en/id/277779-law-on-the-annual-financial-statements-and-consolidated-financial-statements)

A.	**Capital expenditure**		
2.1.	**Depreciation allowances**		
<u>a.</u>	<u>*General Principles*</u>	Latvian approach was that depreciation is allowed based on general tax depreciation (declining balance method) and recognised in general way.	Law on enterprise income tax. Art.13
		<u>Draft Art. 9-3</u> provides: *'In addition to the amounts which are deductible as costs for research and development in accordance with paragraph 2, the taxpayer may also deduct, per tax year, an extra 50% of such costs, with the exception of the cost related to movable tangible fixed assets, that it incurred during that year. To the extent that costs for research and development reach beyond EUR 20 000 000, the taxpayer may deduct 25% of the exceeding amount.'* In addition, the Explanatory Memorandum (**para. 8**) provides: *'R&D costs will be fully expensed in the year incurred (with the exception of immovable property).'* **<u>Draft Art. 10</u>** (Other deductible items) provides: *'A deduction shall be made in respect of the depreciation of fixed assets referred to in Articles 30 to 40. […]'* **<u>Draft Art. 12</u>** (Non-deductible items) provides: *'By way of derogation from Articles 9 and 10, the following items shall be non-deductible:* […] *(i) acquisition or construction costs or cost connected with the improvement of fixed assets which are deductible under Articles 10 and 18, except for the cost related to research and development. The costs referred to in point (a) of Article 33(1) and points (a) and (b) of Article 33(2) shall not be treated as costs related to research and development;* […]' – **<u>For additional context, see Annex</u>**. *Based on your national tax background:*	
2.1.1.	Do you share our understanding that depreciation allowances have to be distinguished depending on the assets concerned, whether they are movable or immovable?	Yes. Distinction is made in accordance with national and EU accounting standards.	
2.1.2.	Do you share our understanding that depreciation allowances are not available for movable fixed assets, because they are fully expensed in the year incurred, and not eligible to the super-deduction?	Yes. In Latvian legislation only remuneration and standardisation costs were subject to 'super-deduction'.	

2.1.3.	Do you share our understanding that depreciation allowances remain available for immovable [property], because it cannot be fully expensed in the year incurred, and is eligible to the super-deduction?	Yes. However, depreciation in Latvia was not subject of super-deduction and immovable property was writed off based on general regulation. Loss-carry forward was allowed so expenses are allowed also in next tax years.	
2.1.4.	What if an asset is used both for research and non-research purposes (such as manufacturing)?	Could be difficult from administration point of view.	
2.1.5.	If eligible, which criteria for proportional eligibility if asset used both for R&D and manufacturing purposes (e.g. an equipment used both to manufacture prototypes and serial products)?	Working hours, value criteria, to be documented and explained by the taxpayer.	
2.1.6.	What if the asset is 'indirectly' used for R&D purposes?	See above.	
2.1.7.	What do you think of the following definition: 'Is considered directly used for R&D purposes an asset permitting, in and of itself, to carry out research programs of the business'?	It solves some problems for administration but allows dual usage of asset.	
2.1.8.	Is the production of the following assets an R&D activity? (i) production of prototypes; (ii) construction of a pilot plant / or pilot facilities	Yes, as the final phase for some R&D activities.	
2.1.9.	Would you characterise the following assets as, potentially, directly used for R&D activities: (i) Handling devices; (ii) Calculation tools; (iii) Computers; (iv) Machines used to manufacture components of a prototype; (v) Telephones, small office appliances, office furniture?	Yes, if properly documented and clarified by the taxpayer.	

b.	*Specific Rules*		
(i)	*Intangible Assets*	Law On the Annual Financial Statements and Consolidated Financial Statements states that intangible investments – intangible properties other than financial assets and complying with both the following classification criteria: a) they can be separated or divided from an undertaking and sold, transferred, licenced, rented out or exchanged (individually or together with another liability or asset) or they have arisen from an agreement or other rights regardless of whether such rights are transferrable or separable from the undertaking or from other rights and obligations, b) an undertaking intends to use them for more than one year and expects that economic benefits will be received from holding of such properties; (Art. 1., p. 15)	Law On the Annual Financial Statements and Consolidated Financial Statements (https://likumi.lv/ta/en/en/id/277779-law-on-the-annual-financial-statements-and-consolidated-financial-statements)
		Draft Art. 33.1(e) provides: *'Without prejudice to paragraph 2 and Articles 37 and 38, fixed assets shall be depreciated individually over their useful lives on a straight-line basis. The useful life of a fixed asset shall be determined as follows: [...] (e) fixed intangible assets: the period for which the asset enjoys legal protection or for which the right has been granted or, where that period cannot be determined, 15 years.'* The problem is that not all intangible items (e.g. intellectual property, brand names), meet the definition of an intangible asset. If an item does meet the definition of an intangible asset, expenditure to acquire it or generate it internally should be recognised as an expense when it is incurred. Therefore, *based on your national tax background*:	
2.1.10.	Should we use the European Union Accounting Rule 6 defining intangible asset (i.e. identifiability, control over a resource, and existence of future economic benefits or service potential)?	Yes.	
2.1.11.	If not, what should be the definition of intangible assets?	N/A.	

2.1.12.	Are intangible fixed assets (including intellectual property (IP)) costs fully expensed in the year incurred and included in the CCTB super-deduction?	Law On enterprise income tax (Art. 13) provided following regulation: 'The value of intangible investments shall be written off as follows: for concessions – over 10 years; for patents, licences and trademarks – over five years. Costs of research and development (also, those pertaining to technical documentation of unrealised projects, if the value of such projects is not included in fixed assets) as relate to economic activity of a taxpayer, except costs of determining the location, quantity and quality of minerals, shall be written off in the year when such costs are incurred.'	Law On enterprise income tax Art.13 part. 5 (https://likumi.lv/ta/en/en/id/34094-on-enterprise-income-tax)
	The inclusion of mere intellectual property costs is not advisable: it may create a bias in favour of patented research compared to that stemming from unpatented technology.		
2.1.13.	Will in practice this provision be limited to patents costs acquired with a view to carry on new experimental research and development?	Yes.	
2.1.14.	What if these patents are (also) used in the manufacturing process?	Latvia had no costs related to the assets included in the super-deduction. Possibly divided based on attribution criteria.	
2.1.15.	Should plant variety rights be treated in the same manner as patents?	Further research is needed.	
2.1.16.	What about outlays incurred to acquire licences or know-how?	If licence or know-how used in specific R&D project could be recognised, however, Latvia is not allowed any costs except for remuneration and standartisation.	
(ii)	*Immovable [property]*	If asset used in specific R&D project could be recognised, however, Latvia is not allowed any costs except for remuneration and standartisation.	
	In any case, not covered by exclusion in Art. 9-3		
	In Austria, building costs and financing expenses related to R&D activity may be taken into account.		

2.1.17.	Should the concept of 'immovable property' (Recital No. 8) be preferred to the one of 'immovable fixed asset' (as opposed to Art. 9.3 CCTB)?	Latvian legislation used 'immovable property objects – parcels of land, buildings, engineering structures, groups of premises, and undivided shares of the abovementioned objects ' from accounting rules.	
2.1.18.	Would building costs and financing expenses related to the acquisition of immovable [property] be eligible to the super-deduction?	If asset used in specific R&D project could be recognised, however, Latvia is not allowed any costs except for remuneration and standartization.	
2.1.19.	What is your understanding of Art. 12(i): <u>1st meaning</u>: that costs related to acquisition or construction of new commercial or second-hand commercial or industrial immovable [property] is excluded from the super-deduction? Or <u>2nd meaning</u>: that costs related to acquisition or construction of new commercial or second-hand commercial or industrial immovable [property] is not fully deductible the year incurred but should be depreciated and such depreciation allowances are eligible to the super-deduction?	First meaning since Latvia was not allowed any costs except for remuneration and standartisation.	
(iii)	*Lease payments*		
2.1.20.	What if equipment is used according to the terms of a leasing-type transaction?	The general rule was that if fixed assets are leased with preemptive rights, the costs of their depreciation and reconstruction, improvement and renewal shall be written off as if the fixed assets were the property of the lessee.	Law On Enterprise Income Tax, Art. 13 part. 5 (https://likumi.lv/ta/en/en/id/34094-on-enterprise-income-tax)
2.1.21.	Are leasing instalments eligible for super-deduction under current wording of Art. 9-3?		

2.1.22.	Should they be?	Personal opinion is yes, but Latvia was not allowed any costs except for remuneration and standartisation	
(iv)	*Alternative readings*		
2.1.23.	Please feel free to add any alternative readings you may have of relevant CCTB provisions and that has not yet been discussed.		
B.	**Current expenditure**		
2.2.	**R&D staff cost**		
a.	*What is meant by R&D staff?*	Scientific staff – scientists who have acquired scientific qualification (a scientific doctoral degree) and professionals with an academic degree or a higher education diploma, who perform research activities in order to acquire new knowledge, products, processes, methods and systems, as well as project managers who are engaged in planning and management of scientific and technical aspects of research activities. Research technical staff – persons who have the necessary technical knowledge and experience in one or several areas and who participate in research activities by performing technical tasks under the guidance of the scientific staff. Engineers, technicians, laboratory assistants, technologists, and operators are included in the research technical staff.	Law On Enterprise Income Tax, Art. 13 part. 5 (https://likumi.lv/ta/en/en/id/34094-on-enterprise-income-tax)
2.2.1.	Should eligibility be limited to staff directly-involved in R&D?	Yes. Every person who is fully or partially included in R&D project and who's involvement can be proved by the taxpayer.	
2.2.2.	In case the staff participates both in R&D and non R&D activities, should the text allow for proportional eligibility based on time spent (or other criteria)?	Yes.	

2.2.3.	How can researchers or scientists be defined? Should the text use black letter criteria (list diplomas (PhDs), qualifications...) or a more open definition?	More open definition, however, Latvian Law On Scientific Activity defines research attending staff – persons who perform assisting functions in the execution of scientific technical works (employees of planning, economic, financial, and scientific technical information structural units, employees of special and scientific technical libraries, patent service specialists, archivists, as well as qualified workers who ensure the assemblage, adjustment, maintenance and repair of the equipment and devices necessary for the performance of scientific activity). A scientist is defined as a natural person who performs scientific activity and who has acquired scientific qualification in accordance with the procedures specified in this Law. But R&D staff should be broader definition.	
2.2.4.	Are research technicians R&D staff?	Yes. Research technical staff – persons who have the necessary technical knowledge and experience in one or several areas and who participate in research activities by performing technical tasks under the guidance of the scientific staff. Engineers, technicians, laboratory assistants, technologists, and operators are included in the research technical staff.	
2.2.5.	What about other employees (not 'official researchers') which still have contributed to a patented invention?	Yes, as persons involved in R&D projects and activities.	
2.2.6.	What about the managers of the business (e.g. running a research program)?	Latvian practice is limited to scientific staff or research technical staff, which are directly attributable to the research and development elaboration works.	
2.2.7.	What about other staff (secretariat, cleaning, etc.)? Can, in the alternative, their compensation be taken into account, proportionally, as other operating R&D expenses (cf. I-3 below)?	Latvian practice is limited to scientific staff or research technical staff, which are directly attributable to the research and development elaboration works.	

b.	*What is meant by R&D staff cost?*		
2.2.8.	Wages, bonuses, benefits in kind?	Yes. Remuneration in tax laws includes salary, premiums, single and regular remuneration and other income in cash or in kind an employee receives on the basis of current or past employment relations	Law On Personal Income Tax (Art. 8) https://likumi.lv/ta/en/en/id/56880-on-personal-income-tax
2.2.9.	Social security contributions (compulsory and/or non-compulsory)?	Yes, as remuneration expenditures includes also social insurance contribution (employer part for Latvia).	
2.2.10.	Employer's contribution to participation of employees in profits of the enterprise by means of profit-sharing plan, employee share-ownership?	No.	
2.2.11.	Can a Member State provide that compensation paid to holders of PhD will count more (e.g. double) for a limited period of time (in order to promote hiring of PhD holders)?	If R&D costs are related to the project there is no any limits for costs.	
2.3.	**Standardisation expenses**		
	Based on your national tax background:		
2.3.1.	Should expenses related to the establishment of technical standards concerning products of the business be eligible for the super-deduction (e.g. expenses incurred on participation of employees in official meetings of standardisation bodies)?	In general, yes but only if they meet attribution requirements and related to business activities. Latvian legislation allowed 'super-deduction' for amount of remuneration for testing, certification and calibration services necessary for the development of a new product or technology and provided by the certification, testing and calibration institution which is accredited at the national accreditation institution or an equivalent institution that is a resident of a European Union Member State or such state of the European Economic Area with which Latvia has entered into a convention on the prevention of imposition of double taxation and tax evasion, provided such convention is in force.	

2.3.2.	If yes, should it still be the case even if these employees are not scientists or research technicians?	Yes, if there is link to the R&D project.	
2.3.3.	How should these expenses be assessed (e.g. as portion of employee compensation related to the time spent in connection with such meetings)?	Yes.	
2.3.4.	Should expenses related to technical monitoring/ technological watch be taken into account?	Yes.	
2.4.	**Patent related expenses**		
2.4.1.	Are expenses linked to patents eligible? Please define NB: *under current French tax law, expenses linked to the filing, the maintenance and the defence of patents incurred in France or in another State (IP consultant's fees, translation costs taxes...) are eligible to the R&D tax credit; insurance costs linked to patents are eligible within a threshold of EUR 60,000. However, under the Frascati criterion, R&D would typically not include administrative and legal work connected with patents, routine tests or data collection.*	Could be eligible if capitalised and depreciated according to the standards. However Latvian incentive did not recognised this expenditures as eligible and applied general depreciation rules. Maintenance costs only if are expenditures related to business activities.	
2.5.	**Other operating expenses related to R&D**		
2.5.1.	Should such category be identified?	Personal opinion is yes, but could raise administration issues e.g. possible different interpretations.	
2.5.2.	Is a detailed list possible of expenses advisable?	Examples are possible and must be for interpretation.	
2.5.3.	Is it appropriate to assess these expenses notionally by reference to other precisely defined eligible expenses (e.g. 15% of immovable [property] depreciation allowances, and/or 50% of eligible staff expenses)?	Yes.	

2.5.4.	Should fees paid to external consultants assisting the company to determine its R&D super deduction be eligible, and to what extent?	Should be deductible as any expenses related to the economic activities.	
C.	**Contracted Expenditure**		
2.6.	**Subcontracting expenses**		
2.6.1.	What if R&D activity is outsourced? *Currently in France, payments to R&D service suppliers, public or private, accredited by the French Ministry of research and located in the EU or the EEA, qualify as eligible expenses.*	Latvian eligible expenditures also was amounts of remuneration for research services received from a scientific institution that is registered in the Register of Scientific Institutions of the Ministry of Education and Science, or equivalent scientific institutions that are a resident of a European Union Member State or such state of the European Economic Area with which Latvia has entered into a convention on the prevention of imposition of double taxation and tax evasion, provided that such convention is in force and the research services are directly related to the research and development work performed by the taxpayer.	
2.6.2.	Should there be a territorial limit to exclude payments to subcontractors outside the EEA (which cannot invoke the freedom to provide services).	No. Latvia extended definition from EU and EEA to the tax treaty countries also.	
2.6.3.	Should there be other limits? *Under current French law for instance, R&D costs invoiced by accredited private subcontractors can be retained within the limit of three times the total amount of all the other R&D eligible expenses incurred by the company; and such expenses can be retained by the company subcontracting R&D works within a yearly limit of EUR 12 or 10 million and EUR 2 million when the parties (i.e. ordering company and R&D supplier) are related companies.*	No.	

B.	**Reimbursed expenditure**		
2.7.	**Treatment of public subsidies**		
2.7.1.	Should governmental and other State agencies subsidies/grants related to R&D eligible projects be deducted from eligible expenses of the year during which these expenses are incurred?	Personal opinion – no. However if included in "superdeduction" also creates additional incentive for the same taxpayer.	

SECTION XII
Luxembourg

The answers are given based on legislation applicable to tax year 2020.

		Answers and comments	Technical source (when necessary)
1.	'RESEARCH AND DEVELOPMENT' – DEFINITION		
1.1.	As indicated in Section I (*supra*), should 'research and development' be excluded if there is no particular application or use in view for the economy or the internal market?	Basic research creates important spillover effects and may benefit the whole economy. The financial risk associated with basic research is, however, high as it does oftentimes not lead to an application or use, which could be exploited by the firm making the investment. R&D should therefore also cover basic research to compensate such financial risk.	Personal opinion
1.2.	Should the level of novelty be new 'to the world', 'to the internal market (EU)', 'to the market', or 'to the firm'?	The European Commission favours the novelty requirement 'new to the world' as it supports R&D with potentially largest social returns. Luxembourg would probably follow this best practice.	European Commission, 'A Study on R&D Tax Incentives (Final Report)', 2014
1.3.	Should R&D be limited to the industrial sector, or also include the service industry (banking and insurance, but also humanities)?	Given the importance of the banking sector for Luxembourg, it is likely that Luxembourg would also include the service sector.	Personal opinion
1.3.1.	In the latter case, which criteria help to identify the presence of R&D in services activities?	The criteria mentioned above could be used to identify the presence of R&D.	Personal opinion
1.3.1.1.	Links with public research laboratories;		
1.3.1.2.	Involvement of staff with PhDs or PhD students;		

1.3.1.3.	Publication of research findings in scientific journals;		
1.3.1.4.	Organisation of scientific conferences;		
1.3.1.5.	Involvement in scientific reviews;		
1.3.1.6.	Others?		
2.	'COSTS' (FOR RESEARCH AND DEVELOPMENT) – DEFINITION		
A.	**Capital expenditure**		
2.1.	**Depreciation allowances**		
<u>a.</u>	<u>*General Principles*</u>	**<u>Draft Art. 9-3</u>** provides: '*In addition to the amounts which are deductible as costs for research and development in accordance with paragraph 2, the taxpayer may also deduct, per tax year, an extra 50% of such costs, with the exception of the cost related to movable tangible fixed assets, that it incurred during that year. To the extent that costs for research and development reach beyond EUR 20,000,000, the taxpayer may deduct 25% of the exceeding amount."* In addition, the Explanatory Memorandum (**para. 8**) provides: '*R&D costs will be fully expensed in the year incurred (with the exception of immovable property).*' **<u>Draft Art. 10</u>** (Other deductible items) provides: '*A deduction shall be made in respect of the depreciation of fixed assets referred to in Articles 30 to 40.* [...]' **<u>Draft Art. 12</u>** (Non-deductible items) provides: '*By way of derogation from Articles 9 and 10, the following items shall be non-deductible:* [...] *(i) acquisition or construction costs or cost connected with the improvement of fixed assets which are deductible under Articles 10 and 18, except for the cost related to research and development. The costs referred to in point (a) of Article 33(1) and points (a) and (b) of Article 33(2) shall not be treated as costs related to research and development;* [...]' – **<u>For additional context, see Annex</u>**. *Based on your national tax background:*	
2.1.1.	Do you share our understanding that depreciation allowances have to be distinguished depending on the assets concerned, whether they are movable or immovable?	Yes, this is also my understanding of the draft directive.	
2.1.2.	Do you share our understanding that depreciation allowances are not available for movable fixed assets, because they are fully expensed in the year incurred, and not eligible to the super-deduction?	I agree that they are not eligible for the super-deduction but why are depreciation allowances not available for fixed assets?	

2.1.3.	Do you share our understanding that depreciation allowances remain available for immovable [property], because it cannot be fully expensed in the year incurred, and is eligible to the super-deduction?	Yes, this is also my understanding of the draft directive.	
2.1.4.	What if an asset is used both for research and non-research purposes (such as manufacturing)?	Luxembourg would probably require a tracking of the use of specific assets to ensure that taxpayers have not inflated the amount of qualifying expenditures, which may benefit from the super deduction.	Personal opinion based on current draft legislation for a new IP box regime
2.1.5.	If eligible, which criteria for proportional eligibility if asset used both for R&D and manufacturing purposes (e.g. an equipment used both to manufacture prototypes and serial products)?	No specific recommendation.	
2.1.6.	What if the asset is 'indirectly' used for R&D purposes?	No specific recommendation.	
2.1.7.	What do you think of the following definition: 'Is considered directly used for R&D purposes an asset permitting, in and of itself, to carry out research programs of the business'?	Alternative: is considered directly used for R&D purposes an asset, which is of such a specialised nature that it permits in and of itself to carry out R&D activities.	
2.1.8.	Is the production of the following assets an R&D activity? (i) production of prototypes; (ii) construction of a pilot plant / or pilot facilities	As mentioned by the EC, such costs may not fit into the general definition of R&D and normally would be excluded from the eligible expenditures of R&D tax incentives, but creation of prototypes and pilot studies are part of the innovation process. A strong capacity for prototyping is cost- and time-efficient way for firms to try and experiment new idea before actually launching them in the market. Building a prototype or a pilot project can also be used as a demonstration tool for investors, which is especially useful for young start-up companies.	European Commission, 'A Study on R&D Tax Incentives (Final Report)', 2014

2.1.9.	Would you characterise the following assets as, potentially, directly used for R&D activities: (i) Handling devices; (ii) Calculation tools; (iii) Computers; (iv) Machines used to manufacture components of a prototype; (v) Telephones, small office appliances, office furniture?	v) should be excluded.	Personal opinion
b.	*Specific Rules*		
(i)	*Intangible Assets*	**Draft Art. 33.1(e)** provides: '*Without prejudice to paragraph 2 and Articles 37 and 38, fixed assets shall be depreciated individually over their useful lives on a straight-line basis. The useful life of a fixed asset shall be determined as follows:* [...] *(e) fixed intangible assets: the period for which the asset enjoys legal protection or for which the right has been granted or, where that period cannot be determined, 15 years.*' The problem is that not all intangible items (e.g. intellectual property, brand names), meet the definition of an intangible asset. If an item does meet the definition of an intangible asset, expenditure to acquire it or generate it internally should be recognised as an expense when it is incurred. Therefore, *based on your national tax background*:	
2.1.10.	Should we use the European Union Accounting Rule 6 defining intangible asset (i.e., identifiability, control over a resource, and existence of future economic benefits or service potential)?	Intangible fixed assets are items without physical substance, which are intended for use on a continuing basis for the purpose of the undertaking's activity. Intangible items are composed of: – Research and development costs; – Concessions, patents, licences, trademarks and similar rights and assets; and – Payments on account and intangible assets under development.	Lux GAAP
2.1.11.	If not, what should be the definition of intangible assets?		
2.1.12.	Are intangible fixed assets (including intellectual property (IP)) costs fully expensed in the year incurred and included in the CCTB super-deduction?	Taxpayers can choose.	Lux GAAP and Luxembourg Income tax Code (Art. 46)
	The inclusion of mere intellectual property costs is not advisable: it may create a bias in favour of patented research compared to that stemming from unpatented technology.		

2.1.13.	Will in practice this provision be limited to patents costs acquired with a view to carry on new experimental research and development?	Question not clear.	
2.1.14.	What if these patents are (also) used in the manufacturing process?	This would require a tracking of use cf. 2.1.4.	
2.1.15.	Should plant variety rights be treated in the same manner as patents?	Yes.	
2.1.16.	What about outlays incurred to acquire licences or know-how?	Question not clear.	
(ii)	*Immovable [property]*		
	In any case, not covered by exclusion in Art. 9-3		
	In Austria, building costs and financing expenses related to R&D activity may be taken into account.		
2.1.17.	Should the concept of 'immovable property' (Recital No. 8) be preferred to the one of 'immovable fixed asset' (as opposed to Art. 9.3 CCTB)?	Question not clear.	
2.1.18.	Would building costs and financing expenses related to the acquisition of immovable [property] be eligible to the super-deduction?	Probably not as the current draft for a new IP Box Regime does also exclude such costs (in accordance with BEPS action 5)	
2.1.19.	What is your understanding of Art. 12(i): 1st meaning: that costs related to acquisition or construction of new commercial or second-hand commercial or industrial immovable [property] is excluded from the super-deduction? Or 2nd meaning: that costs related to acquisition or construction of new commercial or second-hand commercial or industrial immovable [property] is not fully deductible the year incurred but should be depreciated and such depreciation allowances are eligible to the super-deduction?	2nd meaning.	

(iii)	*Lease payments*		
2.1.20.	What if equipment is used according to the terms of a leasing-type transaction?	Not clear.	
2.1.21.	Are leasing instalments eligible for super-deduction under current wording of Art. 9-3?	Not clear.	
2.1.22.	Should they be?		
(iv)	*Alternative readings*		
2.1.23.	Please feel free to add any alternative readings you may have of relevant CCTB provisions and that has not yet been discussed.		
B.	**Current expenditure**		
2.2.	**R&D staff cost**		
a.	*What is meant by R&D staff?*		
2.2.1.	Should eligibility be limited to staff directly-involved in R&D?	Yes.	Personal opinion
2.2.2.	In case the staff participates both in R&D and non R&D activities, should the text allow for proportional eligibility based on time spent (or other criteria)?	Yes proportional eligibility on a time spent basis should be allowed.	Personal opinion
2.2.3.	How can researchers or scientists be defined? Should the text use black letter criteria (list diplomas (PhDs), qualifications…) or a more open definition?	I would favour an open definition.	
2.2.4.	Are research technicians R&D staff?	Yes.	Personal opinion
2.2.5.	What about other employees (not 'official researchers') which still have contributed to a patented invention?	Yes.	Personal opinion
2.2.6.	What about the managers of the business (e.g. running a research program)?	Yes.	Personal opinion

2.2.7.	What about other staff (secretariat, cleaning, etc.)? Can, in the alternative, their compensation be taken into account, proportionally, as other operating R&D expenses (cf. I-3 below)?	Yes, these costs should be taken into account proportionally.	Personal opinion
b.	*What is meant by R&D staff cost?*		
2.2.8.	Wages, bonuses, benefits in kind?	Yes.	Personal opinion
2.2.9.	Social security contributions (compulsory and/or non-compulsory)?	Yes.	Personal opinion
2.2.10.	Employer's contribution to participation of employees in profits of the enterprise by means of profit-sharing plan, employee share-ownership?	Yes.	Personal opinion
2.2.11.	Can a Member State provide that compensation paid to holders of PhD will count more (e.g. double) for a limited period of time (in order to promote hiring of PhD holders)?	No.	Personal opinion
2.3.	**Standardisation expenses**		
	Based on your national tax background:		
2.3.1.	Should expenses related to the establishment of technical standards concerning products of the business be eligible for the super-deduction (e.g. expenses incurred on participation of employees in official meetings of standardisation bodies)?	No.	Personal opinion
2.3.2.	If yes, should it still be the case even if these employees are not scientists or research technicians?		
2.3.3.	How should these expenses be assessed (e.g. as portion of employee compensation related to the time spent in connection with such meetings)?		

2.3.4.	Should expenses related to technical monitoring/ technological watch be taken into account?	No.	Personal opinion
2.4.	**Patent related expenses**		
2.4.1.	Are expenses linked to patents eligible? Please define NB: *under current French tax law, expenses linked to the filing, the maintenance and the defence of patents incurred in France or in another State (IP consultant's fees, translation costs taxes...) are eligible to the R&D tax credit; insurance costs linked to patents are eligible within a threshold of EUR 60,000. However, under the Frascati criterion, R&D would typically not include administrative and legal work connected with patents, routine tests or data collection.*	Luxembourg would probably follow the Frascati-Manuel.	Personal opinion
2.5.	**Other operating expenses related to R&D**		
2.5.1.	Should such category be identified?	No, there should be a certain degree of flexibility.	Personal opinion
2.5.2.	Is a detailed list possible of expenses advisable?	No, there should be a certain degree of flexibility.	Personal opinion
2.5.3.	Is it appropriate to assess these expenses notionally by reference to other precisely defined eligible expenses (e.g. 15% of immovable [property] depreciation allowances, and/or 50% of eligible staff expenses)?	No.	Personal opinion
2.5.4.	Should fees paid to external consultants assisting the company to determine its R&D super deduction be eligible, and to what extent?	No.	Personal opinion

C.	**Contracted Expenditure**		
2.6.	**Subcontracting expenses**		
2.6.1.	What if R&D activity is outsourced? *Currently in France, payments to R&D service suppliers, public or private, accredited by the French Ministry of research and located in the EU or the EEA, qualify as eligible expenses.*	Outsourced R&D should qualify. Excluding outsourced R&D would in particular penalise SMEs. Moreover, one has to keep in mind that the risk associated with outsourced R&D lies normally with the principal. Therefore, outsourced R&D can be put on an equal footing with R&D performed inhouse.	Personal opinion
2.6.2.	Should there be a territorial limit to exclude payments to subcontractors outside the EEA (which cannot invoke the freedom to provide services).	Under the new draft legislation for an IP Box regime, Luxembourg has decided to limit qualifying expenses to those incurred by a PE situated in a EU Member State. In order to increase investments in R&D in Europe it would be advisable to introduce such a limitation.	Personal opinion/draft legislation for a new IP box regime
2.6.3.	Should there be other limits? *Under current French law for instance, R&D costs invoiced by accredited private subcontractors can be retained within the limit of three times the total amount of all the other R&D eligible expenses incurred by the company; and such expenses can be retained by the company subcontracting R&D works within a yearly limit of EUR 12 or 10 million and EUR 2 million when the parties (i.e. ordering company and R&D supplier) are related companies.*	The super-deduction should be limited to the principal of an R&D project; a contractor should not benefit from such an incentive.	
B.	**Reimbursed expenditure**		
2.7.	**Treatment of public subsidies**		
2.7.1.	Should governmental and other State agencies subsidies/grants related to R&D eligible projects be deducted from eligible expenses of the year during which these expenses are incurred?	Yes, a deduction is necessary to prevent a double funding.	Personal opinion

Section XIII
Poland

		Answers and comments	Technical source (when necessary)
1.	'Research and Development' – Definition		
1.1.	As indicated in Section I (supra), should 'research and development' be excluded if there is no particular application or use in view for the economy or the internal market?	No. Basic research, i.e. research carried out without the intention to directly apply the acquired new knowledge for commercial purposes, gives entitlement to the R&D special deduction (see Art. 4a(26 and 27a) CITA and Art. 5a(39a) PITA, below). The definition of of applied research does not refer specifically to application of new knowledge in the economy (see Art. 4a(27b) CITA and Art. 5a(39b) PITA). However, the definitions of industrial research and development works, mention the purpose of devising new products, processes, and services, or introducing significant improvements of existing products, processes, and service (Art. 4a(27c) CITA, Art. 5a(39c) PITA) and the purposes of creating production plans and the creation and design of new, modified, or improved products, processes, and services (Art. 4a(28) CITA, Art. 5a(40) PITA). Moreover, to be eligible for R&D super-deduction, all expenses must meet general criteria for tax deductible expenses, i.e. they must be incurred in order to earn revenue or to maintain or secure a source of revenue (Art. 15(1) CITA and Art. 22(1) PITA) and they cannot be *expresis verbis* lited in the catalogue of non-deductible expenses (see Art. 16 CITA and Art. 22 PITA). Under CITA/PITA (Art. 4a(26-28) CITA and Art. 5a(38-40) PITA) R&D activities are defined as: 'creative activities which involve scientific research or development works performed in a systematic manner for the purposes of increasing the knowledge base and devising new applications of pre-existing knowledge'. Scientific research includes applied research, industrial research and basic research. Basic research is defined as 'original research, experimental or theoretical works performed mostly for the purposes of acquisition of new knowledge about the foundations of phenomena and perceptible facts,	

without the intention to directly apply such knowledge for commercial purposes'. Thus also basic research gives entitlement to the R&D superdeduction.

However, '[e]ligible costs incurred in the course of basic research shall be deducted exclusively on condition that such research is conducted on the basis of an agreement or memorandum of understanding concluded with a research unit within the meaning of the Act of 30 April 2010 on Science Financing'. Applied research is defined as 'applied research – research activities performed for the purposes of acquisition of new knowledge, aimed mostly at the practical application thereof'. Industrial research is defined as 'research intended to acquire new knowledge and skills for the purposes of devising new products, processes, and services, or introducing significant improvements of existing products, processes, and services; the research in question encompasses the creation of constituent parts of complex systems, the construction of prototypes in a laboratory environment or in an environment designed to imitate existing systems, including, in particular, for the purposes of assessment of the suitability of given types of technology, as well as the construction of pilot plants necessary for such research — including for the purposes of producing evidence in case of generic technologies'.

Development works are defined as 'development works — shall refer to the acquisition, compilation, designing, and application of existing knowledge and skills in the area of science, technology, and business, as well as other knowledge and skills for the purposes of creating production plans and the creation and design of new, modified, or improved products, processes, and services, with the exception of works encompassing routine and periodical changes made to products, production lines, manufacturing processes, existing services, and other ongoing operations, even where such changes constitute an improvement — including, in particular: a) designing prototypes and pilot projects as well as demonstrations, testing, and validation of new or improved products,

		processes, and services in an environment which constitutes a model reflecting the conditions of actual functioning, the primary aim of which is the further technical improvement of products, processes, and services whose final shape has not yet been determined, b) designing prototypes and pilot projects which may be used for commercial purposes, where the prototype or pilot project constitutes an end product which is fit for commercial application and the production thereof for demonstration and validation purposes only is excessively costly'.	
1.2.	Should the level of novelty be new 'to the world', 'to the internal market (EU)', 'to the market', or 'to the firm'?	Neither CITA nor PITA provisions relating to the R&D super-deduction (Art. 4a(26-28) and Art. 18d-e CITA, Art. 5a(38-40) and 26e-g PITA) does not expressly state whether R&D involves knowledge new 'to the world', 'to the internal market (EU)', 'to the market', or 'to the firm'. There is also no public ruling explaining this issue. However, before 1 January 2016, Art. 18b(2) CITA and 26c PITA , referring to another, now repealed, R&D incentive, expressly mentioned novelty to the world (referring to a new technology, as technology generally not being applicable for more than 5 years). Since 1 January 2016, the Art. 18b(2) CITA and 26c PITA were deleted and there is no express mention. The only term used is 'new knowledge' in case of research and 'new, modified, or improved products, processes, and services', in case of development works.	
1.3.	Should R&D be limited to the industrial sector, or also include the service industry (banking and insurance, but also humanities)?	No. Even the definition of industrial research (see *supra*) mentions new products, processes, and services, thus refers not only to the production industry, but also to the provision of services. Also, the definition of development works (see *supra*) refers to products, processes, and services.	
1.3.1.	In the latter case, which criteria help to identify the presence of R&D in services activities?	CITA/PITA does not expressly provide any such additional criteria in general. However, in case of development works it is stated that 'works encompassing routine and periodical changes made to products, production lines,	

		manufacturing processes, existing services, and other ongoing operations, even where such changes constitute an improvement' are not considered development works (Art. 4a(28) CITA, Art. 5a(40) PITA).	
1.3.1.1.	Links with public research laboratories;	It is worth mentioning, that expenses incurred in the course of basic research are eligible for R&D super-deduction exclusively on condition that such research is conducted on the basis of an agreement or memorandum of understanding concluded with a research unit within the meaning of the Act of 30 April on Science Financing (Art. 18d(4) CITA and 26e(4) PITA). Also expenses on expert assessments, opinions, consulting services and equivalent services as well as the acquisition of the results of scientific research are eligible for the R&D super-deduction provided that the assessments, opinions, consulting and equivalent services or scientific research are performed by a research unit within the meaning of the Act of 30 April on Science Financing (Art. 18d(2)(5)CITA and Art. 26e(4) PITA) on a basis of an agreement. Research units are units continuously conducting scientific research or development work: a) basic organisational units of the university within the meaning of the statutes of these institutions; b) scientific units of the Polish Academy of Sciences within the meaning of the Act of 30 April on the Polish Academy of Sciences; c) research institutes within the meaning of the Act of 30 April on research institutes; d) international scientific institutes established on the basis of separate regulations, operating in the territory of the Republic of Poland; e) Polish Academy of Arts; f) other organisational units not mentioned in points a) to e), established in the territory of the Republic of Poland, which are organisations conducting research and dissemination of knowledge within the meaning of Art. 2(83) of Commission Regulation (EU)	

		No 651/2014 of 17 June 2014 declaring certain types of aid compatible with the internal market pursuant to Article 2(107) and (108) of the Treaty (Art. 2(9) Science Financing Act). Tax administration applies such a restrictive interpretation (see e.g. Head of Tax Chamber in Katowice, private ruling of 4 January 2017 r. no. 2461-IBPB-1-3.4510.998.2016.1.TS and of 21 November 2016 r. no. 2461-IBPB-1-2.4510.923.2016.1.BG). However, some authors claim that only scientific research must be acquired from a research unit to be eligible, while assessments, opinions, consulting services and equivalent services may be carried also by other persons (see P. WYRWA, *Ulga na działalność badawczo rozwojową*, Lex/el, Warsaw, 2017).	
1.3.1.2.	Involvement of staff with PhDs or PhD students;		
1.3.1.3.	Publication of research findings in scientific journals;		
1.3.1.4.	Organisation of scientific conferences;		
1.3.1.5.	Involvement in scientific reviews;		
1.3.1.6.	Others?		
2.	'COSTS' (FOR RESEARCH AND DEVELOPMENT) – DEFINITION		
A.	**Capital expenditure**		
2.1.	**Depreciation allowances**		
a.	<u>General Principles</u>	**<u>Draft Art. 9-3</u>** provides: *'In addition to the amounts which are deductible as costs for research and development in accordance with paragraph 2, the taxpayer may also deduct, per tax year, an extra 50% of such costs, with the exception of the cost related to movable tangible fixed assets, that it incurred during that year. To the extent that costs for research and development reach beyond EUR 20,000,000, the taxpayer may deduct 25% of the exceeding amount.'* In addition, the Explanatory Memorandum (**para. 8**) provides: *'R&D costs will be fully expensed in the year incurred (with the exception of immovable property).'* **<u>Draft Art. 10</u>** (Other deductible items) provides: *'A deduction shall be made in respect of the depreciation of fixed assets referred to in Articles 30 to 40. [...]'*	

		<u>Draft Art. 12</u> (Non-deductible items) provides: *'By way of derogation from Articles 9 and 10, the following items shall be non-deductible:* [...] *(i) acquisition or construction costs or cost connected with the improvement of fixed assets which are deductible under Articles 10 and 18, except for the cost related to research and development. The costs referred to in point (a) of Article 33(1) and points (a) and (b) of Article 33(2) shall not be treated as costs related to research and development;* [...]' – **<u>For additional context, see Annex</u>**. *Based on your national tax background:*	
2.1.1.	Do you share our understanding that depreciation allowances have to be distinguished depending on the assets concerned, whether they are movable or immovable?	Under CITA/PITA, expenses eligible for R&D super-deduction are included in an exhaustive list (see Art. 18d(2-3) CITA and Art. 26e(2-3) PITA). In case of fixed assets and intangible assets, only depreciation allowances are eligible, however, depreciation allowances on passenger cars, buildings and structures as well as premises which constitute a separate freehold property are excluded from the R&D super deduction (see Art. 18d(3) CITA and Art. 26e(3) PITA). Thus, under Polish rules, there is no general distinction between movable and immovable fixed assets as regards the entitlement to the R&D super deduction. Fixed assets subject to depreciation include tangible movables and certain immovables (generally with the exclusion of land). Also intangible assets (e.g. patents, copyrights) are subject to depreciation). Art. 18d(3) CITA and Art. 26e(3) PITA expressly state that '[e]ligible costs shall also include the depreciation and amortisation write-offs on fixed assets and intangible assets used in the course of the research and development activities performed (with the exception of passenger cars, buildings and structures as well as any premises which constitute a separate freehold property) where such write-offs are made during a given fiscal year [...]'.	
2.1.2.	Do you share our understanding that depreciation allowances are not available for movable fixed assets, because they are fully expensed in the year incurred, and not eligible to the super-deduction?	No. Under CITA/PITA, depreciation allowances regarding movable fixed assets and intangible assets are eligible for the R&D super-deduction (see Art. 18d(3) CITA and 26e(3) PITA, *supra*). However, eligible are only depreciation allowances for the year in which R&D activities are carried out (see Art. 18d(8) CITA and Art. 26e(8) PITA).	

		Under Art. 18d(8) CITA and Art. 26e(8) PITA, '[t]he deduction shall be made in the tax return for the fiscal year during which the relevant eligible costs were incurred. In cases where the taxable person suffered a loss during a given fiscal year or where the amount of the taxable person's income is lower than the amount of deductions to which the taxable person is entitled, the deductions shall – in the entire amount or in the remaining part, respectively – be made in the tax returns for the six successive fiscal years immediately following the year in which the taxable person took advantage of the right to make a deduction or in which the taxable person had such a right'.	
2.1.3.	Do you share our understanding that depreciation allowances remain available for immovable [property], because it cannot be fully expensed in the year incurred, and is eligible to the super-deduction?	No. Under CITA/PITA, expenses eligible for R&D super-deduction are included in an exhaustive list (see Art. 18d(2-3) CITA and Art. 26e(2-3) PITA). In case of fixed assets, including immovables, only depreciation allowances are eligible. However, depreciation allowances on buildings and structures as well as premises which constitute a separate freehold property are excluded from the R&D super deduction (see Art. 18d(3) CITA and Art. 26e(3) PITA). Moreover, land and rights of perpetual usufruct of land are not subject to depreciation (Art. 16c(1) CITA and 22c(1) PITA).	
2.1.4.	What if an asset is used both for research and non-research purposes (such as manufacturing)?	CITA/PITA do not expressly regulate such situation (i.e. proportional eligibility). However, legal doctrine argues for proportional eligibility, pointing out that Art. 18d(3) CITA and Art. 26e(3) PITA do not restrict the scope of R&D special deduction to depreciation allowances on assets used exclusively for R&D activities (see P. Wyrwał, *Ulga na działalność badawczo-rozwojową w praktyce*, Lex/el, Warsaw, 2017). However, as regards, not acquisition but the use for valuable consideration (e.g. under a lease agreements) of scientific and research equipment, R&D super deduction is only applicable in case of exclusive use in the course of R&D activities, thus no proportion eligibility is provided for (see Art. 18d(2)(4) CITA and Art. 26e(2)(4) PITA).	

2.1.5.	If eligible, which criteria for proportional eligibility if asset used both for R&D and manufacturing purposes (e.g. an equipment used both to manufacture prototypes and serial products)?	CITA/PITA do not expressly regulate such situation and do not provide any calculation methods. Tax administration states that time of use of an asset for R&D activities and other activities should be decisive when determining the proportional eligibility of depreciation allowances (see Head of Tax Chamber in Katowice, private ruling of 20 January 2017 No. 2461-IBPB-1-2.4510.1051.2016.1.KP).	
2.1.6.	What if the asset is 'indirectly' used for R&D purposes?	CITA/PITA do not expressly regulate such situation. However, it seems that such an asset is not eligible. Under Art. 18d(2)(2) CITA and Art. 263(2)(2) PITA, only the acquisition of materials (including raw materials) directly linked to the research and development activities performed are eligible. Tax administration refused eligibility in case of electric energy, heating and the like (see Head of Tax Chamber in Bydgoszcz, private ruling of 24 January 2017, No. 0461-ITPB3.4510.724.2016.1.PS). Materials and raw materials used to produce instruments and equipment used in the course of R&D activities are eligible (see Head of Tax Chamber in Warsaw, private ruling of 11 January 2017, No. 1462-IPPB5.4510.1089.2016.1.MR). There is no express condition of direct link in the case of scientific equipment used under lease contracts and the like (see Art. 18d(2)(4) CITA and Art. 26e(2)(4) PITA, *supra*) or in the case of depreciation allowances on fixed assets and intangible assets (see Art. 18d(3) CITA and 26e(3) PITA). However, Polish tax administration would probably require such a link. For example, it has been stated that non-eligible are costs of producing prototypes for the purpose of obtaining certificates enabling the developed products to be introduced to other markets (see Head of Tax Chamber in Katowice, private ruling of 16 December 2016, No. 2461-IBPB-1-2.4510.850.2016.2.MS).	
2.1.7.	What do you think of the following definition: 'Is considered directly used for R&D purposes an asset permitting, in and of itself, to carry out research programs of the business'?	Too narrow.	

2.1.8.	Is the production of the following assets an R&D activity? (i) production of prototypes; (ii) construction of a pilot plant/or pilot facilities	Yes. Art. 4a(28) CITA and 5a(40) PITA provide that 'development works – shall refer to the acquisition, compilation, designing, and application of existing knowledge and skills in the area of science, technology, and business, as well as other knowledge and skills for the purposes of creating production plans and the creation and design of new, modified, or improved products, processes, and services, with the exception of works encompassing routine and periodical changes made to products, production lines, manufacturing processes, existing services, and other ongoing operations, even where such changes constitute an improvement – including, in particular: a) designing prototypes and pilot projects as well as demonstrations, testing, and validation of new or improved products, processes, and services in an environment which constitutes a model reflecting the conditions of actual functioning, the primary aim of which is the further technical improvement of products, processes, and services whose final shape has not yet been determined, b) designing prototypes and pilot projects which may be used for commercial purposes, where the prototype or pilot project constitutes an end product which is fit for commercial application and the production thereof for demonstration and validation purposes only is excessively costly'. For example, the Head of Tax Chamber in Katowice, in private ruling of 4 January 2017 No. 2461-IBPB-1-3.4510.865.2016.2.TS, considered as R&D activities the design and production of matrices and tools necessary for the production of a prototype and the production of a pilot series of products, before a regular production starts.	
2.1.9.	Would you characterise the following assets as, potentially, directly used for R&D activities: (i) Handling devices; (ii) Calculation tools; (iii) Computers; (iv) Machines used to manufacture components of a prototype; (v) Telephones, small office appliances, office furniture?	CITA/PITA do not expressly refer to such expenses. However, assets (i) – (iv) seem to be eligible (see *supra*). According to tax administration, depreciation of a license on computer software used to perform R&D activities are eligible (Head of Tax Chamber in Katowice, private ruling of 21 November 2016, No. 2461-IBPB-1-2.4510.928.2016.1.BG).	

b.	*Specific Rules*		
(i)	*Intangible Assets*	**Draft Art. 33.1(e)** provides: *'Without prejudice to paragraph 2 and Articles 37 and 38, fixed assets shall be depreciated individually over their useful lives on a straight-line basis. The useful life of a fixed asset shall be determined as follows:* [...] *(e) fixed intangible assets: the period for which the asset enjoys legal protection or for which the right has been granted or, where that period cannot be determined, 15 years.'* The problem is that not all intangible items (e.g. intellectual property, brand names), meet the definition of an intangible asset. If an item does meet the definition of an intangible asset, expenditure to acquire it or generate it internally should be recognised as an expense when it is incurred. Therefore, *based on your national tax background*:	
2.1.10.	Should we use the European Union Accounting Rule 6 defining intangible asset (i.e. identifiability, control over a resource, and existence of future economic benefits or service potential)?	The use of a common, already established definition, would provide for more certainty, predictability and uniformity. For example, the definition included in the Art. 3(1)(14) of the Polish Accounting Act states that intangible assets 'shall be understood, subject to the provisions of subparagraph (17), as property rights acquired by a reporting entity and classified as fixed assets, from which economic benefits are expected, to be used by that reporting entity for its purposes, and with the expected useful life of more than one year, including, in particular: a) copyrights and related rights, licenses, concessions, b) rights to inventions, patents, trademarks, utility models and ornamental designs, c) know-how. Intangible assets used on the basis of lease, rental, and similar agreements, including finance or operating lease agreements, are recorded as fixed assets of one of the parties to such an agreement, in accordance with the provisions of par. 4. Intangible assets also include goodwill on acquisition and development costs'.	
2.1.11.	If not, what should be the definition of intangible assets?		
2.1.12.	Are intangible fixed assets (including intellectual property (IP)) costs fully expensed in the year incurred and included in the CCTB super-deduction?	Under Art. 18d(3) CITA and Art. 26e(3) PITA, eligible for R&D super deduction are i.e. depreciation allowances on intangible assets (intangible fixed assets) used in the course of the research and development activities performed, where such depreciation is made during a given fiscal year. As regards, the CCTB super-deduction, they seem to be included in the year they were incurred. The exclusion in Art. 9(3) CCCTB Directive only refers to movable tangible fixed assets.	

	The inclusion of mere intellectual property costs is not advisable: it may create a bias in favour of patented research compared to that stemming from unpatented technology.		
2.1.13.	Will in practice this provision be limited to patents costs acquired with a view to carry on new experimental research and development?	No. In our opinion it seems to refer to intangible fixed assets generally, if used in R&D activities.	
2.1.14.	What if these patents are (also) used in the manufacturing process?	Costs should be eligible even if patents are used in the manufacturing process, if this process if this process is considered R&D activity.	
2.1.15.	Should plant variety rights be treated in the same manner as patents?	Yes. There is no justification for favouring patents over other forms of intangible assets, especially othe forms of intellectual property.	
2.1.16.	What about outlays incurred to acquire licences or know-how?	Yes. There is no justification for favouring patents over other forms of intangible assets, especially other forms of intellectual property.	
(ii)	*Immovable [property]*		
	In any case, not covered by exclusion in Art. 9-3		
	In Austria, building costs and financing expenses related to R&D activity may be taken into account.		
2.1.17.	Should the concept of 'immovable property' (Recital No. 8) be preferred to the one of 'immovable fixed asset' (as opposed to Art. 9.3 CCTB)?	A more coherent solution would be the use of the concept of 'immovable fixed assets', as opposed to 'movable fixed assets', as used in Art. 9(3) CCCTB.	
2.1.18.	Would building costs and financing expenses related to the acquisition of immovable [property] be eligible to the super-deduction?	Yes. The exclusion from R&D super-deduction under CCTB expressly only refers to movable tangible assets.	

2.1.19.	What is your understanding of Art. 12(i): 1st meaning: that costs related to acquisition or construction of new commercial or second-hand commercial or industrial immovable [property] is excluded from the super-deduction? Or 2nd meaning: that costs related to acquisition or construction of new commercial or second-hand commercial or industrial immovable [property] is not fully deductible the year incurred but should be depreciated and such depreciation allowances are eligible to the super-deduction?	1st meaning. They are not considered R&D expenses, thus non-eligible for R&D super-deduction.	
(iii)	*Lease payments*		
2.1.20.	What if equipment is used according to the terms of a leasing-type transaction?	According to Art. 18d(2)(4) CITA and Art. 26e(2)(4) PITA, eligible for R&D super deduction are costs of 'the use – for valuable consideration – of scientific and research equipment used exclusively in the course of the research and development activities performed, where such use takes place otherwise than under an agreement concluded with an entity affiliated with the taxable person within the meaning of Articles 11.1. and 11.4'.	
2.1.21.	Are leasing instalments eligible for super-deduction under current wording of Art. 9-3?	No. Art. 9(3) CCCTB refers generally to costs related to movable tangible fixed assets, and not only to the costs of acquisition of such assets.	
2.1.22.	Should they be?	Yes. According to Art. 18d(2)(4) CITA and Art. 26e(2)(4) PITA, leasing instalments are eligible for R&D super deduction (see *supra*).	

(iv)	*Alternative readings*		
2.1.23.	Please feel free to add any alternative readings you may have of relevant CCTB provisions and that has not yet been discussed.		
B.	**Current expenditure**		
2.2.	**R&D staff cost**		
a.	<u>*What is meant by R&D staff?*</u>	Under Art. 18d(2)(1) CITA and Art. 26e(2)(1) PITA, R&D staff includes 'employees the purpose of whose activities is performing research and development work'. According to tax administration, those persons must be employed for the purposes of performing R&D activities and it should be reflected in their employment agreement or an annex thereto (see Head of the Tax Chamber in Katowice, private ruling of 25 January 2017, No. 2461-IBPB-1-2.4510.934.2016.3.KP). However, the legal doctrine claims that such interpretation is too restrictive and also performing R&D activities on the basis of a direct order of the employer should result in eligibility (see P. Wyrwa, *Ulga na działalność badawczo-rozwojowa w praktyce*, Lex/el, Warsaw, 2017). Moreover, according to tax authorities only employment relationship and similar relationships, result in eligibility, which excludes very popular civil agreements such as a project contract (*umowa o dzieło*) and mandate (*umowa zlecenia*) (see Ministry of Finance, communication: Ulga podatkowa na działalność badawczo-rozwojową – odliczanie kosztów pracowniczych, 18 May 2017, http://www.mf.gov.pl/ministerstwo-finansow/wiadomosci/komunikaty/-/asset_publisher/6Wwm/content/ulga-podatkowa-na-dzialalnosc-badawczo-rozwojowa/pop_up?_101_INSTANCE_6Wwm_viewMode=print [3 September 2017]).	
2.2.1.	Should eligibility be limited to staff directly-involved in R&D?	Yes. According to Art. 18d(2)(1) CITA and Art. 26e(2)(1) PITA, eligible are costs of 'employees the purpose of whose activities is performing research and development work'.	

2.2.2.	In case the staff participates both in R&D and non R&D activities, should the text allow for proportional eligibility based on time spent (or other criteria)?	Yes. CITA and PITA do not refer expressly to such situation. However, even tax administration allows for proportional eligibility (see Head of Tax Chamber in Warsaw, private ruling of 27 December 2016, No. 1462-IPPB5.4510.1087.2016.1.MR). According to tax administration, super-deduction applies only to the extent the staff is actually involved in R&D activities and not in the extent just determined in the employment agreement (see Head of Tax Chamber in Poznań private ruling of 26 January 2017, No. 3063-ILPB2.4510.261.2016.1.AO).	
2.2.3.	How can researchers or scientists be defined? Should the text use black letter criteria (list diplomas (PhDs), qualifications...) or a more open definition?	R&D staff should be defined with a more open definition, with the focus on R&D activities being performed and not in their formal qualifications.	
2.2.4.	Are research technicians R&D staff?	Yes, if the purpose of their activities is performing research and development work (see Art. 18d(2)(1) CITA and Art. 26e(2)(1) PITA, *supra*).	
2.2.5.	What about other employees (not 'official researchers') which still have contributed to a patented invention?	Yes, if the purpose of their activities is performing research and development work (see Art. 18d(2)(1) CITA and Art. 26e(2)(1) PITA, *supra*).	
2.2.6.	What about the managers of the business (e.g. running a research program)?	No, unless they are simultaneously performing research and development work (see Art. 18d(2)(1) CITA and Art. 26e(2)(1) PITA, *supra*), then proportional eligibility should apply.	
2.2.7.	What about other staff (secretariat, cleaning, etc.)? Can, in the alternative, their compensation be taken into account, proportionally, as other operating R&D expenses (cf. I-3 below)?	No (see Art. 18d(2)(1) CITA and Art. 26e(2)(1) PITA, *supra*).	

b.	*What is meant by R&D staff cost?*	According to Art. 18d(2)(1) CITA and Art. 26e(2)(1) PITA, R&D staff costs include: 'receivables payable on the bases specified in Article 12.1 of the Act of 26 July 1991 on Personal Income Tax as well as contributions payable in connection with such receivables, referred to in the Act of 13 October 1998 on the Social Security System, in the part financed by the contribution remitter, where the receivables and contributions in question pertain to employees the purpose of whose activities is performing research and development work". Art. 12(1) PITA provides that "Revenue from a service relationship, employment relationship, outwork and co-operative employment relationship shall mean any type of cash payments and the cash value of in-kind benefits or their equivalents irrespective of the source of financing of these payments and benefits, especially: base pay, overtime pay, supplements, bonuses, equivalents for unused statutory leave and other amounts payable irrespective of whether their amount was agreed in advance or not and cash benefits paid for an employee as well as the value of other gratuitous or partially paid benefits.'	
2.2.8.	Wages, bonuses, benefits in kind?	Yes (see *supra*).	
2.2.9.	Social security contributions (compulsory and/or non-compulsory)?	Yes (see *supra*).	
2.2.10.	Employer's contribution to participation of employees in profits of the enterprise by means of profit-sharing plan, employee share-ownership?	Polish legal system does not recognise such category of payments.	
2.2.11.	Can a Member State provide that compensation paid to holders of PhD will count more (e.g. double) for a limited period of time (in order to promote hiring of PhD holders)?	No. The focus should be on R&D activities being performed and not on formal staff qualifications.	

2.3.	**Standardisation expenses**		
	Based on your national tax background:		
2.3.1.	Should expenses related to the establishment of technical standards concerning products of the business be eligible for the super-deduction (e.g. expenses incurred on participation of employees in official meetings of standardisation bodies)?	CITA/PITA provides for an exhaustive list of eligible expenses for R&D super-deduction (see Art. 18d(2) CITA and Art. 26e(2) PITA). The only category (indirectly) linked with standardisation is 'expert assessments, opinions, consulting services and equivalent services as well as the acquisition of the results of scientific research performed on the basis of an agreement by a research unit within the meaning of the Act of 30 April on Science Financing for the purposes of the research and development activities performed' (Art. 18d(2)(3) CITA and Art. 26e(2)(3) PITA). Moreover, according to tax administration, non-eligible are costs of producing prototypes for the purpose of obtaining certificates enabling the developed products to be introduced to other markets (see Head of Tax Chamber in Katowice, private ruling of 16 December 2016, No. 2461-IBPB-1-2.4510.850.2016.2.MS).	
2.3.2.	If yes, should it still be the case even if these employees are not scientists or research technicians?	No, because eligible are 'employees the purpose of whose activities is performing research and development work' (see Art. 18d(2)(1) CITA and Art. 26e(2)(1) PITA).	
2.3.3.	How should these expenses be assessed (e.g. as portion of employee compensation related to the time spent in connection with such meetings)?		
2.3.4.	Should expenses related to technical monitoring/ technological watch be taken into account?	CITA/PITA provides for an exhaustive list of eligible expenses for R&D super deduction (see Art. 18d(2) CITA and Art. 26e(2) PITA). The only category (indirectly) linked with standardisation is 'expert assessments, opinions, consulting services and equivalent services as well as the acquisition of the results of scientific research performed on the basis of an agreement by a research unit within the meaning of the Act of 30 April on Science Financing for the purposes of the research and development activities performed' (Art. 18d(2)(3) CITA and Art. 26e(2)(3) PITA). Moreover, according to tax administration, non-eligible are costs of producing prototypes for the purpose of obtaining certificates enabling the developed products to be introduced to other markets (see Head of Tax Chamber in Katowice, private ruling of 16 December 2016, No. 2461-IBPB-1-2.4510.850.2016.2.MS).	

2.4.	**Patent related expenses**		
2.4.1.	Are expenses linked to patents eligible? Please define NB: *under current French tax law, expenses linked to the filing, the maintenance and the defence of patents incurred in France or in another State (IP consultant's fees, translation costs taxes...) are eligible to the R&D tax credit; insurance costs linked to patents are eligible within a threshold of EUR 60,000. However, under the Frascati criterion, R&D would typically not include administrative and legal work connected with patents, routine tests or data collection.*	Yes, however, only for micro, small and medium entrepreneurs. According to Art. 18d(2)(5) CITA and Art. 26e(2)(5) PITA, eligible for R&D super deduction are: 'the costs of obtaining and maintaining a patent, a utility model protection right, a right derived from the registration of an industrial design, incurred by a taxable person being a micro-enterprise, a small enterprise, or a medium-sized enterprise within the meaning of the provisions on the freedom of establishment, for: a) preparing application documents and making a submission to *Urząd Patentowy Rzeczypospolitej Polskiej* [the Polish Patent Office] or a competent foreign authority, including the costs of required translations into a foreign language, b) the conduct of proceedings by *Urząd Patentowy Rzeczypospolitej Polskiej* or the competent foreign authority, incurred from the time of the submission, in particular official fees and the costs of legal representation and representation in proceedings, c) countering claims of non-compliance with conditions for being granted a patent, a utility model protection right, or a right derived from the registration of an industrial design, both as part of the application proceedings and after their completion, in particular the costs of legal representation and representation in proceedings, both in *Urząd Patentowy Rzeczypospolitej Polskiej* and in the competent foreign authority, d) regular fees, renewal fees, translations, and undertaking other activities necessary for being granted or maintaining the validity of a patent, a utility model protection right, or a right derived from the registration of an industrial design, in particular the costs of validating a European patent.'	
2.5.	**Other operating expenses related to R&D**		
2.5.1.	Should such category be identified?	No. CITA/PITA provide for an exhaustive list of eligible R&D expenses for super deduction.	
2.5.2.	Is a detailed list possible of expenses advisable?	Yes. It adds clarity and certainty.	

2.5.3.	Is it appropriate to assess these expenses notionally by reference to other precisely defined eligible expenses (e.g. 15% of immovable [property] depreciation allowances, and/or 50% of eligible staff expenses)?	No. Percentage should always be related to actual involvement in R&D activities, not just a lump-sum. However limits may be introduced as regards specific categories of R&D costs, also taking into consideration the size or the status of the taxpayer. For example, under Art. 18d(7) CITA and Art. 26e(7) PITA: 'The amount of eligible costs shall not exceed: 1) where the taxable person is a micro-enterprise, a small enterprise, or a medium-sized enterprise within the meaning of the provisions on the freedom of establishment – 50% of the costs referred to in paragraphs 2 and 3 [all eligible R&D costs]; 2) in the case of other taxable persons: a) 50% of the costs referred to in paragraph 2(1) [eligible R&D staff costs], b) 30% of the costs referred to in paragraphs 2(2) to (4) and paragraph 3. [all other eligible R&D costs]'	
2.5.4.	Should fees paid to external consultants assisting the company to determine its R&D super deduction be eligible, and to what extent?	No.	
C.	**Contracted Expenditure**		
2.6.	**Subcontracting expenses**		
2.6.1.	What if R&D activity is outsourced? *Currently in France, payments to R&D service suppliers, public or private, accredited by the French Ministry of research and located in the EU or the EEA, qualify as eligible expenses.*	Only certain forms of subcontracting to research units is eligible. According to Art. 18d(2)(3) CITA and Art. 26e(2)(3) PITA, eligible costs include 'expert assessments, opinions, consulting services and equivalent services as well as the acquisition of the results of scientific research performed on the basis of an agreement by a research unit within the meaning of the Act of 30 April on Science Financing for the purposes of the research and development activities performed'.	
2.6.2.	Should there be a territorial limit to exclude payments to subcontractors outside the EEA (which cannot invoke the freedom to provide services).	Yes.	

2.6.3.	Should there be other limits? *Under current French law for instance, R&D costs invoiced by accredited private subcontractors can be retained within the limit of three times the total amount of all the other R&D eligible expenses incurred by the company; and such expenses can be retained by the company subcontracting R&D works within a yearly limit of EUR 12 or 10 million and EUR 2 million when the parties (i.e. ordering company and R&D supplier) are related companies.*	Under Art. 18d(6) CITA and Art. 26e(6) PITA: 'A taxable person shall not be entitled to make a deduction where the taxable person in question has, during a given fiscal year, pursued activities within a special economic zone on the basis of a permit granted.' Such taxpayers are exempted from income tax to the extent they perform their activities in the special economic zone under conditions mentioned in so called 'zone permit'.	
B.	**Reimbursed expenditure**		
2.7.	**Treatment of public subsidies**		
2.7.1.	Should governmental and other State agencies subsidies/grants related to R&D eligible projects be deducted from eligible expenses of the year during which these expenses are incurred?	Yes. According to Art. 18d(5) CITA and Art. 26e(5) PITA: 'Eligible costs shall be deducted where they have not been reimbursed to the taxable person in any form.' According to tax administration, if expenses were partially reimbursed, only the remaining (i.e. non-reimbursed) part is eligible (see Head of Tax Chamber in Warsaw, private ruling of 31 March 2016, No. IPPB5/4510-104/16-2/MR).	

Section XIV
Spain

		Answers and comments	Technical source (when necessary)
1.	'Research and Development' – Definition		
1.1.	As indicated in Section I (*supra*), should 'research and development' be excluded if there is no particular application or use in view for the economy or the internal market?	No, because the R&D activity should be detached from the results, in the sense that it does not require the obtaining any particuar application or use in view for the economy or the internal market. The essential characteristic of the R&D activity is the seeking to discover new knowledge.	
1.2.	Should the level of novelty be new 'to the world', 'to the internal market (EU)', 'to the market', or 'to the firm'?	In Spain, on the one hand, tax credits on research and development activities require an objective novelty. New to the world is the level of the novelty that is demanded by tax administration. However, courts of justice have sometimes accepted less novelty for these tax credits. On the other hand, tax credits on technological innovation activities require only subjective novelty. The level of novelty for R&D activities should be new to the EU internal market in the CCTB directive context. New to the world is too restrictive and new to the firm probably too lax to justify tax incentives. New to the market is a difficult and risky concept. For example: What would be the reference market? National market, regional market, or local market.	
1.3.	Should R&D be limited to the industrial sector, or also include the service industry (banking and insurance, but also humanities)?	R&D should include both the manufacturing and service sectors as in the Frascati and Oslo Manuals.	
1.3.1.	In the latter case, which criteria help to identify the presence of R&D in services activities?	For legal certainty reasons the criteria that help to identify the presence of R&D activities in services should be the criteria suggested in Frascati Manual: See rules 2.85, 2.86 and 2.87..	

1.3.1.1.	Links with public research laboratories;	Yes.	
1.3.1.2.	Involvement of staff with PhDs or PhD students;	Yes.	
1.3.1.3.	Publication of research findings in scientific journals;	Yes.	
1.3.1.4.	Organisation of scientific conferences;	Yes.	
1.3.1.5.	Involvement in scientific reviews;	Yes.	
1.3.1.6.	Others?	Any other different criteria that can be inferred of the examples included into the rules 2.85, 2.86 and 2.87.	
2.	'COSTS' (FOR RESEARCH AND DEVELOPMENT) – DEFINITION		
A.	**Capital expenditure**		
2.1.	**Depreciation allowances**		
a.	*General Principles*	**Draft Art. 9-3** provides: *'In addition to the amounts which are deductible as costs for research and development in accordance with paragraph 2, the taxpayer may also deduct, per tax year, an extra 50% of such costs, with the exception of the cost related to movable tangible fixed assets, that it incurred during that year. To the extent that costs for research and development reach beyond EUR 20 000 000, the taxpayer may deduct 25% of the exceeding amount.'* In addition, the Explanatory Memorandum (**para. 8**) provides: *'R&D costs will be fully expensed in the year incurred (with the exception of immovable property).'* **Draft Art. 10** (Other deductible items) provides: *'A deduction shall be made in respect of the depreciation of fixed assets referred to in Articles 30 to 40. […].'* **Draft Art. 12** (Non-deductible items) provides: *'By way of derogation from Articles 9 and 10, the following items shall be non-deductible:* […] *(i) acquisition or construction costs or cost connected with the improvement of fixed assets which are deductible under Articles 10 and 18, except for the cost related to research and development. The costs referred to in point (a) of Article 33(1) and points (a) and (b) of Article 33(2) shall not be treated as costs related to research and development;* […]' – **For additional context, see Annex**. *Based on your national tax background:*	
2.1.1.	Do you share our understanding that depreciation allowances have to be distinguished depending on the assets concerned, whether they are movable or immovable?	Yes, I share your understanding. The depreciation allowances of movable and immovable assets must be distinguished.	

2.1.2.	Do you share our understanding that depreciation allowances are not available for movable fixed assets, because they are fully expensed in the year incurred, and not eligible to the super-deduction?	No, I do not completely share your understanding. I understand that the depreciation allowance is not available for movable fixed assets, because they can/could be fully expensed in the year incurred.	
2.1.3.	Do you share our understanding that depreciation allowances remain available for immovable [property], because it cannot be fully expensed in the year incurred, and is eligible to the super-deduction?	Yes, I share your understanding.	
2.1.4.	What if an asset is used both for research and non-research purposes (such as manufacturing)?	In that case, the depreciation allowances proportional to the using of asset for R&D purposes should be eligible to the super-deduction.	
2.1.5.	If eligible, which criteria for proportional eligibility if asset used both for R&D and manufacturing purposes (e.g. an equipment used both to manufacture prototypes and serial products)?	Any objective criteria could be useful for the proportional eligibility. For example, the time spent by the equipment in each one of these activities.	
2.1.6.	What if the asset is 'indirectly' used for R&D purposes?	In that case, the depreciation allowances of the asset should be not eligible to the super-deduction. What would be the boundary of 'indirectly' used for R&D purposes?	
2.1.7.	What do you think of the following definition: 'Is considered directly used for R&D purposes an asset permitting, in and of itself, to carry out research programs of the business'?	I think that this definition is incomplete, because the development programs should be specifically mentioned. Normally, research and development programs of the business are linked but they are not linked necessarily always.	
2.1.8.	Is the production of the following assets an R&D activity? (i) production of prototypes; (ii) construction of a pilot plant / or pilot facilities	In Spain, the production of a first unmarketable prototype/s and initial demonstration projects or pilots plants are deemed R&D activities, provided they cannot be reconverted or used for industrial application or commercial exploitation. In my opinion, these are correct restrictions.	

2.1.9.	Would you characterise the following assets as, potentially, directly used for R&D activities: (i) Handling devices; (ii) Calculation tools; (iii) Computers; (iv) Machines used to manufacture components of a prototype; (v) Telephones, small office appliances, office furniture?	Handling devices: no. Calculation tools: no. Computers: no. Machines used to manufacture components of a prototype: only the using for this specific application. Telephones, small office appliances, and furniture: no. If the 'indirect' assets used for R&D purposes are not eligible, these excluded assets should not be included through an extensive interpretation of 'directly' assets used for R&D purposes.	
<u>*b.*</u>	<u>*Specific Rules*</u>		
(i)	*Intangible Assets*	**<u>Draft Art. 33.1(e)</u>** provides: '*Without prejudice to paragraph 2 and Articles 37 and 38, fixed assets shall be depreciated individually over their useful lives on a straight-line basis. The useful life of a fixed asset shall be determined as follows:* [...] *(e) fixed intangible assets: the period for which the asset enjoys legal protection or for which the right has been granted or, where that period cannot be determined, 15 years.*' The problem is that not all intangible items (e.g. intellectual property, brand names), meet the definition of an intangible asset. If an item does meet the definition of an intangible asset, expenditure to acquire it or generate it internally should be recognised as an expense when it is incurred. Therefore, *based on your national tax background*:	
2.1.10.	Should we use the European Union Accounting Rule 6 defining intangible asset (i.e., identifiability, control over a resource, and existence of future economic benefits or service potential)?	Yes, in my opinion this using is necessary to achieve legal certainty in EU context.	
2.1.11.	If not, what should be the definition of intangible assets?		
2.1.12.	Are intangible fixed assets (including intellectual property (IP)) costs fully expensed in the year incurred and included in the CCTB super-deduction?	In Spain, the intangible fixed assets affected to R&D activities can be freely amortised, and therefore their fully cost could be included in the CCTB super-deduction.	
	The inclusion of mere intellectual property costs is not advisable: it may create a bias in favour of patented research compared to that stemming from unpatented technology.		

2.1.13.	Will in practice this provision be limited to patents costs acquired with a view to carry on new experimental research and development?	Yes, in practice this provision will be probably limited to patents costs acquired with a view to carry on new experimental research and development.	
2.1.14.	What if these patents are (also) used in the manufacturing process?	In that case, an objective proportional rule would be necessary.	
2.1.15.	Should plant variety rights be treated in the same manner as patents?	Yes, plant variety rights should be treated in the same manner as patents.	
2.1.16.	What about outlays incurred to acquire licences or know-how?	The outlays incurred to acquire licences or know-how should be considered with a view to carry on new experimental research and development. In Spain, the acquisition of advanced technology in form of patents, licences, know-how and designs is expressly deemed a technological innovation activity (in this application, on the one hand, amounts paid by the taxpayer to related persons or entities are not included into deduction basis, and on the other hand, the deduction basis cannot exceed one million of euros).	
(ii)	*Immovable [property]*		
	In any case, not covered by exclusion in Art. 9-3		
	In Austria, building costs and financing expenses related to R&D activity may be taken into account.		
2.1.17.	Should the concept of 'immovable property' (Recital No. 8) be preferred to the one of 'immovable fixed asset' (as opposed to Art. 9.3 CCTB)?	Yes, the concept of 'immovable property' should be preferred to the one of 'immovable fixed asset'. In Spain, the inversions on tangible or intangible assets exclusively affected to R&D activities are eligible to apply tax incentive, but the inversions on buildings and land are specifically excluded.	
2.1.18.	Would building costs and financing expenses related to the acquisition of immovable [property] be eligible to the super-deduction?	No, building costs and financing expenses related to the acquisition of immovable [property] would not be eligible to the super-deduction.	

2.1.19.	What is your understanding of Art. 12(i): <u>1st meaning</u>: that costs related to acquisition or construction of new commercial or second-hand commercial or industrial immovable [property] is excluded from the super-deduction? Or <u>2nd meaning</u>: that costs related to acquisition or construction of new commercial or second-hand commercial or industrial immovable [property] is not fully deductible the year incurred but should be depreciated and such depreciation allowances are eligible to the super-deduction?	My understanding of Art. 12 is coincident with the first meaning.	
(iii)	*Lease payments*		
2.1.20.	What if equipment is used according to the terms of a leasing-type transaction?	I think that the equipment used according to the terms of leasing-type transaction should be treated in the same way that the equipment acquired.	
2.1.21.	Are leasing instalments eligible for super-deduction under current wording of Art. 9-3?	Leasing instalments are not clearly eligible for super-deduction under current wording of Art. 9-3, because there are not acquisition (normally) or construction costs.	
2.1.22.	Should they be?	Yes, they should be eligible for super-deduction.	
(iv)	*Alternative readings*		
2.1.23.	Please feel free to add any alternative readings you may have of relevant CCTB provisions and that has not yet been discussed.		
B.	**Current expenditure**		
2.2.	**R&D staff cost**		
<u>a.</u>	<u>*What is meant by R&D staff?*</u>	Staff directly-involved in R&D activities.	
2.2.1.	Should eligibility be limited to staff directly-involved in R&D?	Yes, in no case general expenses of the business or indirect expenses related to R&D activities should be eligible. In Spain this conclusion is very settled.	

2.2.2.	In case the staff participates both in R&D and non R&D activities, should the text allow for proportional eligibility based on time spent (or other criteria)?	Yes, if the text allows it, the proportional eligibility should be based on an objective criterion like the time spent in R&D and non-R&D activities.	
2.2.3.	How can researchers or scientists be defined? Should the text use black letter criteria (list diplomas (PhDs), qualifications...) or a more open definition?	The text should use a black letter criterion.	
2.2.4.	Are research technicians R&D staff?	The answer depends on the understanding of the R&D staff concept. In Spain, there are a specifically additional tax credit for 'qualified researchers' exclusively dedicated to R&D activities, and tax administration understands that research technicians and other supported staff cannot be considered 'qualified researchers'. Out of this specific context, research technicians may be considered R&D staff. In all case, general rule should be respected: general expenses of the business or indirect expenses related to R&D activities are not eligible.	
2.2.5.	What about other employees (not 'official researchers') which still have contributed to a patented invention?	Their compensation may be eligible only if the general rule were respected.	
2.2.6.	What about the managers of the business (e.g. running a research program)?	Their compensation may be eligible only if the general rule were respected.	
2.2.7.	What about other staff (secretariat, cleaning, etc.)? Can, in the alternative, their compensation be taken into account, proportionally, as other operating R&D expenses (cf. I-3 below)?	Their compensation may be eligible only if the general rule were respected, and off course taken into account proportionally.	

b.	*What is meant by R&D staff cost?*	All emoluments satisfied to R&D staff, not only wages.	
2.2.8.	Wages, bonuses, benefits in kind?	Yes.	
2.2.9.	Social security contributions (compulsory and/or non-compulsory)?	Yes.	
2.2.10.	Employer's contribution to participation of employees in profits of the enterprise by means of profit-sharing plan, employee share-ownership?	Only if these contributions are deemed an emolument in national tax law.	
2.2.11.	Can a Member State provide that compensation paid to holders of PhD will count more (e.g. double) for a limited period of time (in order to promote hiring of PhD holders)?	It will depend on what the CCTB directive final text was, but it does not seem that a Member State could provide this treatment by its own decision.	
2.3.	**Standardisation expenses**		
	Based on your national tax background:		
2.3.1.	Should expenses related to the establishment of technical standards concerning products of the business be eligible for the super-deduction (e.g. expenses incurred on participation of employees in official meetings of standardization bodies)?	No, these expenses should not be eligible for the super-deduction. In Spain, these expenses are not eligible for the tax credits.	
2.3.2.	If yes, should it still be the case even if these employees are not scientists or research technicians?	In that case, only if these employees are scientists or research technicians.	
2.3.3.	How should these expenses be assessed (e.g. as portion of employee compensation related to the time spent in connection with such meetings)?	In that case, only a portion of employee emoluments related to time spent in connection with these activities.	
2.3.4.	Should expenses related to technical monitoring/ technological watch be taken into account?	No, these expenses should not be eligible for the super-deduction, except in case that these technical monitoring/technological watch lead to a new R&D activities ('R & D retroactive').	

2.4.	**Patent related expenses**		
2.4.1.	Are expenses linked to patents eligible? Please define NB: *under current French tax law, expenses linked to the filing, the maintenance and the defence of patents incurred in France or in another State (IP consultant's fees, translation costs taxes...) are eligible to the R&D tax credit; insurance costs linked to patents are eligible within a threshold of EUR 60,000 However, under the Frascati criterion, R&D would typically not include administrative and legal work connected with patents, routine tests or data collection.*	In Spain, these expenses are not eligible to the R&D tax credits as under Frascati criterion.	
2.5.	**Other operating expenses related to R&D**		
2.5.1.	Should such category be identified?	Yes, such category should be identified.	
2.5.2.	Is a detailed list possible of expenses advisable?	Yes, it is possible with an 'open' close clause. For example: any other expenses related to R&D activities that cannot deemed as a general expense of the business or indirect expense related to R&D activities.	
2.5.3.	Is it appropriate to assess these expenses notionally by reference to other precisely defined eligible expenses (e.g. 15% of immovable [property] depreciation allowances, and/or 50% of eligible staff expenses)?	It is appropriate in that sense.	
2.5.4.	Should fees paid to external consultants assisting the company to determine its R&D super deduction be eligible, and to what extent?	No, these fees should be not eligible, but if these fees were eligible, they should be limited to a small maximum amount.	

C.	**Contracted Expenditure**		
2.6.	**Subcontracting expenses**		
2.6.1.	What if R&D activity is outsourced? *Currently in France, payments to R&D service suppliers, public or private, accredited by the French Ministry of research and located in the EU or the EEA, qualify as eligible expenses.*	Currently, in Spain, payments related to R&D activities contracted (or subcontracted), individually by the company or in collaboration with other companies and carried out in Spain or in another Member State of the EU or EEA, qualify as eligible expenses.	
2.6.2.	Should there be a territorial limit to exclude payments to subcontractors outside the EEA (which cannot invoke the freedom to provide services).	Yes, the tax incentive is justified if it promotes R&D activities into EU or EEE territorial limits, not outside of them.	
2.6.3.	Should there be other limits? *Under current French law for instance, R&D costs invoiced by accredited private subcontractors can be retained within the limit of three times the total amount of all the other R&D eligible expenses incurred by the company; and such expenses can be retained by the company subcontracting R&D works within a yearly limit of EUR 12 or 10 million and EUR 2 million when the parties (i.e. ordering company and R&D supplier) are related companies.*	Only other limit seems necessary: the acquisition of the rights to the eventual results of the R&D activity by the contractor and payer company, in order to avoid unjustified double or multiple tax incentives for the same R&D activity.	

B.	**Reimbursed expenditure**		
2.7.	**Treatment of public subsidies**		
2.7.1.	Should governmental and other State agencies subsidies/grants related to R&D eligible projects be deducted from eligible expenses of the year during which these expenses are incurred?	Yes, governmental and other State agencies subsidies/grants related to R&D eligible projects should be deducted from eligible expenses of the year during which these expenses are incurred. It seems a better option that the two public channels existing to promote R&D activities were not mixed. In Spain, 65% of the governmental and other State agencies subsidies/grants related to R&D eligible projects were deducted from eligible expenses of the year. This percentage was the reverse of the general rate in the Corporate Income Tax, but it was not adapted in its successive modifications. But the currently Corporate Income Tax law excludes 100% of the governmental and other State agencies subsidies/grants related to R&D eligible projects.	

Section XV
Switzerland

The Swiss report reflects the state of the legislation by 2017. The author however indicates that the *Conférence Suisse des Impôts* issued a document on 4 June 2020 entitled *'Analyse de la déduction supplémentaire des dépenses de recherche et développement selon les art. 10a et 25a de la loi fédérale sur l'harmonisation des impôts directs'*.[166]

		Answers and comments	Technical source (when necessary)
1.	'Research and Development' – Definition		
1.1.	As indicated in Section I (*supra*), should 'research and development' be excluded if there is no particular application or use in view for the economy or the internal market?	There is currently no clear definition of R&D for tax purposes in Switzerland, either at the federal level or at the cantonal level. In the CTR III, this notion had to be defined by the Federal Council in the Ordinance of the Federal Tax Harmonisation Act which was never made public. The currently available information on the new Tax Proposal 17 is silent on this point. Therefore, this notion has not yet been defined.	
1.2.	Should the level of novelty be new 'to the world', 'to the internal market (EU)', 'to the market', or 'to the firm'?	There is currently no clear definition of R&D for tax purposes in Switzerland, either at the federal level or at the cantonal level. In the CTR III, this notion had to be defined by the Federal Council in the Ordinance of the Federal Tax Harmonisation Act which was never made public. The current information on the new Tax Proposal 17 is silent on this point. Therefore, this notion has not yet been defined but must respect the principle of proportionality in particular the ability principle.	See proposals made by Robert Danon in R. Danon, *La constitutionnalité des mesures fiscales proposées par la troisième réforme de l'imposition des entreprises (RIE III)*, Lausanne, 2015, p. 81.
1.3.	Should R&D be limited to the industrial sector, or also include the service industry (banking and insurance, but also humanities)?	This notion has not yet been defined but must respect the principle of access neutrality.	R. Danon, *La constitutionnalité des mesures fiscales proposées par la troisième réforme de l'imposition des entreprises (RIE III)*, Lausanne, 2015, p. 78.

166. Available at: https://www.ssk-csi.ch/fileadmin/dokumente/Analysen/analyse_Forschung_Entwicklung_FR_2020.pdf.

1.3.1.	In the latter case, which criteria help to identify the presence of R&D in services activities?	Not yet defined.	
1.3.1.1.	Links with public research laboratories;	Not yet defined.	
1.3.1.2.	Involvement of staff with PhDs or PhD students;	Not yet defined.	
1.3.1.3.	Publication of research findings in scientific journals;	Not yet defined.	
1.3.1.4.	Organisation of scientific conferences;	Not yet defined.	
1.3.1.5.	Involvement in scientific reviews;	Not yet defined.	
1.3.1.6.	Others?		
2.	'Costs' (For Research and Development) – Definition	There is currently no clear definition of R&D expenses in Switzerland, either at the federal level or at the cantonal level. In the CTR III, this notion had to be defined by the Federal Council in the Ordinance of the Federal Tax Harmonisation Act which was never made public. The new Tax Proposal 17 simply provides that the additional super deduction for R&D (50%) shall take more account of personnel costs. Therefore, this notion has to be more precisely defined.	
A.	**Capital expenditure**		
2.1.	**Depreciation allowances**	No particular depreciation allowances in favour of R&D exists in Switzerland.	
a.	General Principles	**Draft Art. 9-3** provides: '*In addition to the amounts which are deductible as costs for research and development in accordance with paragraph 2, the taxpayer may also deduct, per tax year, an extra 50% of such costs, with the exception of the cost related to movable tangible fixed assets, that it incurred during that year. To the extent that costs for research and development reach beyond EUR 20 000 000, the taxpayer may deduct 25% of the exceeding amount.*" In addition, the Explanatory Memorandum (**para. 8**) provides: '*R&D costs will be fully expensed in the year incurred (with the exception of immovable property).*' **Draft Art. 10** (Other deductible items) provides: '*A deduction shall be made in respect of the depreciation of fixed assets referred to in Articles 30 to 40. [...]*'	

		Draft Art. 12 (Non-deductible items) provides: *'By way of derogation from Articles 9 and 10, the following items shall be non-deductible:* [...] *(i) acquisition or construction costs or cost connected with the improvement of fixed assets which are deductible under Articles 10 and 18, except for the cost related to research and development. The costs referred to in point (a) of Article 33(1) and points (a) and (b) of Article 33(2) shall not be treated as costs related to research and development;* [...]' – **For additional context, see Annex**. *Based on your national tax background:*	
2.1.1.	Do you share our understanding that depreciation allowances have to be distinguished depending on the assets concerned, whether they are movable or immovable?	In Switzerland, depreciation allowance depends on the sectors of activity and the assets. Therefore the relevant Federal tax administration guidelines distinguish for instance between 'commercial enterprises', 'entreprises active in the electric sectors', 'entreprises active in the agricultural sector', etc. on the one hand and between 'machine', 'commercial real estate', 'computers', 'intellectual property', etc. on the other hand.	Notice AFC A 1995 – Entreprises électriques; Notice AFC A 1995 – Entreprises commerciales; Notice AFC A 1995 – Téléférique; Notice AFC A 1995 – Navigation; Notice AFC A 2001 – Agriculture/Sylviculture.
2.1.2.	Do you share our understanding that depreciation allowances are not available for movable fixed assets, because they are fully expensed in the year incurred, and not eligible to the super-deduction?	Depreciation allowance for movable fixed assets are authorised in Switzerland but the Swiss lawmaker has not yet decided if they are eligible or not as qualified R&D expenses to the R&D 'super-deduction'.	
2.1.3.	Do you share our understanding that depreciation allowances remain available for immovable [property], because it cannot be fully expensed in the year incurred, and is eligible to the super-deduction?	Depreciation allowance for immovable fixed assets are authorised in Switzerland but the Swiss lawmaker has not yet decided if they are eligible or not as qualified R&D expenses to the R&D 'super-deduction'.	
2.1.4.	What if an asset is used both for research and non-research purposes (such as manufacturing)?	In Switzerland, no distinction exists if an asset is used or not for R&D activities. The lawmaker or the tax administration has not yet edited specific Guidelines permitting to qualify this dual-use assets as eligible R&D expenses or not for the 'super-deduction' purposes.	

2.1.5.	If eligible, which criteria for proportional eligibility if asset used both for R&D and manufacturing purposes (e.g. an equipment used both to manufacture prototypes and serial products)?	Switzerland doesn't have specific allocation rule for this case.	
2.1.6.	What if the asset is 'indirectly' used for R&D purposes?	Currently, the fate of the assets indirectly used for R&D purposes is still undecided.	
2.1.7.	What do you think of the following definition: 'Is considered directly used for R&D purposes an asset permitting, in and of itself, to carry out research programs of the business'?	No definition of asset directly used for R&D purposes exists in current Swiss tax law or practice.	
2.1.8.	Is the production of the following assets an R&D activity? (i) production of prototypes; (ii) construction of a pilot plant / or pilot facilities	Not yet defined.	
2.1.9.	Would you characterise the following assets as, potentially, directly used for R&D activities: (i) Handling devices; (ii) Calculation tools; (iii) Computers; (iv) Machines used to manufacture components of a prototype; (v) Telephones, small office appliances, office furniture?	Not yet defined.	
<u>b.</u>	<u>*Specific Rules*</u>		
(i)	*Intangible Assets*	**<u>Draft Art. 33.1(e)</u>** provides: '*Without prejudice to paragraph 2 and Articles 37 and 38, fixed assets shall be depreciated individually over their useful lives on a straight-line basis. The useful life of a fixed asset shall be determined as follows:* [...] *(e) fixed intangible assets: the period for which the asset enjoys legal protection or for which the right has been granted or, where that period cannot be determined, 15 years.*'	

		The problem is that not all intangible items (e.g. intellectual property, brand names), meet the definition of an intangible asset. If an item does meet the definition of an intangible asset, expenditure to acquire it or generate it internally should be recognised as an expense when it is incurred. Therefore, *based on your national tax background*:	
2.1.10.	Should we use the European Union Accounting Rule 6 defining intangible asset (i.e. identifiability, control over a resource, and existence of future economic benefits or service potential)?		
2.1.11.	If not, what should be the definition of intangible assets?	Because the Swiss tax law doesn't have a special treatment for Intangible asset, there is currently no clear definition of intangible asset for tax purposes in Switzerland, neither at the federal level nor at the cantonal level.	
2.1.12.	Are intangible fixed assets (including intellectual property (IP)) costs fully expensed in the year incurred and included in the CCTB super-deduction?	The expenses are tax-deductible as long as they are considered to be business-related (*'justifiées par l'usage commercial'*).	Notice AFC A 1995 – Entreprises commerciales
	The inclusion of mere intellectual property costs is not advisable: it may create a bias in favour of patented research compared to that stemming from unpatented technology.		
2.1.13.	Will in practice this provision be limited to patents costs acquired with a view to carry on new experimental research and development?	Not yet defined.	
2.1.14.	What if these patents are (also) used in the manufacturing process?	Not yet defined.	
2.1.15.	Should plant variety rights be treated in the same manner as patents?	Not yet defined.	
2.1.16.	What about outlays incurred to acquire licences or know-how?	Not yet defined.	
(ii)	*Immovable [property]*		
	In any case, not covered by exclusion in Art. 9-3		

	In Austria, building costs and financing expenses related to R&D activity may be taken into account.		
2.1.17.	Should the concept of 'immovable property' (Recital No. 8) be preferred to the one of 'immovable fixed asset' (as opposed to Art. 9.3 CCTB)?	Not yet defined.	
2.1.18.	Would building costs and financing expenses related to the acquisition of immovable [property] be eligible to the super-deduction?	Not yet defined.	
2.1.19.	What is your understanding of Art. 12(i): 1st meaning: that costs related to acquisition or construction of new commercial or second-hand commercial or industrial immovable [property] is excluded from the super-deduction? Or 2nd meaning: that costs related to acquisition or construction of new commercial or second-hand commercial or industrial immovable [property] is not fully deductible the year incurred but should be depreciated and such depreciation allowances are eligible to the super-deduction?	As we cannot find R&D 'super-deduction' in current Swiss tax law, the interpretation is still open from a Swiss perspective.	
(iii)	*Lease payments*		
2.1.20.	What if equipment is used according to the terms of a leasing-type transaction?	Not yet defined.	
2.1.21.	Are leasing instalments eligible for super-deduction under current wording of Art. 9-3?	As there is no R&D 'super-deduction' in the current Swiss tax law, the interpretation is still open from a Swiss perspective.	

2.1.22.	Should they be?	As there is no R&D 'super-deduction' in the current Swiss tax law, the relevance of this expense as qualified R&D 'super-deduction' expense is still open from a Swiss perspective. So theoretically, we can extend the scope of the R&D qualified expense to R&D 'super deduction' but we have a general limitation to 70% of taxable profit in the Tax Proposal 17.	
(iv)	*Alternative readings*		
2.1.23.	Please feel free to add any alternative readings you may have of relevant CCTB provisions and that has not yet been discussed.		
B.	**Current expenditure**		
2.2.	**R&D staff cost**	For the time being, the only information available about the new outfit of R&D 'super-deduction' Tax Proposal 17 is that the additional super-deduction for R&D (50%) shall take more account of personnel costs. However, at the same time, the overall tax relief of all tax measures shall be limited to only 70% of a business year's corporate income before deduction of previous years' losses carried forward. So if theoretically we can extend the scope of the R&D qualified expense to R&D 'super-deduction', we have however a general limitation to 70% of taxable profit in the Tax Proposal 17.	
a.	*What is meant by R&D staff?*		
2.2.1.	Should eligibility be limited to staff directly-involved in R&D?	Not yet defined.	
2.2.2.	In case the staff participates both in R&D and non R&D activities, should the text allow for proportional eligibility based on time spent (or other criteria)?	Not yet defined.	
2.2.3.	How can researchers or scientists be defined? Should the text use black letter criteria (list diplomas (PhDs), qualifications...) or a more open definition?	Not yet defined.	

2.2.4.	Are research technicians R&D staff?	Not yet defined.	
2.2.5.	What about other employees (not 'official researchers') which still have contributed to a patented invention?	Not yet defined.	
2.2.6.	What about the managers of the business (e.g. running a research program)?	Not yet defined.	
2.2.7.	What about other staff (secretariat, cleaning, etc.)? Can, in the alternative, their compensation be taken into account, proportionally, as other operating R&D expenses (cf. I-3 below)?	Not yet defined.	
b.	*What is meant by R&D staff cost?*		
2.2.8.	Wages, bonuses, benefits in kind?	Not yet defined.	
2.2.9.	Social security contributions (compulsory and/or non-compulsory)?	Not yet defined.	
2.2.10.	Employer's contribution to participation of employees in profits of the enterprise by means of profit-sharing plan, employee share-ownership?	Not yet defined.	
2.2.11.	Can a Member State provide that compensation paid to holders of PhD will count more (e.g. double) for a limited period of time (in order to promote hiring of PhD holders)?	Not yet defined.	
2.3.	**Standardisation expenses**		
	Based on your national tax background:		
2.3.1.	Should expenses related to the establishment of technical standards concerning products of the business be eligible for the super-deduction (e.g. expenses incurred on participation of employees in official meetings of standardisation bodies)?	Not yet defined.	

2.3.2.	If yes, should it still be the case even if these employees are not scientists or research technicians?	Not yet defined.	
2.3.3.	How should these expenses be assessed (e.g. as portion of employee compensation related to the time spent in connection with such meetings)?	Not yet defined.	
2.3.4.	Should expenses related to technical monitoring/ technological watch be taken into account?	Not yet defined.	
2.4.	**Patent related expenses**		
2.4.1.	Are expenses linked to patents eligible? Please define NB: *under current French tax law, expenses linked to the filing, the maintenance and the defence of patents incurred in France or in another State (IP consultant's fees, translation costs taxes...) are eligible to the R&D tax credit; insurance costs linked to patents are eligible within a threshold of EUR 60,000. However, under the Frascati criterion, R&D would typically not include administrative and legal work connected with patents, routine tests or data collection.*	Not yet defined.	
2.5.	**Other operating expenses related to R&D**		
2.5.1.	Should such category be identified?	Not yet defined.	
2.5.2.	Is a detailed list possible of expenses advisable?	No.	
2.5.3.	Is it appropriate to assess these expenses notionally by reference to other precisely defined eligible expenses (e.g. 15% of immovable [property] depreciation allowances, and/or 50% of eligible staff expenses)?	Not yet defined.	

2.5.4.	Should fees paid to external consultants assisting the company to determine its R&D super deduction be eligible, and to what extent?	Not yet defined.	
C.	**Contracted Expenditure**		
2.6.	**Subcontracting expenses**		
2.6.1.	What if R&D activity is outsourced? *Currently in France, payments to R&D service suppliers, public or private, accredited by the French Ministry of research and located in the EU or the EEA, qualify as eligible expenses.*	In the CTR III, R&D activity outsourced in Switzerland were included in the R&D 'super-deduction'. Thus this super deduction was limited to expenses incurred in Switzerland by Swiss resident taxpayers or paid to third parties for R&D activities performed within the Swiss territory.	
2.6.2.	Should there be a territorial limit to exclude payments to subcontractors outside the EEA (which cannot invoke the freedom to provide services).	In the CTR III, it was only the expenses related to R&D activities performed abroad that were excluded from the increased tax deduction. Expenses for foreign (i.e. outside of Switzerland) R&D activities did not qualify for the super-deduction.	
2.6.3.	Should there be other limits? *Under current French law for instance, R&D costs invoiced by accredited private subcontractors can be retained within the limit of three times the total amount of all the other R&D eligible expenses incurred by the company; and such expenses can be retained by the company subcontracting R&D works within a yearly limit of EUR 12 or 10 million and EUR 2 million when the parties (i.e. ordering company and R&D supplier) are related companies.*	According to the CTR III, if assignor of a mandate of research and of development ('*mandant*') can benefit from the super deduction, the assignee ('*mandataire*') is not entitled to any super deduction. We do not know yet whether this rule will be taken over in the PF 2017 but we think it will be since preparatory work of the Federal department in charge of the legislative bill mentioned that the super deduction can not benefit both the assignee and the assignor.	

B.	**Reimbursed expenditure**		
2.7.	**Treatment of public subsidies**		
2.7.1.	Should governmental and other State agencies subsidies/grants related to R&D eligible projects be deducted from eligible expenses of the year during which these expenses are incurred?	Not yet defined.	

Chapter 5
Annexes

SECTION I
Questionnaire

		Answers and comments	Technical source (when necessary)
1.	'RESEARCH AND DEVELOPMENT' – DEFINITION		
1.1.	As indicated in Section I (*supra*), should 'research and development' be excluded if there is no particular application or use in view for the economy or the internal market?		
1.2.	Should the level of novelty be new 'to the world', 'to the internal market (EU)', 'to the market', or 'to the firm'?		
1.3.	Should R&D be limited to the industrial sector, or also include the service industry (banking and insurance, but also humanities)?		
1.3.1.	In the latter case, which criteria help to identify the presence of R&D in services activities?		
1.3.1.1.	Links with public research laboratories;		
1.3.1.2.	Involvement of staff with PhDs or PhD students;		
1.3.1.3.	Publication of research findings in scientific journals;		
1.3.1.4.	Organisation of scientific conferences;		
1.3.1.5.	Involvement in scientific reviews;		
1.3.1.6.	Others?		

2.	'COSTS' (FOR RESEARCH AND DEVELOPMENT) – DEFINITION		
A.	**Capital expenditure**		
2.1.	**Depreciation allowances**		
<u>a.</u>	<u>*General Principles*</u>	**<u>Draft Art. 9-3</u>** provides: *'In addition to the amounts which are deductible as costs for research and development in accordance with paragraph 2, the taxpayer may also deduct, per tax year, an extra 50% of such costs, with the exception of the cost related to movable tangible fixed assets, that it incurred during that year. To the extent that costs for research and development reach beyond EUR 20 000 000, the taxpayer may deduct 25% of the exceeding amount.'* In addition, the Explanatory Memorandum (**para. 8**) provides: *'R&D costs will be fully expensed in the year incurred (with the exception of immovable property).'* **<u>Draft Art. 10</u>** (Other deductible items) provides: *'A deduction shall be made in respect of the depreciation of fixed assets referred to in Articles 30 to 40. [...]'* **<u>Draft Art. 12</u>** (Non-deductible items) provides: *'By way of derogation from Articles 9 and 10, the following items shall be non-deductible:* [...] *(i) acquisition or construction costs or cost connected with the improvement of fixed assets which are deductible under Articles 10 and 18, except for the cost related to research and development. The costs referred to in point (a) of Article 33(1) and points (a) and (b) of Article 33(2) shall not be treated as costs related to research and development;* [...]' – **<u>For additional context, see Annex</u>**. *<u>Based on your national tax background:</u>*	
2.1.1.	Do you share our understanding that depreciation allowances have to be distinguished depending on the assets concerned, whether they are movable or immovable?		
2.1.2.	Do you share our understanding that depreciation allowances are not available for movable fixed assets, because they are fully expensed in the year incurred, and not eligible to the super-deduction?		
2.1.3.	Do you share our understanding that depreciation allowances remain available for immovable [property], because it cannot be fully expensed in the year incurred, and is eligible to the super-deduction?		

2.1.4.	What if an asset is used both for research and non-research purposes (such as manufacturing)?		
2.1.5.	If eligible, which criteria for proportional eligibility if asset used both for R&D and manufacturing purposes (e.g. an equipment used both to manufacture prototypes and serial products)?		
2.1.6.	What if the asset is 'indirectly' used for R&D purposes?		
2.1.7.	What do you think of the following definition: 'Is considered directly used for R&D purposes an asset permitting, in and of itself, to carry out research programs of the business'?		
2.1.8.	Is the production of the following assets an R&D activity? (i) production of prototypes; (ii) construction of a pilot plant / or pilot facilities		
2.1.9.	Would you characterise the following assets as, potentially, directly used for R&D activities: (i) Handling devices; (ii) Calculation tools; (iii) Computers; (iv) Machines used to manufacture components of a prototype; (v) Telephones, small office appliances, office furniture?		

b.	*Specific Rules*		
(i)	*Intangible Assets*	**Draft Art. 33.1(e)** provides: *'Without prejudice to paragraph 2 and Articles 37 and 38, fixed assets shall be depreciated individually over their useful lives on a straight-line basis. The useful life of a fixed asset shall be determined as follows: [...] (e) fixed intangible assets: the period for which the asset enjoys legal protection or for which the right has been granted or, where that period cannot be determined, 15 years.'* The problem is that not all intangible items (e.g. intellectual property, brand names), meet the definition of an intangible asset. If an item does meet the definition of an intangible asset, expenditure to acquire it or generate it internally should be recognised as an expense when it is incurred. Therefore, *based on your national tax background*:	
2.1.10.	Should we use the European Union Accounting Rule 6 defining intangible asset (i.e. identifiability, control over a resource, and existence of future economic benefits or service potential)?		
2.1.11.	If not, what should be the definition of intangible assets?		
2.1.12.	Are intangible fixed assets (including intellectual property (IP)) costs fully expensed in the year incurred and included in the CCTB super-deduction?		
	The inclusion of mere intellectual property costs is not advisable: it may create a bias in favour of patented research compared to that stemming from unpatented technology.		
2.1.13.	Will in practice this provision be limited to patents costs acquired with a view to carry on new experimental research and development?		
2.1.14.	What if these patents are (also) used in the manufacturing process?		
2.1.15.	Should plant variety rights be treated in the same manner as patents?		

2.1.16.	What about outlays incurred to acquire licences or know-how?		
(ii)	*Immovable [property]*		
	In any case, not covered by exclusion in Art. 9-3		
	In Austria, building costs and financing expenses related to R&D activity may be taken into account.		
2.1.17.	Should the concept of 'immovable property' (Recital No. 8) be preferred to the one of 'immovable fixed asset' (as opposed to Art. 9.3 CCTB)?		
2.1.18.	Would building costs and financing expenses related to the acquisition of immovable [property] be eligible to the super-deduction?		
2.1.19.	What is your understanding of Art. 12(i): 1st meaning: that costs related to acquisition or construction of new commercial or second-hand commercial or industrial immovable [property] is excluded from the super-deduction? Or 2nd meaning: that costs related to acquisition or construction of new commercial or second-hand commercial or industrial immovable [property] is not fully deductible the year incurred but should be depreciated and such depreciation allowances are eligible to the super-deduction?		
(iii)	*Lease payments*		
2.1.20.	What if equipment is used according to the terms of a leasing-type transaction?		

2.1.21.	Are leasing instalments eligible for super-deduction under current wording of Art. 9-3?		
2.1.22.	Should they be?		
(iv)	*Alternative readings*		
2.1.23.	Please feel free to add any alternative readings you may have of relevant CCTB provisions and that has not yet been discussed.		
B.	**Current expenditure**		
2.2.	**R&D staff cost**		
a.	*What is meant by R&D staff?*		
2.2.1.	Should eligibility be limited to staff directly-involved in R&D?		
2.2.2.	In case the staff participates both in R&D and non R&D activities, should the text allow for proportional eligibility based on time spent (or other criteria)?		
2.2.3.	How can researchers or scientists be defined? Should the text use black letter criteria (list diplomas (PhDs), qualifications…) or a more open definition?		
2.2.4.	Are research technicians R&D staff?		
2.2.5.	What about other employees (not 'official researchers') which still have contributed to a patented invention?		
2.2.6.	What about the managers of the business (e.g. running a research program)?		
2.2.7.	What about other staff (secretariat, cleaning, etc.)? Can, in the alternative, their compensation be taken into account, proportionally, as other operating R&D expenses (cf. I-3 below)?		

b.	*What is meant by R&D staff cost?*		
2.2.8.	Wages, bonuses, benefits in kind?		
2.2.9.	Social security contributions (compulsory and/or non-compulsory)?		
2.2.10.	Employer's contribution to participation of employees in profits of the enterprise by means of profit-sharing plan, employee share-ownership?		
2.2.11.	Can a Member State provide that compensation paid to holders of PhD will count more (e.g. double) for a limited period of time (in order to promote hiring of PhD holders)?		
2.3.	**Standardisation expenses**		
	Based on your national tax background:		
2.3.1.	Should expenses related to the establishment of technical standards concerning products of the business be eligible for the super-deduction (e.g. expenses incurred on participation of employees in official meetings of standardisation bodies)?		
2.3.2.	If yes, should it still be the case even if these employees are not scientists or research technicians?		
2.3.3.	How should these expenses be assessed (e.g. as portion of employee compensation related to the time spent in connection with such meetings)?		
2.3.4.	Should expenses related to technical monitoring/ technological watch be taken into account?		

2.4.	**Patent related expenses**		
2.4.1.	Are expenses linked to patents eligible? Please define NB: *under current French tax law, expenses linked to the filing, the maintenance and the defence of patents incurred in France or in another State (IP consultant's fees, translation costs taxes...) are eligible to the R&D tax credit; insurance costs linked to patents are eligible within a threshold of EUR 60,000. However, under the Frascati criterion, R&D would typically not include administrative and legal work connected with patents, routine tests or data collection.*		
2.5.	**Other operating expenses related to R&D**		
2.5.1.	Should such category be identified?		
2.5.2.	Is a detailed list possible of expenses advisable?		
2.5.3.	Is it appropriate to assess these expenses notionally by reference to other precisely defined eligible expenses (e.g. 15% of immovable [property] depreciation allowances, and/or 50% of eligible staff expenses)?		
2.5.4.	Should fees paid to external consultants assisting the company to determine its R&D super deduction be eligible, and to what extent?		
C.	**Contracted Expenditure**		
2.6.	**Subcontracting expenses**		
2.6.1.	What if R&D activity is outsourced? *Currently in France, payments to R&D service suppliers, public or private, accredited by the French Ministry of research and located in the EU or the EEA, qualify as eligible expenses.*		

2.6.2.	Should there be a territorial limit to exclude payments to subcontractors outside the EEA (which cannot invoke the freedom to provide services).		
2.6.3.	Should there be other limits? *Under current French law for instance, R&D costs invoiced by accredited private subcontractors can be retained within the limit of three times the total amount of all the other R&D eligible expenses incurred by the company; and such expenses can be retained by the company subcontracting R&D works within a yearly limit of EUR 12 or 10 million and EUR 2 million when the parties (i.e. ordering company and R&D supplier) are related companies.*		
B.	**Reimbursed expenditure**		
2.7.	**Treatment of public subsidies**		
2.7.1.	Should governmental and other State agencies subsidies/grants related to R&D eligible projects be deducted from eligible expenses of the year during which these expenses are incurred?		

SECTION II
EU Technical Resources (extracts)

European Parliament (2018) Report on the Proposal for a
COUNCIL DIRECTIVE
on a Common Corporate Tax Base

Proposal for a directive

Recital 8

Text proposed by the Commission	*Amendment*
(8) Taxable revenues should be reduced by business expenses and certain other items. Deductible business expenses should normally include all costs relating to sales and expenses linked to the production, maintenance and securing of income. To support innovation in the economy and modernise the internal market, deductions should be provided for research and development ***costs***, including super-deductions, and those should be fully expensed in the year incurred (with the exception of immovable property). ***Small starting companies without associated enterprises which are particularly innovative (a category which will in particular cover start-ups) should also be supported through enhanced super-deductions for research and development costs.*** In order to ensure legal certainty, there should also be a list of non-deductible expenses.	(8) Taxable revenues should be reduced by business expenses and certain other items. Deductible business expenses should normally include all costs relating to sales and expenses linked to the production, maintenance and securing of income. To support innovation in the economy and modernise the internal market, deductions should be provided ***and taxpayers should receive a tax credit for genuine expenses of research and development relating to expenses in respect of staff, subcontractors, agency workers and freelancers***, and those should be fully expensed in the year incurred (with the exception of immovable property). ***A clear definition of the genuine expenses of research and development is needed to avoid misuse of the deductions.*** In order to ensure legal certainty, there should also be a list of non-deductible expenses.

Article 4

Définitions

[...]

(6) 'expenses' means decreases in net equity of the company during the accounting period in the form of outflows or a reduction in the value of assets or in the form of a recognition or increase in the value of liabilities, other than those relating to monetary or non-monetary distributions to shareholders or equity owners in their capacity as such.

[...]

(11) 'research and development' means experimental or theoretical work undertaken primarily to acquire new knowledge of the underlying foundations of phenomena and observable facts, without any particular application or use in view (basic research); original investigation undertaken in order to acquire new knowledge but directed primarily towards a specific, practical aim or objective (applied research); systematic work, drawing on knowledge gained from research and practical experience and producing additional knowledge, which is directed to producing new products or processes or to improving existing products or processes (experimental development);

[...]

(19) 'fixed assets' means tangible assets acquired for value or created by the taxpayer and intangible assets acquired for value that are capable of being valued independently and that are used in the business for producing, maintaining or securing income for more than 12 months, except where their acquisition or construction cost is less than EUR 1,000. Fixed assets shall also include financial assets, with the exception of financial assets held for trading in accordance with to Article 21;

[...]

Article 7

Elements of the tax base

The tax base shall be calculated as revenues less exempt revenues, deductible expenses and other deductible items.

[...]

Article 9

Deductible expenses

1. Expenses shall be deductible only to the extent that they are incurred in the direct business interest of the taxpayer.
2. The expenses referred to in paragraph 1 shall include all costs of sales and all expenses, net of deductible value added tax, that the taxpayer incurred with a view to obtaining or securing income, including costs for research and development and costs incurred in raising equity or debt for the purposes of the business.

Proposal for a directive

Article 9 – Paragraph 3 – Subparagraph 1

Text proposed by the Commission	*Amendment*
In addition to the amounts which are deductible as costs for research and development in accordance with paragraph 2, the taxpayer may also deduct, per tax year, an extra 50% of such costs, with the exception of the cost related to movable tangible fixed assets, that it incurred during that year. To the extent that costs for research and development reach beyond EUR 20 000 000, the taxpayer may deduct 25% of the exceeding amount.	***For research and development costs not exceeding EUR 20 000 000 and that relate to staff including wages, subcontractors agency workers and freelancers, the taxpayer shall receive a tax credit of 10% of the costs incurred.***

Proposal for a directive
Article 9 – Paragraph 3 – Subparagraph 2

Text proposed by the Commission	*Amendment*
By way of derogation from the first subparagraph, the taxpayer may deduct an extra 100% of its costs for research and development up to EUR 20 000 000 where that taxpayer meets all of the following conditions: ***(a) it is an unlisted enterprise with fewer than 50 employees and an annual turnover and/or annual balance sheet total that does not exceed EUR 10 000 000;*** ***(b) it has not been registered for longer than five years. If the taxpayer is not subject to registration, the period of five years may be taken to start at the moment that the enterprise either starts, or is liable to tax for, its economic activity;*** ***(c) it has not been formed through a merger;*** ***(d) it does not have any associated enterprises.***	***Deleted***

Article 10

Other deductible items

A deduction shall be made in respect of the depreciation of fixed assets referred to in Articles 30 to 40.

[...]

Article 12

Non-deductible items

By way of derogation from Articles 9 and 10, the following items shall be non-deductible:

[...]

(i) acquisition or construction costs or cost connected with the improvement of fixed assets which are deductible under Articles 10 and 18, except for the cost related to research and development. The costs referred to in point (a) of Article 33(1) and points (a) and (b) of Article 33(2) shall not be treated as costs related to research and development;

[...]

Article 18

Costs related to non-depreciable assets

Acquisition or construction costs of fixed tangible assets as referred to in Article 38, or costs for the improvement of those assets, shall be deductible in the tax year in which those assets are disposed of, provided that the disposal proceeds are included in the tax base.

Article 33

Individually depreciable assets

1. Without prejudice to paragraph 2 and Articles 37 and 38, fixed assets shall be depreciated individually over their useful lives on a straight-line basis. The useful life of a fixed asset shall be determined as follows:
   (a) commercial, office and other buildings, as well as any other type of immovable property in use for the business, with the exception of industrial buildings and structures: 40 years;
   (b) industrial buildings and structures: 25 years;
   [...]
2. Second-hand buildings and other types of immovable property, second-hand long-life fixed tangible assets, second-hand medium-life fixed tangible assets and second-hand fixed intangible assets shall be depreciated in accordance with the following rules:
   (a) second-hand commercial, office or other buildings, as well as any other type of immovable property in use for the business, with the exception of industrial buildings and structures: 40 years, unless the taxpayer demonstrates that the estimated remaining useful life of the asset is shorter than 40 years, in which case it shall be depreciated over that shorter period.
   (b) second-hand industrial buildings and structures: 25 years, unless the taxpayer demonstrates that the estimated remaining useful life of the asset is shorter than 25 years, in which case it shall be depreciated over that shorter period;

*

* *

EXPLANATORY MEMORANDUM

[...]

5. OTHER ELEMENTS

[...]

Detailed explanation of the specific provisions of the proposal

[...]

'Tax base: it is designed broadly. All revenues will be taxable unless expressly exempted. Income consisting in dividends or proceeds from the disposal of shares held in a company outside the group will be exempt for participations of at least 10 percent, in order to prevent the double taxation of foreign direct investment. In the same vein, the profits of permanent establishments will also be exempt from tax in the state of the head office.

Taxable revenues will be reduced by business expenses and certain other items. The new proposal for a common corporate tax base will also replicate, with some necessary adjustments to ensure consistency, the list of non-deductible expenses that features in the proposal of 2011. To support innovation in the economy, this re-launch initiative will introduce a super-deduction for R&D costs into the already generous R&D regime of the proposal of 2011. The baseline rule of that proposal on the deduction of R&D costs will thus continue to apply; so, R&D costs will be fully expensed in the year incurred (with the exception of immovable property). In addition, taxpayers will be entitled, for R&D expenditure up to EUR 20 000 000, to a yearly extra super-deduction of 50%. To the extent that R&D expenditure reaches beyond EUR 20 000 000, taxpayers may deduct 25% of the exceeding amount.

Considering that one of the key policy initiatives relating to the functioning of the single market is to support small and innovative entrepreneurship, the re-launch proposal for a common corporate tax base will grant an enhanced super-deduction for small starting companies without associated enterprises which are particularly innovative (a category that will in particular cover start-ups). In that context, taxpayers who qualify, according to the directive, may deduct 100% of their R&D costs in so far as these do not exceed EUR 20 000 000 and provided that these taxpayers do not have any associated enterprises.'

Afterword

Knowledge creation and its utilisation are key factors for achieving economic prosperity and people's well-being. State support is, in this respect, generally recognised as a key element to stimulate research and development (R&D) by business enterprises. Among the main features of such State intervention are tax incentives. Such incentives are applicable at the stage of conducting R&D operations (super deduction or tax credit) or upon receipt of income from the sale or licence of technology.

The definition of qualifying R&D expenditures is a major point which tax administrations, business enterprises and tax courts have to address. While the OECD Frascati and Oslo manuals provide helpful guidance for such definition, the concept of novelty may vary from one country to another, and questions arise of the scope of expenses (current expenditure and asset investments) to be taken into account.

The present book, which covers fourteen EU countries and Switzerland, proposes solutions to these issues in order to provide a legal environment conducive to R&D investments as well as to EU tax harmonisation. Its developments are of direct interest to those involved in business taxation matters, in particular in the European Union. Georges Cavalier lead the conceptualisation and editing efforts of this study. He can be thanked for this major contribution.

Jean-Luc Pierre

Professor Emeritus, Jean-Moulin (Lyon 3) University

www.ingramcontent.com/pod-product-compliance
Ingram Content Group UK Ltd.
Pitfield, Milton Keynes, MK11 3LW, UK
UKHW051905290926
8980IPUK00017B/1782

9 781839 705625